Star Babies

a&b

Star Babies

JUDY FLOWER

First published in Great Britain in 2006 by
Allison & Busby Limited
13 Charlotte Mews
London W1T 4EJ
www.allisonandbusby.com

A catalogue record for this book is available from
the British Library.

10 9 8 7 6 5 4 3 2 1

ISBN 0 7490 8190 2
978-0-7490-8190-4

Printed and bound in Wales by
Creative Print and Design, Ebbw Vale

JUDY FLOWER gained the Diploma of the Faculty of Astrological Studies in 1985. As well as writing the early horoscope columns for *Mizz* and articles for *Surrey Occasions* and various in-house magazines, she scripted daily horoscopes for the BT Starcall Line and forged a successful radio career with both the British Forces Broadcasting Services and LBC. She became a respected voice with her horoscopes for both stations and at LBC a favourite contributor with her phone-ins, especially one devoted to astrological guidance on relationships. Judy also maintains a private consultancy, advising on individual charts for clients from the UK and overseas. She has brought up four children and is now enjoying a new generation as her grandchildren start to grow up. After thirty years in Surrey she has recently moved to Cambridgeshire.

For
my grandchildren
and
in memory of Monty Flower

Acknowledgements

Writing is a solitary business but at the same time one is never alone as the chapters take shape and the finished work eventually emerges. *Star Babies* has experienced a rather protracted birth, during which I have been extremely grateful to a first class midwifery team. First of all, heartfelt thanks to my agent, Vanessa Holt, and to Susie Dunlop and her team at Allison & Busby. I am also most appreciative of the wisdom and guidance of Deryn Lake and Georgina Jones, with whom I spent a memorable evening and who started me on this venture. In addition, Maureen Woollett's supportive friendship, wicked sense of humour and (in true Sagittarian style) honest comments about my tendency to procrastinate definitely kept the project moving forward. Thank you, too, to Annette Shaw who volunteered the title when she commissioned a short article on babies and their sun signs. Last, but by no means least, my thanks to my children for so kindly producing the grandchildren who have given me both enormous pleasure and much food for thought about astrological parent/child relationships. Labours of love indeed!

Judy Flower

Contents

Introduction

Some years ago I took part in a local radio station's weekly phone-in on astrological relationships. Whilst many of the questions concerned adult partnerships, there was always one query along the lines of 'we're thinking of starting a family: which star sign would be the most compatible for us?' Whilst it is a strange phenomenon, but an astrological truth, that a baby's own horoscope, whenever it is born, invariably has significant links with the birth charts of its parents, that is not to say an immediate rapport will instantly develop. My interest in the relationship between parent and child was particularly rekindled when my Cancerian daughter, about to give birth to an Aquarian, wondered how she would get along with her firstborn. She realised she didn't have any close Aquarian friends and usually found the sign rather cool and unapproachable. Instinctively she had picked up on the difficulties surrounding any relationship between the over-sensitive, emotional Cancer and the logical, sometimes rather aloof Aquarius and was keen to understand how she could avoid any pitfalls that could mar the mother/baby bond. Most mothers are fortunate enough to form an amazingly deep connection with their baby at birth, but a true appreciation of the similarities that will unite, and the differences that will require patience, perception and tolerance to overcome, can only enhance those strong protective ties.

We all love our children, but whether we really know them or, from time to time even like them, is a totally different matter. Every Sun sign has the ability to get along with every other. Some find it very easy to establish an immediate rapport; others struggle to find common ground and to value each other's qualities. A little knowledge of astrological characteristics can make a huge and beneficial difference to family harmony.

With two or more children born to the same parents there is a good probability that love, hate, indifference and all emotions in between will go into the melting pot. My four children are all very different and each connects with the other siblings in a unique and special way. That does not mean it is, or has been, all sweetness and light! In all families rivalry, or a total unwillingness to understand a sister or brother's way of thinking or behaving, can put a temporary (or sometimes permanent) blight on the relationship. Learning to appreciate the other's qualities rather than fret about the differences can often haul a potentially stressful sibling relationship from the brink.

Once I started to think about the early interaction between parent and child and between siblings, I also remembered how differently my own children had developed in their first five years. Each astrological sign has its innate gifts and talents, which will develop quickly and easily, and its more challenging characteristics that will take time to encourage or tame. By the time the five- year-olds reach the school gates they have more or less attained the same goals, albeit by somewhat different routes, and the birth sign could have a lot to do with it. Much worry can frequently be alleviated if it is accepted, for example, that Geminis are likely to master words and movement quickly but Taureans will win hands down when it comes to creating masterpieces in the sandpit. As for the Piscean ability to hold a tune and tap to the rhythm, Handel, Chopin and Rimsky Korsakov are testament to that!

I hope this book will not only be informative but also help you to enjoy your relationship with the youngest members of the family and their own alliances within the home. If it can also throw a new light on your child's development, allowing you to take pride in his or her talents and, equally, not to worry too much if other milestones take longer to achieve, then I have answered not only one Cancerian's questions but perhaps those from every member of the zodiac's family.

Judy Flower
Mother of four and grandmother of eight

The Signs Of The Zodiac

Sign	Dates	Symbol	Element
Aries	March 21st – April 19th	The Ram	Fire
Taurus	April 20th – May 20th	The Bull	Earth
Gemini	May 21st – June 20th	The Twins	Air
Cancer	June 2lst – July 21st	The Crab	Water
Leo	July 22nd – August 22nd	The Lion	Fire
Virgo	August 23rd – September 22nd	The Virgin	Earth
Libra	September 23rd – October 22nd	The Scales	Air
Scorpio	October 23rd – November 21st	The Scorpion	Water
Sagittarius	November 22nd – December 21st	The Archer	Fire
Capricorn	December 22nd – January 19th	The Goat	Earth
Aquarius	January 20th – February 17th	The Water Bearer	Air
Pisces	February 18th – March 20th	The Fish	Water

Astrological Note

There can be a slight variance from year to year in the day the Sun changes from one sign to the next, usually more in the way of hours rather than days. However, those few hours can be very significant and if you have a child born on any of the following dates, it could be very helpful to read both the birth sign and the next-door sign. If you are in doubt as to whether your son or daughter is one sign or another, the characteristics and, more importantly, the relationship sections, could make it all much clearer.

Date	Signs
January 20	Capricorn and Aquarius
February 18	Aquarius and Pisces
March 20	Pisces and Aries
April 20	Aries and Taurus
May 20	Taurus and Gemini
June 21	Gemini and Cancer
July 22	Cancer and Leo
August 23	Leo and Virgo
September 22	Virgo and Libra
October 23	Libra and Scorpio
November 22	Scorpio and Sagittarius
December 21	Sagittarius and Capricorn

Aries

The Aries Child 0-5 Years

The Aries baby makes its presence felt the moment it arrives in the world. Just as a newborn lamb rarely wastes any time lying around in the straw, keen to get to its feet and to explore its surroundings, so it is with a newborn Aries. Eager and alert, this baby arrives with a 'go-go-go' attitude, ready to fulfil its designated role in life as leader, adventurer and all-action hero. As the first sign of the zodiac, Aries knows it holds an important position in the world and the baby Ram, from day one, just wants to ensure that everyone knows that it is definitely a cut above the rest. 'Me first' is its motto and through a combination of dynamic energy, great enthusiasm, warm smiles and a sheer joy of living, manages to have everyone at its beck and call.

Patience may well be a virtue in many people's eyes, but this concept is totally lost on the Aries child. With a general fixation about speed, it wants everything NOW, whether it's a feed, a clean nappy, a present it's seen waiting in the wings, general attention or a change of scene – and it will be highly vociferous in making its views known. And talking of presents: don't bother too much with the wrapping. Aries young and old just rip off the packaging! Temper tantrums – usually caused by sheer frustration – are an innate part of the Aries character and it doesn't take until the 'terrible twos' for them to manifest. Puce in the face and angry beyond belief, even a young baby can demonstrate the Aries fiery nature in a quite alarming way. However, just as a parent, childminder or grandparent is starting to panic at not being able to calm this slightly hysterical baby, the noise suddenly stops, the baby beams and behaves as though nothing has happened (leaving the poor adult shattered and confused). From an early age, Aries learns to control its environment and if the fire doesn't work it can turn on the ice. Being studiously ignored by a toddler can be just as unnerving to a carer as the hot-headed dramatics!

Encouraging an Aries youngster into new ventures is never going to be a problem. A good social life, lots of interests and plenty of interaction with the world at large will keep it extremely happy. In keeping, too, with its inclination to be ahead of the pack, never let Aries arrive late for anything: it likes to be early or at least on time. With its go-getting attitude to life and a careless disregard for danger, it's much more likely that reining back is going to be far more necessary. Its 'leap before you look' attitude to life is both endearing and worrying, and finding the right place on that fine dividing line between encouragement and pouring cold water on its initiative is never easy. Being accident-prone, particularly bumps and bruises to the head, is almost a rite of passage during the early Aries years. However, wrapping this bundle of dynamic energy in cotton wool is probably going to make matters worse: anger at being denied the rough and tumble of life could make the little Ram even more impulsive and headstrong and far less likely to listen to any kind of reason.

Supreme self-confidence often oozes out of an Aries youngster: even babies are usually fully aware that they rule the roost and are fazed by nothing. The other side of the coin is a rather selfish attitude to life: consideration for others has to be taught as it is not, and never will be, something that comes naturally! Tact and diplomacy, the forté of a Libran for example, is also rather alien to its nature and speaking before thinking starts early for Aries. Friendships can come and go for these children, some ending through thoughtless and unkind remarks made to more sensitive members of the zodiac. It is often through unhappy events, such as a best friend moving on to another individual or group, that the little Ram comes to realise that forthright comments are not always appreciated. Also behind its noisy, quick-witted (not quite on a par with Gemini but coming close!) and occasionally bumptious persona lies a much more fragile ego than is realised. The Aries child can be easily crushed: it needs much more reassurance and morale boosting than would appear.

Whilst all Aries children are usually keen to acquire any game or toy that is currently in vogue or take up a sport or pastime, many of their parents know just how much their child's short-lived enthusiasms have cost them! Starting a hobby or interest is so very exciting: staying with it for months, weeks or even days is quite another story and usually becomes boring within a very short space of time. Finishing projects of any kind can also be a problem for Aries. Learning to put toys away, completing a puzzle or a drawing, finishing a story, anything in fact which rounds off an activity, is a very useful lesson and will help enormously when it faces the routines of the classroom. The Aries child is naturally ambitious and sometimes best learns the basic skills in a competitive situation. It won't like to be beaten and seeing contemporaries getting ahead is a spur to anything from walking, talking, feeding itself, learning letters and numbers or kicking a football.

There are some signs in the zodiac who are comfortable with the idea of rules and regulations: Aries is not and finds it very difficult to cope with strict discipline. Having room to manoeuvre is very important. However, it does respond well to sensible limitations when they are explained and seem to have validity. Rules for rule's sake will just encourage the little Ram to head butt them all, thus ditching the good with the unnecessary. With enterprise and initiative strong in its character, taking charge of situations is a natural Aries talent and one that shouldn't be discouraged. It will probably always be at the forefront of any escapade and can be guaranteed to have a large retinue of admiring followers. In order to ensure that adventures have a safe outcome, young Aries have to learn early on about responsibility. Whilst never being in Capricorn's league, faced with a duty of any kind even the youngest Ram will perform admirably and, given enough reminders, with a certain amount of forethought.

Many Aries children have a love/hate relationship with hats and a great affinity with red, the colour associated with their ruler, Mars. Whether it's red clothes or the hint of Titian colours in the hair, they frequently feel comfortable in the vibrant tones that are an anathema to their more retiring or conservative little friends. Getting an Aries out of its rather dashing wardrobe and into what it sees as a relatively dull school uniform can cause major upsets!

From the start the Aries child will be assertive: woe betide the parent who ignores its demands or, even worse, its presence! However, that assertiveness can sometimes become something akin to aggression and this always has to be watched. With their association with Mars, Aries are naturally courageous warriors with an innate feeling for protecting the weak. When and where to use that more bellicose nature has to be learned, probably in the nursery, when it feels an injustice has occurred! It takes time for the Aries youngster to realise that literally fighting its corner isn't always necessary. And it's not just the boys who will go into battle. The girls might be more subtle about it, but whether it's pinching, biting, pulling hair or a quick kick under the table, they have their own very effective ways of dealing with trouble.

No one can fail to be enchanted by the ebullience and generally sunny and positive demeanour of an Aries child, but seeing it through the early years is always going to be a challenge. It thrives on action and adventure and a high energy level is often fruitfully spent in the sporting arena: its attention span is fairly limited and left to its own devices for a minute or two it'll surely be into something that spells trouble. However, its willingness to help, its confidence and courage at tackling anything new, its understanding of what is really important in life and its thoroughly affectionate nature are just a few of its most endearing qualities. Behind the sometimes rumbustious nature there also lies a spirit of idealism and heroism and every little Aries sees itself as a knight in shining armour. It's easy to get this particular child involved in charities, fund-raising and helping other people: in their own little way they are personally saving the world. Aries children constantly fall down (literally and metaphorically) but are classically good at dusting themselves down and starting all over again. It's that brave spirit – it rarely deserts them.

Aries, more than some of the other signs, reaches the school gates having had anything but a dull and uneventful start in life. This lively, confident and assured five-year-old, so eager to please, will soon make its mark for all the right reasons. More importantly, many will see him or her as their champion – a title usually richly deserved.

Aries and Aries

Aries Child/Aries Mother

The noisy, ecstatic duo in the maternity ward is very likely to be the Aries mother with her Aries baby and the little Ram will be overjoyed to find its mother full of such warmth and brio. That she relishes a challenge is also obvious as they bowl out of the hospital on a bit of a wing and a prayer. The Aries mother will be equally delighted with her baby. Full on and determined to take all the limelight, this baby is entirely in her own mould. However, as with all same sign combinations, mother and baby have similar attributes and the same weaknesses. Neither is particularly patient or tolerant, and for the Aries mother, whose self-confidence is often more brittle than it appears, her demanding, short-tempered baby can become trying in the extreme. Equally, her baby requires a great deal of her attention and she just has so many other things to do. Hence, screams of frustration from her offspring and feelings of exasperation for her. On the plus side, these two thrive on a busy life and a good social scene and mother and baby will fully understand the other's low boredom threshold. Both will go through life with much enthusiasm and optimism and the mother will just adore her small child's initiative and wholehearted commitment to being centre stage. However, she often fails to see in her child that fragile ego of which she herself is so conscious. Through thoughtless remarks and sometimes rather selfish behaviour she can unwittingly crush his or her spirit. In turn, as the Aries child grows up, the mother can be the recipient of some stinging verbal blows. Sometimes this relationship turns out to be quite combustible, with mother and child trying to out-do each other and a self-centred attitude leading to misunderstandings and feelings of inadequacy in both. At best, this can be a wonderfully positive and dynamic relationship, with each egging the other on to greater heights and both fully understanding each other's vulnerabilities.

Aries Child/Aries Father

The Aries male is one of the most ambitious and competitive in the zodiac and expects his Aries son or daughter to be exactly the same. Whilst both father and child will want to be involved in all sorts of ventures, the innate Aries assertiveness can bring a lot of problems. Very often the father will decide (because of his own preferences) the sports, interests and hobbies that are suitable for his child. Unfortunately, his Aries offspring will have its own ideas, and rows and often a total impasse ensue! The father can also feel quite threatened by the success of his child in any arena, whether it's school work, sport or a real talent for friendships. Criticism and undermining his child's confidence are often his weapons of choice in any stand off. However, the father's own child-like eagerness to please usually makes him avoid the ego-orientated pitfalls and makes him a wonderful companion for his little Ram. Together they can make an extrovert and lively duo. An Aries daughter often has cause to be particularly grateful to an Aries father. He'll have no notions at all of what is 'suitable' for his daughter and will usually offer enormous encouragement in all her ambitions.

Aries Siblings

To the outside world Aries siblings seem to enjoy a shared sense of humour and an active lifestyle and are often very supportive of each other's aims and ambitions. Behind closed doors, however, it's very often a case of who can show the most bravado. It takes much self-knowledge and quite a bit of courage for these two to admit to their weaknesses. They merely see each other's selfishness and monumental egotism! However, with a bit of encouragement, these two can be of enormous help to each other. No one realises better than another Aries how vulnerable each feels and how easy it is to be selfish and thoughtless. Each can be the other's greatest morale booster while at the same time not being afraid to pull him or her up short. In nurturing the other's ambitions, their competitive edge can be used positively to push each other to greater achievement. Aries children desperately want to be liked and, with that agenda in mind, both often make a supreme effort to get along and to develop a genuine affection for each other.

Aries and Taurus

Aries Child/Taurus Mother

Taurus is an earth sign, Aries fire. Earth is safe when it's still: fire needs to move to survive. To the Taurean mother whose whole purpose in life is to establish stability and security for herself and her family is born the greatest risk-taker in the zodiac. She is in no way attuned to the 'it'll be all right on the night' philosophy, just as her Aries baby will never be comfortable if denied its pioneering spirit. Initially, of course, Taurus will be totally enamoured of her active and engaging baby and Aries will thrive in the limelight shone on it by a reliable, patient and generally placid mother. But, the routine in which Taurus thrives quickly becomes stifling for Aries whose boredom is shown in wails and restlessness. Taurus, in turn, cannot fathom her baby's distress and probably retreats into even safer pastures rather than doing something totally different on the spur of the moment and giving her baby new fields to conquer. Aries is very sociable and loves company and its Taurean mother is usually very hospitable, but Taurus can be quite possessive and can easily feel jealous and rejected as Aries happily gurgles its way around a crowded room, being passed from one admirer to the next. The essence of Aries is its daring and its confidence and as it grows older it can feel thwarted at every turn by an over-protective mother. Anger and a sense of impotence build up as Aries is constantly pushed into the safety zone of all activities. Much understanding of how the other ticks is needed if this relationship is going to develop well. At worst, Aries feels discouraged and foiled and Taurus stick-in-the-mud and harried. Spectacular arguments are not unknown. With plenty of give and take, however, these two can learn a lot from each other: Aries gently encourages Taurus out of her comfort zones and she, in turn, teaches Aries about consideration for others and what can be achieved with steady persistence rather than dare-devil antics.

Aries Child/Taurus Father

Aries is the natural entrepreneur of the zodiac and Taurus hopes for a job for life. Aries wants to be out there doing things while Taurus frets over his pension, his savings and making life comfortable and secure for his family. Whilst the Taurean father will always provide a wonderfully stable home in which Aries will be able to prosper, he often fails to get truly involved with his child's activities and certainly doesn't appreciate his little Ram's confidence. Try as he might, Taurus will not be able to stop Aries from leading (at age six or sixteen) what he considers to be a totally irresponsible existence which could be anything that doesn't fit in with his view of what is sensible! Clashes over spending will definitely fall into that category. He can either give in gracefully and become entirely supportive of his child or refuse to budge, thus surely bringing about a monumental clash of personalities. With a little flexibility Taurus could thoroughly enjoy the exploits of his Aries son or daughter, who, in turn, would benefit from the secure environment from which to sally forth and to which safely return.

Aries/Taurus Siblings

With two such different personalities and both having their own special game plan for life, these two often get on extremely well. Taurus can be king or queen of the domestic scene and extrovert Aries centre stage in every other arena. The worst these two, as youngsters, can think about each other is that Taurus is unadventurous and Aries reckless. Generally, Aries is extremely good at easing its Taurean sibling out of a rut just as Taurus can pour effective cold water on some of Aries' crazier notions. However, the Taurean stubbornness can bring out the worst in Aries who will tend to prod and irritate until the desired reaction is achieved – and then doesn't like the end result at all. The Taurean temper, when ignited, is awesome. Taurus is very loving and warm-hearted and is often appalled at the Arian insensitivity and yet Aries sees its Taurean sibling as greedy, self-indulgent and possessive – the latter a trait Aries finds particularly difficult to cope with. They are usually very supportive of each other all through life although neither truly gets to grips with the other's way of thinking.

Aries and Gemini

Aries Child/Gemini Mother

The Gemini mother, who never has enough time in the day to fit in everything she has planned, will be utterly charmed by her energetic and restless Aries baby who, itself, is in a seventh heaven with this busy and, sometimes slightly chaotic, lifestyle. Both thrive on action: neither is happy with time on their hands. So, from the start, this is potentially an astrological relationship that is destined to be fun, exciting and very rewarding. In the early months of the Aries' life, it will meet everyone, do everything and be encouraged to explore as well as to face challenges and overcome them. This is good practice for later years when out-of-school activities will become as important as time spent in the classroom. Where Gemini also works well with her Aries baby is in her ability to defuse its anxieties and, more often that not, its tantrums. Gemini is the master of cool logic and it is through stating the obvious rather than indulging in heated argument that saves not only her child from itself, but stops the relationship getting bogged down in unnecessary hostility. Both, however, are known for their blunt speaking and the Gemini mother can unwittingly dampen her Aries child's innate enthusiasms with a few withering or critical comments. Because she only sees the supreme Aries self-confidence and doesn't always fathom things at a deeper level, she invariably misses out on her child's uncertainties and certainly fails to realise how much encouragement and praise it needs. (Aries, as it gets older, can be just as forthright and unthinking.) A sense of humour is the saving grace for the two of them and any tensions tend to be short-lived. Whilst these two will never truly understand each other's inner feelings and sensibilities, as both tend to be appallingly bad listeners, they will always have a very strong bond and many common interests. Where a busy life, lots of chat and much laughter are concerned, the Gemini mother and Aries baby will have it all.

Aries Child/Gemini Father

An Aries child is always full of enterprise and enthusiasm and desperate to tell everyone about his or her latest adventures and achievements. The Gemini father, whilst never uninterested in what his child is up to, is often too busy to listen properly or much keener to tell of his own activities or to give everyone the benefit of his views. Aries can also find it difficult to get a firm sense of guidance from a Gemini father who thrives on a fairly haphazard existence and whose thoughts tend to change from hour to hour. Despite this small problem, these two usually enjoy a tremendously good companionship and are both open to new experiences, egging each other on in sport, intellectual achievement and creative endeavours. Gemini also loves having his Aries child with him on the social scene. Aries is not as versatile as Gemini and sometimes the father becomes impatient with what it sees as the Aries inability to change tack quickly. Aries resents the criticism and the temper boils over, often to be met with the father's studied indifference. On the whole these two are friends for life, vying to outdo each other as they get older with their exploits and ideas.

Aries/Gemini Siblings

This relationship is usually characterised by non-stop chatter and much laughter. Whether they actually know a great deal about each other would be a moot point: neither tends to look too much beneath the surface of situations, or people, and neither is known for its ability to understand or empathise with the human condition. Mutual interests, a good social scene and the acquisition of knowledge definitely unite these siblings, plus the Gemini verbal skills which invariably get them both out of trouble when an Aries escapade has not gone quite to plan. Gemini is also very good at defusing the Aries hot-headed ideas, and certainly at ignoring the explosions of temper, and bringing some kind of logic to the situation. Equally, Aries tends to encourage Gemini to give things a whirl rather than always looking at situations from a totally rational perspective. These two invariably like each other a lot. They will always enjoy spending sprees (neither can be considered miserly) and can often end up as best mates as well as siblings.

Aries and Cancer

Aries Child/Cancer Mother

The fundamental differences between Aries and Cancer, which tend to cause problems in an adult relationship, are writ large from the start. The Aries baby is determined to be noticed. Noisy, alert, raring to go and embarking on its naturally adventurous role in life, the little Ram tends to lead the home-loving, cautious and protective Cancerian mother a right dance. Cancerian mothers, especially first-timers, are a very nervous bunch, totally convinced that they are not getting things right and worrying about every minute of their new baby's existence. Being landed with an Aries is probably tantamount to having her shaky self-confidence shattered, as her baby seems to be calling all the shots and is never just quietly content with life. Fairly early on she'll be faced with a son or daughter who might feel it's got better things to do than just be cuddled or be the centre of her world, and it'll be a wise mother who neither gets too possessive about her Aries child nor tries to crush its enterprising attitude to life. Aries have a low boredom threshold and a high activity level and, born to a Cancerian mother who probably favours a gentle and safe existence focused around the home, can mean immediate frustration for the child and excess stress for the parent. For the Cancer/Aries relationship to succeed, Cancer has to recognise not only the wonderfully warm and loving Aries spirit but also its need to explore, to take risks and to be a leader. An over-protective mother for this most exciting and dynamic sign of the zodiac can cause great difficulties, first for the child and later for the mother when Aries asserts its independence. If Cancer can let Aries off the lead, whilst at the same time providing a refuge to which her child can return at the end of the day (when saving the world was top of its 'to do' list), then later on she'll feel invigorated by the activities and zest of her young Arian. In turn, the Ram will feel its Cancerian mother always listens, understands and encourages. Best of all, of course, is for Cancer to have the courage never to hold Aries back.

Aries Child/Cancer Father

Cancer men, just like their female counterparts, tend to hold their mother in high esteem, and a Cancerian father's first duty to an Aries will be to instil respect for the child's mother. Although the Cancer man can be just as protective as the woman (particularly if a daughter is concerned), he will find it much easier to understand the go-getting streak in his Aries child. Cancer, after all, is one of the zodiac's most ambitious signs. The problems arise because of their totally different attitudes towards achieving goals. The Cancer father will take a cautious route, having thoroughly checked the way ahead, whilst his Aries offspring will leap before it looks and delight in taking the more risky road. In order not to dampen the wonderful Aries enthusiasm for life and ultimately find himself father to a youngster who has become demoralised, Cancer has to grit his teeth and just be ready with the safety net while Aries flings itself into life with gusto and daring.

Aries/Cancer Siblings

A Cancer child can feel seriously threatened by the arrival of a new baby, especially an Aries one that is going to make its presence felt in a very obvious way. As it will have already developed a very close bond with its mother (and will feel that relationship to be at risk), one of the best ways to harness its naturally tender nature is to involve it very closely with the care of the new arrival. The early years of an Aries/Cancer sibling relationship can be quite difficult with the naturally boisterous Aries tending to clatter all over Cancer's finer feelings. Cancer, in return, can become secretive, quite devious and extremely economical with the truth, getting its own back in a far more subtle way. It probably won't take parents long to learn that the Cancerian's tears and wide-eyed innocence should not always be taken at face value, and that the Aries noise is very often whistling in the dark or a cover for vulnerability. As they get older the siblings tend to gain a lot from each other: Aries learns from Cancer about consideration for others and a more caring approach, while Cancer is chivvied by Aries to be slightly more daring and positive about life.

Aries and Leo

Aries Child/Leo Mother

Two fire signs tend to get on well together, although not enough control over the flames can lead to spectacular pyrotechnics! Whilst none of this looks likely as the Leo mother takes in the wonder of her newly arrived Aries, it doesn't take them long to jostle for position as numero uno in the relationship. Leo sees herself as queen bee and Aries as first among equals. Who is going to get the more attention: Leo for producing this wonderful baby, or Aries for endearing itself to all and sundry? Both, however, have an innate generosity and warm-heartedness, and, even more important, both brim with enthusiasm for life. The Aries baby will thrive in its mother's well-organised, busy but stable routine, and Leo will get enormous satisfaction from showing off her sunny-natured and outgoing little Ram. As time goes on Aries will probably realise that a lot of its activities are much more to do with its mother's whims and her tendency to hold centre stage than with its own abilities, but will still be very appreciative of everything she arranges. Leo, of course, knows best about everything, can be bossy in the extreme and is not averse to pressurising her child: coming up against the Aries toddler who certainly knows his or her own mind can be quite an experience. It often takes a short, sharp and very heated row to find an answer to the problem, and the Leo mother soon recognises that Aries cannot be pushed around and responds best to persuasion rather than orders. Both mother and child can be impatient and intolerant, and, at worst, this relationship can become a battle of egos, neither willing to give in and characterised by highly dramatic arguments. At best, and this is much more usual, these two enjoy a very close relationship. While both are happily putting the world to rights, Aries profits from its mother's broad-minded attitude and zealous encouragement, while Leo basks in her child's adoration and gratitude.

Aries Child/Leo Father

The Leo father, more than anything else, will want to take pride in his child, and an Aries will certainly give him cause to do so. He'll admire his young Ram's pioneering spirit, ambition and energy and will do his utmost to encourage every aspect of his child's character. The Aries confidence and innate intelligence will also chime nicely with Leo's creative mind and expansive attitude to life. Where he could come unstuck is by being more interfering in his child's life than is welcomed, whether it's over its social life, hobbies or at nursery school. Sometimes Leo's rather snobbish attitude can cause much unhappiness for his more open-minded child. There could be many fiery disagreements before Leo abandons trying to over-manage his child's life. Where these two will gel is in enjoying the good things in life. Both tend to be spendthrifts and even the youngest Aries' more extravagant suggestions will be indulged by the Leo father. If Leo can stand back and let his headstrong child make its own successful way in life, this relationship can be a joy for both. Too much control and Aries is likely to find its own path and there's no return passage.

Aries/Leo Siblings

These two fire signs will probably spend much time pushing each other on to bigger and better things. Aries and Leo have very warm and loving natures as well as large egos and a flair for drama. Leo is invariably mesmerised by its sibling's devil-may-care and headstrong approach to life and Aries by Leo's big personality and grand plans. Neither, however, is particularly perceptive when it comes to what lies behind the Leo bombast and the Aries overweening self-confidence. With Aries blind to Leo's sensitivity and Leo unappreciative of Aries' vulnerabilities, much trampling over the other's emotions is definitely on the agenda. At worst, both can see the other as insufferable, aggressive and bossy, but at best they share a great sense of humour, a real love of life and a huge sense of loyalty to each other. If some crazy scheme has gone wrong, it will often be very difficult for a parent to work out who is to blame. It is sometimes easier in this relationship if Leo is the elder sibling: managing people is one of its strengths and Aries respects a peer who can talk it out of its own worst follies.

Aries and Virgo

Aries Child/Virgo Mother

There are some sun sign combinations that are inherently more difficult than others and this is one of them. Aries and Virgo are radically different but, as with all chalk and cheese relationships, the attraction at the start is astonishing. At first the Virgo mother will be utterly enchanted with her baby's outgoing, happy and demanding personality. Aries, in turn, will feel it has truly landed on its feet in such a very well-ordered household (Gina Ford books much in evidence) and with a mother who attends to its every whim. However, Aries from an early age looks to wide vistas and excitement around every corner while Virgo concentrates on the minutiae of life, practical necessities and imaged dangers everywhere. Virgo is a worrier par excellence and Aries the natural risk-taker. It doesn't take long for the child, who is desperate to get to grips with life and to develop its natural leadership talents, to feel thwarted and restless at being held back 'for its own good' – or more accurately for its mother's peace of mind. This fiery, positive spirit becomes a complete mystery to the more modest Virgo, and frequently these two come to exist in a state of high anxiety: Aries is constantly champing at the bit and Virgo is totally stressed at not being able to either control or understand her child. At worst Virgo resorts to nit-picking or even outright criticism in the hope that she can put a brake on her child's actions. In turn Aries feels it more and more necessary to break the rules. However, all is not lost in this relationship. Aries often benefits from its Virgo mother's pragmatic approach to life, common sense and total reliability. Virgo's life is also enhanced by the liveliness, good humour, eagerness to please and confidence of her Aries child. Much compromise and understanding is needed for this relationship to prosper, and Virgo is usually intelligent enough to see where the problems lie and how to solve them. In letting go of the reins, she learns to bask in her child's achievements.

Aries Child/Virgo Father

The Virgo father, who puts providing for his family as a top priority, can often seem rather distant to his ebullient little Aries who is an attention-seeker of the first order. In his generally busy life he fails to register or nurture the bright-eyed Aries enthusiasm and also finds it difficult to understand his child's selfishness, let alone its tendency to rush in where angels fear to tread. Without its father's interest, Aries can either withdraw or find dramatic ways to take centre stage. On the plus side, Virgo is usually a wonderful teacher and Aries gains greatly from its father's knowledge and these two often end up sharing a hobby. Virgo can be pleasantly chivvied into slightly more exciting ventures by the eagerness and dynamism of his son or daughter. Neither sign really wants to get into the realm of heart to hearts, but Virgo, faced with what he sees as bullish self-confidence, thinks Aries can easily brush off criticism. Not so: the Aries child is easily crushed. At worst father and child can retreat into their own corners for a lifetime. At best they appreciate each other's qualities and make real efforts to benefit from them.

Aries/Virgo Siblings

Because Aries and Virgo children are so different they either get on extremely well, because neither feels threatened by the other, or are perpetually at loggerheads. The rather boisterous Aries behaviour can unnerve Virgo who often resorts to illnesses of one kind or another to keep its sibling out of the way. Aries can also become exasperated by Virgo's rather fussy and perfectionist tendencies, usually resorting to destroying something that has taken hours of painstaking Virgoan work to complete! In return Virgo can play the role of 'Mummy's pet' and spill the beans on Aries' latest misadventure. It's inevitable with these two that Aries is going to lead Virgo into all sorts of trouble and Virgo will get them both out of it through its ability to talk its way out of difficulty! Aries will probably never understand Virgo's analytical approach any more than Virgo will favour the Aries inconsiderate behaviour, but these two often learn a lot from each other. Aries is brilliant at pushing its more reluctant sibling out onto the social scene and Virgo encourages Aries to tone down the ego and the forthright remarks.

Aries and Libra

Aries Child/Libra Mother

Libra is charm personified, peaceable and diplomatic and loves to be in refined and beautiful surroundings. Having given birth to an Aries she has brought into her life a noisy, impulsive and forthright baby who may love the home she has created but is so busy getting out into the world and moving on to new things that it never has time to notice. Like all opposite signs of the zodiac this mother and child approach life from totally different directions but at the same time need each other's skills and attributes. For a start, Aries needs Libra's tact and Libra could do with a goodly dollop of the Ram's get-up-and-go. Libra's laid-back, indecisive and rather changeable daily routine can be thoroughly perplexing to the little Aries who is so much more sure of what it wants – and when. The mother then frets because her baby doesn't seem to like her loving and gentle maternal role, and soon falls into the trap of being manipulated and outwitted by a very shrewd operator. Aries can easily make its Libran mother feel used and put-upon as she gives in to its endless demands. Whilst both Libra and Aries are innately sociable and together will enjoy getting out and about, entertaining and being entertained, Aries tends to thrive in a noisy, busy environment which makes Libra feel quite discomfited. Even the youngest Aries will ginger up proceedings if it all goes too quiet! Libra is never going to be gung-ho about anything and generally finds it difficult to indulge all the Aries enthusiasms, to say nothing of understanding the Ram's insistence on speaking its mind. As with all opposites this can be an all or nothing relationship. At worst, these two make no effort to bridge the gap between them and fail to comprehend the other's personality at all. At best, however, they rub off beautifully on each other: Aries learns to tone down the impatience and foolhardiness and to bring harmony into its life while Libra learns from her child about taking both action and the initiative.

Aries Child/Libra Father

For the assertive Aries child, a Libran father comes as something of a pushover. Definite though his views might be about discipline, it is just so much easier to give in to the delightfully winning Aries. Only when his headstrong offspring gets into all sorts of hot water will he possibly start to wonder if he went wrong. An Aries child needs firm and fair handling but the Libran father is desperate to be liked and doesn't want to cause upset. He will either resort to bribery to get his own way or call in judge and jury in the form of the mother, either option not going down brilliantly with an Aries who would far prefer it if its father could fight his own battles. Aries will always love its Libran father, but whether the Ram will always respect him is a different matter. On the plus side, the little Aries can spur Libra into action and many a father has been eternally grateful to the more forceful child for opening up his life. Libra can teach Aries about subtlety and compromise and as a team these two can work very well together. Even the youngest Aries will reluctantly admit that its Libran father smoothes its path in life.

Aries/Libra Siblings

This can be an exhausting relationship for both: Aries is constantly having to chivvy its Libra sibling into action while Libra is forever trying to save Aries from the consequences of his or her latest impulsive decision. Aries can also become exasperated at the time Libra takes to make up its mind about anything, whilst the Libran gets fed up with sorting out its brother or sister's playground battles. However, both are ambitious and want to do well in the world: they have a good understanding of each other's long-term goals and do much to encourage them. Aries is usually very protective of what it sees as the more vulnerable Libran and yet is also aware that it's Libra who has the charm and the larger social circle. Becoming Libra's champion makes entry to that particular group so much easier! Libra is fully aware of its sibling's good-hearted personality and will quickly forgive most of Aries' selfish behaviour. With time and patience this relationship can go from strength to strength but intolerance and vacillation can mean a distance that never lends enchantment.

Aries and Scorpio

Aries Child/Scorpio Mother

The Aries/Scorpio relationship is one of the zodiac's most powerful, for better or worse. The moment Scorpio first sets her piercing and beautiful gaze on her Aries baby she already has plans for its success. Unfortunately, she hasn't reckoned on an equally determined child. At the start, Aries benefits wonderfully from the Scorpio routine and disciplined lifestyle, and its mother delights in the warmth of her baby's strong personality. She won't be daunted, either, at the prospect of curbing its leap before you look attitude to life. These two, however, are eventually bound to clash. Aries will chafe against the rather rigid rules and will soon realise that impulsive action and a bit of daring behaviour are not going to be encouraged. Thus, the little Aries' natural bravado is gradually crushed. Ambition is a mutual Aries and Scorpio trait but Scorpio doesn't trust her Aries child to travel the right path. Her views will be paramount and she'll have no qualms about manipulating Aries around to her way of thinking. Scorpio is also emotionally needy but often keeps those deep feelings very private. Aries is not highly attuned to its feelings and vents worry and insecurities in a display of temper rather than looking for demonstrative affection. Thus Scorpio feels unloved and unappreciated and racks up the control. Before long this relationship reaches a crisis. By letting her child have its head a bit more, putting some flexibility into its upbringing and refraining from prying into every Aries move, Scorpio can save the situation. In turn, Aries needs to tone down the impetuousness and selfishness and understand that its mother isn't quite so confident as she might appear. The worst case scenario for these two is a battle royal, with Scorpio becoming more devious and Aries more belligerent. At best, they can be mutually supportive, Aries appreciating its mother's strong guidance and constant loyalty and Scorpio wondrous at her child's energy, confidence and courage – and ultimate success on its own terms.

Aries Child/Scorpio Father

Where a Scorpio father and an Aries son are concerned, this can frequently be a case of an irresistible force and an immovable object. Both will want their own way and Aries will resent what it sees as its father's rather controlling behaviour. Aries is not going to be pushed around by anyone, let alone by a father who in no way appreciates its entrepreneurial approach to life. With an Aries daughter, the Scorpio is very protective and can often be shattered by her assertive behaviour. She knows she can take care of herself, but he can't or won't see it. After all, she's only five! Aries is one of the most open signs in the zodiac and often finds it difficult to communicate with a Scorpio father who is adept at hiding his feelings. This relationship often prospers when the father/child chatter is based on everyday matters rather than any kind of emotional hiatus. With both signs having an affinity with Mars, father and child frequently enjoy the same sports and hobbies and both are quite competitive. Trouble starts if Scorpio always insists on winning: the Aries ambitions need to be nurtured and a sensible father learns to give in – just occasionally!

Aries/Scorpio Siblings

With Aries and Scorpio children under the same roof, it can either be blissful hush or a domestic war zone. Sometimes these two are so little interested in each other, and understand each other even less, that they lead independent lives with moody silences, and pertinent but often hurtful remarks as their means of interaction. More often, however, this is an extremely volatile relationship. Whilst Aries will fight heroically for its Scorpio sibling in return for Scorpio's deep and abiding loyalty, both tend to want to occupy the same part of the playground and can be intransigent in the extreme. Scorpio will invariably have the upper hand because it is naturally more cunning and has more staying power, but not before it has been at the receiving end of the Aries quick temper and impulsive action. The Aries ego can be exasperating to Scorpio but its own jealous and secretive nature equally irritates the more transparent Aries. At best Aries learns about persistence from Scorpio who, in turn, is helped out of any potential ruts by its quick-witted and go-ahead sibling.

Aries and Sagittarius

Aries Child/Sagittarius Mother

These two fire signs are likely to develop a wonderfully joyous relationship. Both epitomise warmth, generosity and action and share a huge enthusiasm for life. The Sagittarian mother is going to be enchanted with her alert, noisy and rather demanding Aries baby, who, in turn, will be thrilled to be with a parent who does not try to smother it with affection and gives it time and space to explore its amazing new world. Being the zodiac's natural adventurer and averse to being held back, the baby Ram will soon be smiling in the company of its engaging and positive mother who will be more than keen for her child to take note of its surroundings and to practise its social skills. From the very first, these two will have a lot of fun together and a real sense of companionship will quickly develop which will just get better as they get older. Sagittarius understands the Aries need to be 'first' and will certainly encourage its competitive edge while at the same time instilling ideas of fair play, justice and good judgment. The child will benefit from his or her mother's endless good humour, philosophical outlook (which will do much to help Aries deal with its innate short, sharp temper!) and frank opinions. Neither sign shilly-shallies around issues. Where the Sagittarian mother could come unstuck with an Aries child is in trying to enforce an element of discipline into its life. She is not that great at getting her own life together and she's probably not going to lose a great deal of sleep over whether the homework's done or the daily timetable's been adhered to. If her Aries child is going to achieve its potential, it needs some kind of order and structure in the home, to say nothing of learning to finish tasks and cope with the more boring bits in life, not just the excitement. Impatience with each other could also be a problem for these two. Generally, however, this is a great relationship, much appreciated by both.

Aries Child/Sagittarius Father

The Sagittarian father will ensure that his child benefits from a very stimulating home environment and in an Aries he's found a member of the family who will take full advantage of it. Both father and child will probably also enjoy all sorts of outdoor pursuits together, particularly sports, and as long as the father is wise enough to let Aries win, they'll have a thoroughly rewarding time. Away from the sporting arena, the competitive Aries nature is not always understood by a Sagittarian father and sometimes he finds it hard to fathom his child who must, it seems, always come first. He can do much to help his Aries child become less egocentric and more considerate of others. Intellectually, the Sagittarian father can either instil a real love of learning in his Aries child or, through being over-eager for his son or daughter's academic success, become too pushy and crush the natural Aries enthusiasm and confidence. If the father plays the game correctly, then he will foster a lifetime of lively debate and a marvellously questioning mind in his child. These two will spur each other on and bring out the best in each other.

Aries/Sagittarius Siblings

When these two get on they will do so famously, both enjoying an adventurous approach to life, living very much for the moment and sharing a good sense of humour. Often, however, the Aries tendency to put itself first, its impatience and its aggression can irritate Sagittarius, who, fed up with such overt selfishness, cuts off from the relationship. The lack of commitment in Sagittarius and its restlessness equally annoy Aries and trigger a possible temper tantrum. Both siblings, however, will usually enjoy many of the same activities and a little competition can bring out the best in both of them. Aries is definitely action personified in its whole approach to life and has to be 'on the go'. Sagittarius, while enjoying an outdoor and active life, is far more intellectually inclined and relishes time spent with books and in learning generally. It takes time for these two to understand this difference. An Aries/Sagittarius sibling relationship will never be dull and each can be an inspiration to the other.

Aries and Capricorn

Aries Child/Capricorn Mother

Both Capricorn and Aries are ambitious, enterprising and ready for action, but go about achieving their goals in totally different ways. The Aries baby, all noise, sunshine and a me-first attitude can come as a bit of a shock to the Capricorn mother who likes to take a more discreet and orderly approach to getting on in life. In fact, she can often be run ragged by the demands of her insistent and attention-seeking baby who has no plans whatsoever to fit in with her efficient routines, sensible plans and busy daily timetable. However, the Aries smile, alertness, quick mind and sheer joy in the business of living absolutely enchant its mother. Capricorn, in turn, manages to provide her baby with the firm boundaries and practical daily lifestyle that it badly needs and within which it can thrive. For the Capricorn mother, who sees life as a series of steady steps forward, the Aries notions of leaping before it looks and embracing the new are both incomprehensible and alarming. It is therefore easy for the more cautious Capricorn to stifle her child's sense of adventure. She can also be amazed at the Aries impatience and temper tantrums (often brought on through sheer frustration) that are so alien to her forbearing and controlled nature. There will also be a huge gulf between these two where money matters are concerned, and at an early age Aries will astound its mother with its grand financial plans! At best these two have a lot to offer each other: Capricorn actively encourages Aries to develop his or her myriad talents, to persevere and to appreciate that some things are worth waiting for. Aries, in turn, injects excitement, courage and a sense of adventure into its mother's psyche and makes her realise that a rigid outlook isn't always justified. At worst, these two jog along together in total disharmony until the Aries has made its mark in the world. Then, of course, Capricorn truly understands her child, though will still be confused as to how it got to the top of the ladder!

Aries Child/Capricorn Father

The arrival of an Aries child with its go-getting, adventurous attitude beautifully combined with a wonderfully trusting and sunny nature is a joy to a Capricorn father who sees in his baby his own ambitious traits and determination. Although both signs want to get to the top they are, however, inherently very different. The Aries' self-centredness, to say nothing of its frequent insensitivity to people and situations, can cause major embarrassment to the Capricorn father who, in turn, can seem overly pessimistic, controlling and heavy-handed with his ebullient son or daughter. An Aries child thrives on fun, laughter and challenge: the Capricorn father, although possessing a dry wit, often finds it difficult to put pleasure before business and prefers a steady climb up life's ladder to a series of perilous undertakings. Capricorn also becomes exasperated at his Aries child's inability to stick at anything for very long and, in Aries' eyes, the Capricorn father is often just 'boring'. Personality clashes are inevitable between these two (as much with a son as a daughter), but a real respect for each other's achievements ultimately keeps this relationship on the road.

Aries/Capricorn Siblings

To Capricorn, life is a serious business and it often loses patience with the more happy-go-lucky Aries who, in turn, sees its sibling as a wet blanket and probably rather prissy. Aries thrives on the social scene where Capricorn, who usually rates diligence and hard work way above pleasure, tends to be slightly more diffident. Both also tend to be bossy and want their own way, which means there is little give and take in the relationship. With the right encouragement Capricorn and Aries can do much to bring out the best in each other. Capricorn has the ability to channel the Aries enthusiasms down more fruitful paths and Aries is absolutely brilliant at dissolving a black Capricorn mood. Capricorn can also learn much from Aries about living for the moment and, in turn, is able to encourage Aries to give thought to the consequences of its often ill-considered actions. This relationship often works best if Capricorn is the older of the two, when it can take a parental view of its more irrepressible sibling.

Aries and Aquarius

Aries Child/Aquarius Mother

The air and fire combinations in astrology tend to work well and the Aries baby will certainly not come as a complete culture shock to its Aquarian mother. The little Ram starts as it means to go on – headstrong, noisy and adventurous – all qualities the Aquarian can not only cope with but, in many ways, admires, and both will thrive on plenty of activity and lots of distractions. Aries, whose first instinct is to be leader of the pack and to get on in life, will love the fact that its mother is an excellent teacher and is keen for her baby to learn and to progress quickly. As neither sign places great importance on either physical or emotional closeness, Aries will flourish with a mother who values independence and is keen to allow her child to socialise and to develop its pioneering spirit. These two will chat endlessly, have a lot of fun together as they explore the world, and probably share a great sense of humour. The 'me first' Aries attitude will be nicely balanced by its Aquarian mother's more humanitarian approach and she'll be an excellent tutor in gently guiding her child towards the understanding that there are other people in the world who need to be considered. However, it is this same Aries self-centredness, the constant need for attention and the 'in-your-face' enthusiasm that can become a problem for the cooler and more rational Aquarian mother as her child gets older. Equally, the Aries offspring can feel that she is not nearly involved enough in its life and should more ebullient. Her fixed opinions can also jar with the more exuberant and 'can do' Aries mind set. In general, however, these two find it relatively easy to understand each other's idiosyncrasies, Aquarius benefiting from the boundless Aries enthusiasm and the child from its mother's rational outlook and abundant kindness.

Aries Child/Aquarius Father

In theory this should be an excellent relationship. The Aquarian father will be enchanted by his child's enormous enthusiasm for life, its constant questions and its adventurous spirit. In turn, the little Ram will have as a father a wonderful friend and mentor who will both encourage and challenge its physical and intellectual abilities. As neither sign is totally at home in the realm of emotions, the closeness between them is demonstrated in a constant airing of views and many joint activities. This works particularly well with an Aries son, but sometimes an Aries daughter would like a little more in the way of demonstrative affection from her Aquarian father. Problems also occur in this relationship when the father's ideas and opinions are questioned, and at worst disregarded, by his Aries offspring. The Aquarian then tends to become almost autocratic whilst the Aries, scenting that a battle has been won, can become rebellious and wilful. On balance, however, this relationship works well and a great friendship usually develops between the two.

Aries/Aquarius Siblings

Both these children thrive in a busy environment and long to get involved with whatever is going on. They are an enormous support to each other on the social scene, enjoy endless chatter and often develop a very close companionship as they go through life. However, there are a few potential problems that can make this relationship a little strained from time to time. The more pushy and devil-may-care Aries can fail to understand the Aquarian's more detached and rational temperament, let alone its stubbornness, and in turn Aquarius finds the Aries selfishness and lack of self-discipline thoroughly irritating. With Aquarius always being right about everything and Aries knowing best, quarrels are inevitable. Neither sign, however, is prone to sulks: disagreements, therefore, are usually short, sharp, heated and quickly forgotten. At best these two will be brilliant at nurturing and encouraging each other's finer qualities and one thing is certain – this sibling relationship will never be dull.

Aries and Pisces

Aries Child/Pisces Mother

Most Piscean mothers are totally unprepared for the arrival of a little Aries, not in a lack of readiness for its birth (although that can sometimes be a bit haphazard!) but for the strong personality that has joined the family. On the one hand she'll secretly delight in her child's zeal and eagerness to please and yet, on the other, wonders why she never seems to hold much authority in the relationship. Aries, from the start, needs firm guidelines and a canny mixture of encouragement and caution. Pisces will probably have great difficulty in establishing the ground rules and boundaries within which her child will best develop, let alone know how and when to haul it back from the brink. Thus Aries can run out of control while Pisces flounders around, frantically trying to work out why her gentle, accommodating approach is yielding such questionable results. In keeping with the idea of the Pisces symbol of two fish swimming in opposite directions, she can then make matters worse by changing her mind about everything, leaving her little Aries even more confused. Aries' low boredom threshold and need for attention is in direct contrast to the Piscean escapist tendencies and ability to live in her imagination. However, Pisces is very creative and she'll have a head start in the wonders of glue, pasta, leaves, shells and everything else that goes into picture making and will invariably come up with the best costume for the school play or fancy dress party, talents not lost on her Aries who likes to be top dog at all times. Pisces is compassionate, kind and easily reduced to tears: as her Aries baby grows older and develops its forthright approach, the mother is often devastated by her child's remarks. This relationship can founder in a whirlpool of anger, crossed lines and hurt feelings. At best, however, and with a great deal of work, Aries learns about sensitivity and the needs of others while Pisces will bask in her child's derring-do and generally protective approach to its mother.

Aries Child/Pisces Father

The Aries child is extremely trusting and likes to believe its father's promises will be kept. Realising, time after time, that Pisces has something better to do or has made last minute changes to the plans, is devastating to Aries, whose enthusiasms need to be nurtured not dashed. In turn, the father is flummoxed by the selfishness and overt ambition of Aries and cannot understand its thoughtlessness. Aries loves the rough and tumble of life: Pisces hates confrontation. The positive, confident Aries, therefore, finds it easy to dominate its less assertive father who, rather than argue, swims away from the battleground. Aries, having won, then frets about losing an imaginative and kind companion and learns fast about hollow victories. At worst, the child grows intolerant of a seemingly weak-willed father, while Pisces abhors his child's impatient egotism. At best, after many tribulations, Pisces gets more out of life by becoming involved in the Aries adventures and Aries learns much about the effectiveness of the softly-softly approach to life.

Aries/Pisces Siblings

Once Aries has fathomed that it hasn't got an all-action playmate and Pisces has realised its sensitivities are always going to be trampled under foot, these two either decide to stick firmly to their own corner or manage to develop a wary respect for each other and, eventually, a good friendship. Pisces is one of the zodiac's great listeners and, although not averse to investing in a good set of earplugs while its sibling goes on and on and on, is often a fount of sensitive advice and gentle reproach. Its winning and gentle ways tend to defuse parental anger far better than an Aries on the war path. Aries proves excellent at encouraging Pisces to swim out of the shallows, whether into a busier social life or new interests, and throws a very protective arm around its sibling from playground to teenage angst. The bugbear for Aries is the copious Piscean tears, which get the Ram wrongly blamed for all manner of incidents. Pisces, in turn, gets maddened by its sibling's constant interference and thoughtless attitude. These two do best with each other 'on side', but it sometimes takes time for them to realise it.

TAURUS

The Taurus Child 0-5 Years

Contentment and abundant charm ooze from every pore of the newly arrived Taurus baby. Its basic loving and warm-hearted temperament is obvious from the start and the little Bull's liking for all the good things in life soon becomes apparent. The youngest Taurean fully appreciates cashmere, silk and other expensive materials next to its skin, will forego the carrots for the avocado and will grumble menacingly if it doesn't have the most comfortable baby seat around. This is one of the most tactile and sensuous members of the zodiac who thrives on cuddles, snuggling into the neck, skin-to-skin contact, handholding and anything else that ministers to its highly developed sense of touch. In return for such demonstrative affection, the Taurus child will give a marvellous impression of being a good listener, a steadying presence and a shoulder to cry on.

Unlike its astrological neighbours, Aries and Gemini, it makes no real effort to rush into the world, just does what it has to do at its own steady pace. At first it seems that there's a wonderfully placid member of the family, enthusiastic about feeding and an absolute pleasure to look after: its parents can seem to do no wrong. A false dawn has broken, however, because it's not long before the Taurean stubbornness emerges and it becomes clear that this baby has a mind of its own – and a very strong one at that. Forget about coaxing this little individual into anything, whether it's a hobby, new clothes or going to a party: just remember it's a Bull and when it's decided to dig in its heels, it's probably best to walk away from the situation rather than risk a headlong charge or an eruption of the earth-shattering Taurean temper. It takes time for Taurus to lose its rag: this is not a child who will throw a tantrum at the slightest setback to its plans and many parents make the mistake of thinking their Taurean will put up with anything and is bothered by nothing. Like a volcano, however, slights, injustices and anger are all building up below the surface and it'll be the proverbial straw that triggers the explosion. A bellowing little Bull is awesome and usually involves a bit of rampaging around the home as well!

Taurus is a thoroughly conventional sign: in order to thrive in its early months and years it really needs firm routines, sensible rules and a thoroughly stable environment. It will soon feel mightily put out and become extremely tetchy with a lifestyle that is either subject to constant changes or within which there are no solid boundaries. This baby definitely needs to know what is, and what is not, allowed, and from an early age frequently displays a common sense approach to situations that can leave adults open-mouthed with astonishment. As a toddler, Taurus becomes extremely reliable and develops a sense of responsibility that means it can be trusted to help around the home and to be protective of a younger sibling. As a budding leading light on the social scene it also enjoys company, being both a brilliant host and an enchanting guest from its earliest years.

It is rare for a Taurean baby to be ahead in the walking and talking stakes. It instinctively knows that it's so much easier to be ferried in a buggy or carried around and who wants to make all that effort to learn so many sounds? That is not to say that Taurus loves to live in a world of silence – far from it. It's a singer by nature, and music to this baby is a joy forever. Humming or joining in with nursery rhymes or with a favourite video/CD is something it will indulge in far earlier than its contemporaries and music is often a very useful key to Taurean learning. It doesn't have the innate curiosity of a Gemini, nor the quest for knowledge of a Sagittarian, but will often learn well by rote and repetition and through songs and musical games. Where it does win hands down over the other signs is in its practical abilities. Most Taureans are builders par excellence: they know how to stack the building blocks, make mud pies and sandcastles and create masterpieces with anything that comes to hand. This is the child who teaches a parent how to construct the Lego model! Taurus is often very green-fingered as well, and in keeping with an earth sign, loves to get its hands in the soil. Giving a little Bull a packet of seeds and its own patch of ground is probably the best present ever: this child will never forget to weed or water.

The Taurean's biddable and charming nature can easily hide its determination and persistence. Not easily distracted from a course of action, Taurus needs a very good reason if it is not to continue down a forbidden track. It responds well to sensible argument but rarely to high-handed orders: in the face of the latter the child can become intractable and almost enjoys the impasse. Jealousy also tends to fire the Taurean determination. Taurus is very possessive and even as a baby finds it very difficult to share anything. 'It's mine' are often the first words it feels compelled to utter as it moves heaven and earth to retain or regain its favourite toy or its place nearest to its mother. Friendships can also suffer, especially at nursery or in the early days in the school playground when the little Taurean learns the hard way that it doesn't own anyone. Watching a favourite companion giving his or her attention to someone else can be devastating, and it's a wise parent who tackles this problem early on. Learning about the bigger picture in all aspects of life can be invaluable for Taurus.

For a Taurean to be picky over food is most unusual. This is a sign that champs at the bit to get at its meals and is often the first to move on from the baby menus and onto more grown-up fare. At best this child is a joy to feed, ready to experiment with new tastes and textures and making sure that nothing is left on the plate. Greed, however, is not far from the little Bull's mind and it's all too easy to succumb to its ideas on grazing its way through the day as well as sitting down to breakfast, lunch and tea. Many Taureans ultimately suffer from weight problems that have their origin in a childhood fascination with food coupled with an equal dislike of exercise. Lethargy and laziness are often part and parcel of the Taurean character, not helped by the fact that their interests in life rarely involve great activity. Taurus is essentially a sensible plodder and sees no reason to go rushing through life, let alone jump through hoops.

A natural acumen for business is usually obvious very early on in a Taurean's life. Bartering in the nursery is often quickly followed by selling its own homemade cookies and buns (Taurus not only loves its food but invariably loves cooking it too), flowers grown in the garden or brooches made from the jewellery kit. Conducting tough negotiations over pocket money at the age of five is the next step and he or she is no slouch at getting what it wants! A natural aptitude for figures puts Taurus ahead of the class in maths although its literary skills might still be mediocre. Cancer might be the greatest squirrel of the zodiac when it comes to putting money away, but Taurus takes top spot for saving and investment. Many a little Taurean has probably marched into a bank or building society to open up an account with the best interest rate. Paradoxically, Taurus loves to spend money on life's luxuries.

Whilst good routines and a certain amount of necessary discipline make all baby Bulls feel safe in their home environment and give them the confidence to explore other territory, it's often difficult for a Taurean child to develop any kind of adaptability. It can easily become inflexible and obstinate not only in its actions but also in its thinking. From the first, a Taurean youngster often startles the adults around by the sheer force of its opinions and benefits enormously from being encouraged to look at another point of view. Without this wider look at issues, Taurus can become a didactic five-year-old who will be in danger of becoming a bore of the first order.

Taurean children are unlikely to be blazing beacons of innovation, leadership or daring (except perhaps in the market place!) but in their steady, pragmatic and cautious way will become rocks to which the more erratic people in the Zodiac can safely cling. They make loyal and loving friends, are exceptionally patient with people and situations that would make other signs scarper, and are frequently generous with their time and hospitality. Many a parent of a little Bull has found itself entertaining a houseful of nursery playmates on the say-so of her four-year-old! The safe but sure Taurean approach to all things in life shouldn't be a cause for worry: eventually it'll reach its goals and, having attained them, won't abandon them in a hurry. 'Everything that is worth having is worth waiting for' is as good a motto for Taurus as it is for Capricorn. Above all, Taurus exudes charm and, like Libra, frequently gets away with all manner of misdemeanours by dint of a few well-chosen words and that beautiful smile.

Taurus and Aries

Taurus Child/Aries Mother

The Aries mother probably can't believe her luck when she realises that she's given birth to a wonderfully calm and accommodating baby, thus leaving her so much more time for her own busy schedule. What she hasn't yet twigged is that once her little Taurean realises that its mother lives for the moment and has no real game plan for this whole child-rearing business, things are going to be very different. The lack of routine and firm boundaries suddenly sets off the formidable Taurean obstinacy and temper, throwing its seemingly confident mother into a state of confusion and even panic. Mother and child are totally different. Aries needs variety and must shine on her particular stage while Taurus just wants to feel grounded and safe. It takes much self-knowledge and understanding for the Aries mother to give her little Bull just what it needs and frequently she has to put the brakes on her own indulgences while she settles her baby onto sure foundations. Taurus is also extremely tactile and needs much cuddling and comfort. Aries is certainly not cool in her affections but frequently finds better things to do with her time than snuggle up with her baby. These two are generally very comfortable on the social scene, although Aries needs to be aware of the fact that her little Taurean is not nearly as brave about facing new situations as she is. Taurus likes everything to be taken at a relatively slow pace whilst Aries thrives on speed and a very busy timetable. Thus, Taurus often feels harried and insecure and Aries frustrated that her child seems unable to enjoy everything she's taken the time to organise. Aries' exasperation at the Taurean's slower mind-set and inability to get out of a rut, together with Taurus' distaste for its mother's quest for novelty and risk, can lead these to into a relationship cul-de-sac before too long. With much understanding on both sides, however, Aries learns to rely on the Taurean stability whilst Taurus admires its mother's can-do attitude.

Taurus Child/Aries Father

Aries is one of the most ambitious signs in the zodiac and expects to get to the top. Taurus is happy just to be on life's ladder and certainly doesn't want to take any risks which might involve falling off. From the beginning this father/child combination tends to suffer from Aries chivvying his child to move onwards and upwards and Taurus digging in its heels and becoming more and more wary about any new ventures. Taurus needs a lot of patience and gentle encouragement at an early age if it is going to develop its self-confidence, and the poor Aries father just doesn't understand that his own slightly gung-ho attitude is really quite terrifying to his child. The Aries and Taurus interests are usually very different too: the artistic and creative Taurean is happy indoors or in its garden while its Aries father thrives in a very competitive environment, especially sport. Eventually, with an element of understanding between the two, they can develop a good relationship. Aries is soon in awe of the Taurean business acumen and Taurus takes advantage of its father's entrepreneurial skills. However, without careful nurturing, these two often come to grief in the face of the Taurean inflexibility and the Aries ego.

Taurus/Aries Siblings

This sibling relationship works best if neither is forced to become too involved in the other's lifestyle. Taurus probably secretly admires its rather dare-devil sibling although gets fed up at having to cover for its escapades and sort out the mess, while Aries wishes it could possess a dose of the Taurus common sense, yet at the same time loathing the Bull's opinionated views and sometimes resentful attitude. There could be many arguments too about who owns what. Taurus doesn't share at the best of times, and Aries feels there are more important things in life than taking care of toys and other people's possessions. Aries' complete disregard for anyone's finer feelings can bring out the worst in the loving Taurean and the Aries sibling usually learns the hard way that it's foolish to ignite the Bull's temper. As they grow older they either learn to appreciate each other's qualities or grow apart, impatience, selfishness, jealousy and self-indulgence proving insurmountable barriers to the relationship.

Taurus and Taurus

Taurus Child/Taurus Mother

All same sign combinations tend to be either a match made in heaven or a disaster waiting to happen. Each loves seeing the other's positive traits writ large in the other, but at the same time resents the character flaws being displayed in glorious Technicolor. Certainly at the start of the relationship when mother and baby are developing the daily routines that will become part and parcel of the baby's life, they definitely sing very happily from the same hymn sheet. The mother provides that vital sense of security and the baby thrives in her tactile, patient and usually rather placid care. Both relish a relatively slow pace of life and neither is going to put the other under stress through differing needs in any shape or form. Mother and baby will love making things together, gardening, going shopping (especially when it's for clothes), entertaining friends and acting out every nursery rhyme in the book. The older child will learn to save money and to work methodically and, taking a leaf out of its mother's book, to give comfort and practical advice. Many a Taurean youngster comes up with the blindingly obvious! However, that stubborn streak and jealousy can cause havoc with these two. Both tend to take very entrenched positions and, rather than rationally discuss problems, build up all sorts of resentments. Differences of opinion, which at worst turn into hostility, usually remain well hidden for a long time (it could be years) – but when the dam breaks and tempers flare, the needle on the Richter scale can go right off the chart. Neither is particularly forgiving and a very unsettled peace sometimes turns into a permanent coolness in the relationship. Thankfully, this is a relatively rare scenario: for most Taurean mothers with a Taurean child, there is usually much love, understanding and mutual support together with an appreciation of the good things in life. Eating out together is something these two always enjoy and it's often over a good meal that problems can be aired and solved before an impasse becomes inevitable.

Taurus Child/Taurus Father

The Taurean father, who wants nothing more than to provide a comfortable and secure environment for his family, is absolutely delighted to find that he has a child who thrives in the cocoon he has created and seems to have no inclination towards dare-devilry or risk-taking. Father and child will develop a good routine and frequently have the week (or possibly month) mapped out as to when they spend time together and what they will be doing. Problems develop when the father, who works all hours to provide his family with the best of everything, has to cancel some arrangement. His Taurean child is not that flexible and doesn't look at the situation particularly rationally. What to another child is a slight disappointment becomes an issue of enormous importance to the little Bull. Jealousy can also rear its ugly head in this relationship, especially if the child starts to outshine the father. For the most part, however, these two usually plod along happily together, both appreciating the other's need for stability and a conservative approach to life.

Taurus Siblings

Taurus is very conventional and it's most unlikely that these siblings will ever be looking to break rules or to cause chaos. In fact, they'll probably make up all sorts of additional regulations for themselves so each knows exactly where the other stands and what is and isn't allowed. They are also very possessive and sharing anything from toys to knowledge is never going to be a feature of this relationship. Innate obstinacy is the major problem with these two: it is not unknown for two Taureans to carry on some minor feud for days or even weeks and to refuse to listen to any wise counsel. Neither has the ability, either, to pull the other out of negative thinking and the classic Taurean rut. On the plus side, their determination to succeed and their persistence in the face of difficulties make them formidable allies when they decide to work together. Their abundant charm, too, can melt opponents and give them the upper hand in negotiations. With many shared interests and a love of midnight feasts and a full fridge, these two usually jog along happily together, but often complain that the other is 'boring'!

Taurus and Gemini

Taurus Child/Gemini Mother

Earth and air together can generate an awful lot of dust after the initial attraction is over. Earth (Taurus) is fascinated by air's (Gemini) wit, logic and general busyness, while air admires earth's common sense and practical attitude to life. And there it quickly ends, both soon finding the other both a mystery and an annoyance. For the Taurean, who needs routine and a very steady and peaceful path through babyhood, it comes as a shock to realise that its mother is most unlikely to be on the same wavelength at all. Geminis rarely understand the meaning of timetables and a quiet life and are certainly not the most tactile people in the zodiac. For the Gemini mother who talks endlessly to her baby, has arranged a buzzing social life and much to-ing and fro-ing generally, it's depressing in the extreme to find that the more she arranges for her little Taurean the more distressed it seems to get. Taurus, however, just wants regular mealtimes, lots of cuddles and made to feel extremely safe rather than being rushed from pillar to post. On a basic level, Taurus needs to be swaddled whilst the Gemini mother can't imagine anything worse than being constrained. The Gemini mind is very quick but the attention span is invariably limited. With Taurus tending to learn at a slow and thorough pace and wanting to spend hours with the same toys, problems are likely even where play is concerned. Gemini loses patience and interest while Taurus becomes frustrated and then loses confidence. On the plus side Gemini is brilliant at encouraging Taurus to widen its interests and in dealing with her child's stubborn streak, usually by ignoring it. She's also able to teach Taurus that change isn't always to be feared. Gemini can also learn much from her child about consistency and perseverance. At worst, this relationship can suffer later on because Taurus sees its mother as slightly superficial and Gemini, despite her child's winning charm, thinks it's old before his or her time.

Taurus Child/Gemini Father

Whilst not in the Virgo league where it comes to dishing out criticism, the Gemini father can be both sharp tongued and quite damning in the face of his Taurean youngster's slightly pedantic approach. Taurus thus becomes unnerved and even more reluctant to take any kind of step into the dark. The Gemini thought patterns and action plans veer about all over the place, but if he can just slow down a bit, he'll find his little Taurean a very willing pupil and agog at its father's knowledge of seemingly everything, to say nothing of the witty manner in which he imparts these zillion interesting facts. Equally, Gemini should be thrilled at the painstaking way Taurus takes in this knowledge, committing it to paper and intent upon reading more about it. Taurus is never going to go through life at the Gemini pace and the more the father pressurises Taurus into running rather than walking, the more difficult this relationship will become. In later life, Taurus often takes on the role of parent in the face of what it sees as its Gemini father's inability to grow up!

Taurus/Gemini Siblings

These two either enchant or exasperate each other. Gemini stirs up and upsets all the Taurean routines and well-laid plans, and Taurus pours cold water on its Gemini sibling's inventive ideas. On the other hand, Taurus often enjoys and admires Gemini's lively approach to life whilst in turn Gemini comes to rely on Taurus' common sense and practicality to get it out of a scrape. With totally different interests, neither tends to tread on the other's toes. Both, in their own way, have the gift of the gab and the Taurean charm can be just as winning as the Gemini eloquence. Long silences and stalemate situations are rarely found in this relationship, which doesn't preclude deep and noisy disagreements. Gemini will be good at defusing the Taurean head of steam before it builds up too much whilst Taurus will hold Gemini to account and stop its sibling from promising more than he or she can deliver. Despite Taurus taking life too seriously and Gemini being too flippant, they usually maintain a friendship for life. This relationship often works better if Taurus is the older sibling.

Taurus and Cancer

Taurus Child/Cancer Mother

This is very often a supremely comfortable relationship for both mother and child. The Taurean baby, like any member of the sign, is extremely tactile and the Cancer mother likes nothing better than to hold her child. In fact the more they can be really close to each other, the better both will like it. Taurus craves a sense of security and with a Cancerian it's certainly found someone who will see that the home is an absolute haven of stability. The Cancer mother and her Taurean baby will happily establish a daily routine, which will involve lots of cuddles, excellent nourishment (Taureans are the 'foodies' of the zodiac and it starts young!) and plenty of sleep. On the whole Taureans look on exercise as a necessity rather than a pleasure, and most baby Bulls aren't bothered with the business of giving their lungs that much of a work out. Angered or frustrated, however, they can bellow with the best of them, but it's never their first line of attack! The nervous Cancerian mother has her self-esteem enormously boosted by her generally contented and placid baby, which in turn makes her confident in dealing with his or her needs. Between these two there is often a mutual admiration society. Like her, the Taurean child has no wish to rush headlong through life and prefers a gentler, more sure-footed approach. These two can happily spend time together, whether cooking, making all sorts of decorations, or encouraging the Taurean's latent creative skills, which normally manifest as anything from sculpting the best mud pies to being a naturally good singer. Both Cancer and Taurus are extremely green-fingered and often find a great sense companionship and fun in the garden. Later in life, the Taurean child will feel it has always been carefully nurtured by its Cancerian mother, and in return will prove to be extremely understanding of her deep emotions and her worries (real or imagined) and be ready with a great deal of practical support.

Taurus Child/Cancer Father

Cancer can be one of the most changeable signs of the zodiac and Taurus one of the most stubborn and these negative characteristics often emerge in this relationship. Most baby Bulls thrive in a thoroughly stable environment where they are encouraged to develop slowly but surely. Cancer is ambitious by nature but also very protective, so his Taurean feels slightly nonplussed when it's almost too molly-coddled one minute and then shoved onto a grown-up stage the next. The Taurean reaction is to stop being accommodating in any way and the Crab is no match for the Bull in that kind of mood! Attitudes to money can also be a bone of contention between father and child. Cancer is a natural hoarder and rarely enters the financial zone marked 'extravagant' and Taurus is born to save and then spend, preferably in the luxury market. Both, however, have an innate love of home and family and the domestic scene will always give them a very strong bond. When the Cancer father and Taurus child get along well, as they usually do, each becomes a source of pride and comfort to the other and strong emotional ties hold the relationship together if it goes through any testing times.

Taurus/Cancer Siblings

In their own way each of these two is possessive: Cancer about the mother and Taurus about his or her belongings. Both need to learn to share, and the sooner they realise that there are plenty of possessions, and above all enough love, to go around, the better. The other potential problems with these two are the rather fixed opinions of the Taurean (which tend to surface at a very early age) and the over-sensitivity of the Cancerian, which is masked by cutting remarks but can lead to tearful dramas. Both, in their own way, also remember slights and grievances, which, if not dealt with quickly, can lead to all sorts of long-term problems. Generally, however, these two usually rub along quite happily together, are very supportive of each other and, as they get older, the Taurean can be a beacon of pragmatism and practicality for the more emotional and insecure Cancer, who, in turn, is a haven of kindness and comfort for Taurus.

Taurus and Leo

Taurus Child/Leo Mother

The Leo mother and her Taurus baby are both warm-hearted and abundantly loyal and, as long as the little Bull never forgets that its mother knows best in all things and Leo remembers that Taurus just can't be pushed around, this relationship happily prospers. Leo will certainly provide Taurus with exactly the desired element of comfort together with the security blanket that comes from a well-organised environment. Taurus repays the compliment by being a wonderfully placid and appreciative baby. After all, Leo needs to be able to show off her offspring in the best possible light: she doesn't want an attention-seeking child stealing all her best scenes, unless it's on her terms! Both mother and child possess a very creative streak and often spend much time together producing artistic masterpieces with pasta, leaves and various sparkly shapes. She'll also be very encouraging of her child's efforts but forgets that her baby likes to do things slowly and thoroughly. In her efforts to propel her Taurean to the top of the class she can become very pushy. The baby then feels pressurised and digs in its heels. Leo is just as determined and, because she sees non-compliance as a total affront to her authority and won't drop the issue, suddenly there's stalemate. Taurus is opinionated and Leo dogmatic, so it's not surprising that there are often blazing rows between the two. Neither, however, tends to sulk. Leo will certainly get over the drama long before Taurus and is often adept at jollying her child out of its trenchant mood. Anything that upsets the Taurean's daily rhythm, however small, could be a cause for an outburst just as much as defying her wishes brings out Leo's intolerance. As Taurus gets older it's much more trusting of Leo's skills at taking her child down the right path. In return, Leo sets smaller tests for her child and is enthusiastic about all its achievements. Spending sprees are the lifeblood of both signs and many a teenage Taurean has been thankful for a Leo mother!

Taurus Child/Leo Father

In keeping with the idea of the King of the Jungle, the Leo father likes to see himself as the alpha male. He struts his stuff, often with much roaring, which he likes to think is really quite intimidating. It could be alarming to, perhaps, a Pisces, but his Taurean child is pretty good at bellowing back and there can be some fairly spectacular disagreements, particularly with a Taurus son who won't be pushed around or asked to make his father look good. A daughter is better at dealing with her sometimes bossy father: the Taurean charm and generally placid nature, together with her ability to see that much of her father's bombast is just a cover for a more sensitive nature, can turn the Lion into a cuddly domesticated moggy! On the plus side, these two often share creative interests and both love the social scene. Leo will also find even the smallest Taurean appreciative of his often rather glamorous lifestyle. If no effort is made to find a way through two entrenched viewpoints, father and child can end up miles apart, each seeing the other as didactic and self-indulgent.

Taurus/Leo Siblings

On the surface, these two have much in common. Both are very loving and enjoy spending money. Neither copes with change that easily and, although Leo often gives the impression of being ready to leap into new ventures, it's all a front. Whilst Leo will always be very protective of its Taurus sibling, it can be insufferably interfering, something the Taurean really resents. Equally the Taurus practicality and common sense will frequently bail Leo out of trouble but its jealousy and possessiveness can irk the more open and generous Lion. However, rigid thinking and a certain amount of intolerance are inherent in both. They will probably spend hours talking *at* each other and disagreements often abound. Much door slamming and long silences can mark this relationship, and it is invariably Leo, whose temper is sharper but shorter, who has to end the hostilities. Very often these two enjoy a lasting friendship, helped no end by numerous shopping sprees! If, however, they remain strongly and stubbornly opinionated, and they can't agree to differ, then both, later on, will probably choose to meet only when necessary.

Taurus and Virgo

Taurus Child/Virgo Mother

Two earth signs are a great source of comfort to each other, and the Virgo/Taurus relationship is often one of the best where mother and baby are concerned. Virgo runs a very efficient ship and her little Taurean not only feels totally cosseted but also instinctively realises that Virgo magically anticipates its every wish and whim. Her own need for order and a good routine is exactly that of her baby and both tend to thrive in a cosy togetherness, which allays her own fears of not coming up to scratch and her baby's worries about a lack of stability. Just as important for Taurus is the fact that its mother has no wish to rush through life at a hectic pace. They both like to take things at a sensible rate and Virgo, an excellent teacher, gives her baby time to take in anything new, thus giving the Taurean great confidence. Her intelligent and flexible attitude to life also deflects her child's stubbornness: she'll always appeal to its innate pragmatism. Into every perfect relationship a little rain must fall and for these two it's the Virgo tendency to worry and fuss, which can be slightly unnerving to Taurus who then sees its mother as not quite so capable as it thought. She can, from time to time, get her priorities wrong, putting housework and keeping the place clean and tidy way ahead of the needs of her baby. With the Taurean, a trencherman from birth and eager to feed itself, Virgo loses patience with her baby's efforts to decorate the walls, floor and itself. Soon, her fretting over the state of the chairs, carpets or anything else makes her child feel insecure. Virgo equally can become irritated by her child's possessiveness and sometimes rather clinging approach and she can also be surprised by the Taurean determination. Her baby has staying power which is both admirable and yet annoying, especially when she wants to change tack quite quickly. Despite these relatively small problems, this is usually an enriching relationship for both and, as Taurus grows up, they often become great friends.

Taurus Child/Virgo Father

The Virgo father and his Taurean child are both relatively conservative by nature so neither is going to have to cope with any over-the-top behaviour from the other, let alone outlandish ideas and liberal attitudes. Virgo will certainly appreciate his child's slow and diligent approach to learning and, as both have a very practical streak, will enjoy making and building things – anything from a tower of wooden bricks to the latest complicated construction kit. Virgo, however, can be over-critical, and it comes easily to the father to correct his child and to set quite ridiculously high standards. Rather than let his youngster make its own model, rough edges and all, Virgo constantly seeks perfection. To start with, Taurus appreciates the lesson, but after a time gets fed up and opts out of any joint endeavour. Taurus also sets great store by a secure domestic scene and can often feel let down by a workaholic father it rarely sees, but, on the whole, this is usually a loving and sound relationship that improves with age and mutual understanding.

Taurus/Virgo Siblings

As with other Taurus/Virgo relationships, these two tend to get on very well, despite the Virgo sibling's rather fussy approach to life and the Taurean's rigid thinking and possessiveness. Each has loads of common sense and a down to earth attitude and neither wants to become involved in emotional dramas. Sometimes Virgo can think its Taurus sibling is a bit of a bore, as it doesn't accommodate sudden change and a different way of thinking all that quickly. Taurus, in turn, gets irritated by Virgo's sometimes prissy and carping behaviour, to say nothing of its endless worries. In times of difficulty, it's often Virgo's quicker mind that gets them both out of trouble, but Taurus usually proves an absolute rock when it comes to calming the Virgo fears and coming up with practical solutions to a problem. Within the family each has a its own need. Taurus appreciates demonstrative affection while Virgo thrives on verbal communication. If Virgo criticism and Taurean jealousy don't ruin this relationship, then these two are friends for life.

Taurus and Libra

Taurus Child/Libra Mother

Taurus and Libra are ruled by Venus. Therefore, harmony, beauty and love are important to both signs, a wonderful starting point for this mother and baby relationship. For the placid little Taurean, coming to an environment which is probably very stylish and calm is just bliss, to say nothing of the fact that its mother is going to do her utmost to ensure that her baby thinks she is just the very best in the world. Early on, mother and baby seem to bathe each other in charm, smiles and eagerness to please, although it's not long before Taurus starts to sense that its mother finds it difficult to make decisions and tries to juggle far too many balls in the air. Libra, who is friendly to everyone, equally finds it hard to cope when Taurus gets fretful if she's out of sight or devoting her attention to someone else. Because she has a wonderful ability to float through life in a thoroughly easy-going and sociable manner, she fails to understand her baby's need for firm foundations and boundaries as well as endless reassurance in the form of close contact with its mother. Taurus also thrives in a fairly disciplined environment, which Libra usually finds difficult to establish. She wants to be liked and fears that rules and regulations will put her at odds with her Taurean. It's quite the opposite; it's a lack of direction that upsets the Taurean! Libra can also find herself being outmanoeuvred and almost bullied by her very determined two-year-old Taurean who soon senses that her 'anything for a quiet life' approach allows the toddler all sorts of licence. Both Libra and Taurus can be self-indulgent in the extreme and revel in the 'naughty but nice' ethos. The Taurean can be assured of treats galore from babyhood onwards. Sometimes Taurus wishes for a mother with a slightly more 'feet on the ground' attitude and frequently Libra hopes her child's obdurate attitude will mellow, but it's rare for this relationship to come to grief.

Taurus Child/Libra Father

The Taurus child, who is both persistent and determined, frequently needs a father who is firm, fair and more than able to deal with his youngster's obstinate stance. Fair the Libran father certainly is, but whether he's able to stand up to Taurus in one of its more inflexible moods, let alone show who's calling the shots, is quite another story. Whilst there will always be much mutual love and affection in this relationship, as father and child will delight in each other's generally charismatic and relaxed nature, the Libran can easily find that his wishes are ignored and idealism trampled on. In turn, Taurus becomes unnerved by a lack of firm guidance and resorts to underhand tactics to get his or her own way. Jealousy can also be a problem in this relationship: Taurus just doesn't understand its father's genuine liking for all and sundry and often feels less than special; this can be a particular problem for the Libran father and Taurean daughter. From the earliest years these two will resolve their differences in the nearest shopping mall. Call it bribery or the joy of giving, father and child love to spend money!

Taurus/Libra Siblings

Sometimes the placid, immovable Taurean feels it's trying to chase an ethereal sibling who doesn't commit to anything and has no firm ideas. Libra, on the other hand, thinks Taurus is devoid of any lightness of touch and takes life far too seriously. Although bound by a sociable nature, an abundance of charm and financial extravagance, these two often find that they function better in separate arenas. Taurus finds it very difficult to cope with the Libran changeability and gets fed up with having to deal with the practical realities of the subsequent problems. Libra gets annoyed at constantly having to sweet talk Taurus out of its intransigence or jealousy and then having to use its innate diplomacy to explain away its sibling's moody behaviour. Both, however, hate conflict and often suffer in silence whilst at the same time reluctantly appreciating how much they benefit from the other's qualities. As they grow older, the arts, good food and a little bit of luxury keep these two thinking along the same lines.

Taurus and Scorpio

Taurus Child/Scorpio Mother

Taurus and Scorpio are opposite signs in the zodiac and, as with all oppositions, there is an enormous attraction between the two. Scorpio loves the gurgling contentment that radiates from her little Taurean, whilst her baby instinctively knows its mother will provide a thoroughly stable and ordered environment in which it will flourish. There'll certainly be no lack of firm rules from Scorpio. To start with Taurus feels thoroughly comfortable with these clear guidelines and the very obvious support it gets from its mother. Problems start to arise once Taurus wants to make its own decisions and set out its own stall: Scorpio hasn't bargained for a two-year-old whose determination is more than a match for her own forcefulness. When in difficulty, Scorpio tends to retreat into her own private world of very deep feelings, which probably include resentment at being ignored and plans to assert authority. Taurus understands and prefers the sensible, common sense approach and becomes unnerved by its mother's silent and secretive nature, let alone the sometimes convoluted route she takes to getting her own way. She will never, of course, rush her little Bull into anything it's not ready for: she recognises her child's need for security. Her magnetic personality is also very exciting to Taurus who laps up her passionate approach to life and benefits hugely from the excitement she generates. This will never be a totally easy relationship: each is uncompromising and Scorpio hates coming up against the protective brick wall built by her Taurean child when the going gets tough. Taurus can't fathom its mother's extremely deep emotions, whilst she often believes her child has no feelings at all. Jealousy and possessiveness from both can result in each becoming its own worst enemy. Sometimes these two drift apart in later years, but more often they stick together and become quite a team. Each realises that the other's star qualities far outweigh their maddening faults.

Taurus Child/Scorpio Father

The Scorpio father frequently has its child's life mapped out from the moment of birth, setting up a game plan for his young Taurean sooner rather than later. Taurus, whilst admiring its father's sheer force of personality, loving his involvement with its interests and basking in a lot of attention, soon comes to realise that it's often being pushed down a path it doesn't want to travel. Stand offs between this father and child can be earth shattering and the more difficult the situation, the more Scorpio becomes didactic and Taurus digs in its heels. On the plus side, each admires the other's persistence and perseverance and the warm-hearted Taurean, with its broad shoulders, is usually most forgiving of its father's emotional outbursts or stony silences. The Scorpio father and Taurean son, however, often go through life in a permanent state of readiness for war: a Taurean daughter is usually better at coping with her father's manipulation and powerful feelings.

Taurus/Scorpio Siblings

Like all opposite signs of the zodiac Taurus and Scorpio share many of the same characteristics. Both can be jealous, resentful and possessive, and each can be as obstinate and fixed in opinion as the other. They also have an inbuilt dislike of change. Each, therefore, understands where the other is coming from and, although the rigidity and inability to share can lead to endless squabbles when they are young, they often operate a mutual support system and develop an amazingly loyal bond as they get older, becoming each other's closest confidante. Their chief problems arise through Scorpio's very private nature, which Taurus sees as secretive and vengeful, and the Taurean self-indulgence which Scorpio regards as appalling and totally unnecessary. Taurus also finds it difficult to comprehend its sibling's strong intuition, whilst Scorpio gets tired of the Taurean common sense. At worst these two hate what they see in each other and keep out of their sibling's way, though never forgetting to throw in a frequent barbed comment about the other's failings. At best, Taurus learns a lot from Scorpio about people's finer feelings whilst Scorpio comes to rely on the Bull's practicality.

Taurus and Sagittarius

Taurus Child/Sagittarius Mother

Astrologically, Sagittarius and Taurus are radically different and this mother and baby relationship is not always easy for either of them. The Taurean baby has come into the world hoping for the security of an established routine, plenty of good food, slow and steady progress through life and, most importantly of all, a thoroughly tactile mother. The Sagittarian mother is not too hot on the organisational skills, rarely considers cooking as her most cherished activity, expects everyone to move at quite a pace and values good conversation way above hugs and general closeness. There is clearly a potential problem from the start! The lack of a structured timetable can soon make the Taurean baby quite fractious as it immediately feels somewhat unsure about everything. The sense that it is being rushed into things, or being asked to live at a faster rate than is to its liking, inevitably brings out the Taurean stubbornness. That, in turn, triggers the Sagittarian impatience. Her skills are in reasoning and in an intellectual approach to problems: her child's needs are much more physical – food, cuddles, and a bit of crooning in the ear! However, despite an often rocky start, these two can eventually develop an excellent relationship. Thanks to a Sagittarian mother, Taurus will never be allowed to get into a rut, let alone take a plodding and over-cautious approach to life. She will benefit from her child's common sense, pragmatism and responsible nature. Some Sagittarian mothers feel with a Taurean child that the roles are reversed: in many ways the child becomes the parent! Taureans are also extremely affectionate and it is a rare baby Bull who does not love its bright and extrovert mother just as much as Sagittarius is charmed by her warm-hearted and determined child. A fine line exists in this relationship between complete misunderstanding and an appreciation of each other's qualities. It often takes time and skill on both sides to judge the situation accurately.

Taurus Child/Sagittarius Father

This is an astrological relationship that has the potential for success or disaster and a lot will depend on how the Sagittarian father handles his baby Bull in the early stages. It's easy to forget, when the Taurean child is a fund of charm, gentleness and affection, that it can also be stubborn in the extreme, opinionated, lazy and, when goaded beyond endurance, prone to a fearsome temper. All this is at odds with the much more active and easy-going father, who prides himself on his energy, open-mindedness and adaptability. It is important for Sagittarius to understand that his Taurean responds best to slow and patient teaching, and, as Sagittarius is one of the zodiac's natural educators, this should be well within the father's capabilities. Taurus thrives on routines and 'immovable' situations, whether it's a chess game every Friday or an outing on Sunday, and a wise Sagittarian father will move heaven and earth to keep these dates. Given a secure base, the Taurean child will blossom and start to appreciate its father's wide interests and positive approach to life. A thoughtless Sagittarian will quickly alienate the Taurean and they'll struggle to develop a relationship at all.

Taurus/Sagittarius Siblings

The jovial and versatile Sagittarian will find it very difficult to understand the possessive and obstinate Taurean, who in turn will see its Sagittarius sibling as irresponsible and restless and, even worse, rather disrespectful about the security of home and family. On the plus side, because these two will have totally different attitudes to life, both will have the possibility of being kings of their own particular empires which will be mutually satisfactory. Problems tend to come about if they are encouraged to join in the same activities and pit themselves against each other in any way. Handled well, these two can be a great help to each other. The pragmatic Taurean can ground its Sagittarian sibling and save it from its worst excesses, and Sagittarius can open up a more exciting lifestyle for the more circumspect Taurean. Both ultimately enjoy the good things in life and, if this relationship is properly nurtured when they are young, as adults they often find each other to be excellent company.

Taurus and Capricorn

Taurus Child/Capricorn Mother

Capricorn and Taurus value stability and security, are conservative by nature and are concerned with the practicalities of life. In its Capricorn mother, the little Taurean will have found a perfect ally and these two feel naturally attuned to each other. She truly appreciates its tactile sense, its need for a settled routine and its dislike of being rushed through the day – or life generally for that matter. In turn, Capricorn is utterly charmed by her placid, contented baby, who thinks she is efficiency, understanding and love personified. The affectionate Taurean invariably warms the mother's cooler emotions and Capricorn often seems to develop a softer side through contact with her little Bull. Although the Capricorn mother and Taurus child are never likely to reach a major impasse, as with every relationship there will be some stickier moments. It will soon dawn on the mother that her baby perhaps doesn't share her diligence. From an early age the Taurean can show signs of laziness: even in a pre-school group Capricorn will want her child to do well while Taurus will just want to be popular! It can also be incredibly stubborn and from an early age Taurus is quite happy to stand up to its mother's authority. Whilst on the one hand she will admire her child's strong will, on the other she'll be exasperated at its inflexibility. The Taurean temper, slow to get going but thunderous when it comes to the boil, is completely foreign to the more self-contained Capricorn. Taurus also tends to gravitate at the earliest age towards good food and luxury. The mother, with thrift and prudence her watchwords, can find it very annoying to think her child is becoming obsessed with things she thinks are unimportant: money, and how it is spent, often becomes an issue between these two. Generally, however, this mother/child relationship is one of shared values and affections and a mutual determination to build sound foundations for the future.

Taurus Child/Capricorn Father

From the start, Capricorn is delighted with his affectionate and very contented child, who clearly thinks the world of its father. Both are determined, patient and persevering by nature and therefore tend to have much in common, including shared interests. Taurus is also comforted by the idea that its father takes a fairly cautious approach to most things and is not likely to rush it into new ventures. Nevertheless, it will soon become apparent to the father that his baby Bull is far more social than he is and is far more concerned with the good things in life. Capricorn is often dismayed to see a rather hedonistic attitude developing at a very young age. In contrast, Taurus views its father as stuffy and miserly and the father's concepts of duty and discipline often fall on stony ground. Because both tend to have a rather rigid outlook, these two can also have major disagreements: a mediator is often needed. These are glitches, however, in a relationship that is usually a very happy one (particularly between a Capricorn father and Taurean daughter). This duo has much fun together and understands each other all too well.

Taurus/Capricorn Siblings

The Capricorn/Taurus sibling relationship often produces this scenario: Capricorn does all the hard work and the Taurean, sitting back and smiling sweetly and affectionately, takes all the credit and praise! Capricorn often finds it very difficult to compete with its sibling's natural charm and usually rather envies its more laid-back style. Taurus secretly admires the Capricorn ambition but becomes irritated with its pessimism and overly cautious approach to life. There is also a problem with the Taurean possessiveness. Capricorn can often feel pushed aside by Taurus when it comes to its mother's affections and parental attentions generally. However, on the plus side, these two have a genuine understanding of each other and are thankful that neither is particularly adventurous. Taurus can definitely bring Capricorn out of its sometimes rather bleak shell whilst Capricorn can teach its sibling about making the most of its talents. They both also have a good sense of humour and laughter can often break a stalemate situation.

Taurus and Aquarius

Taurus Child/Aquarius Mother

The baby Taurean is one of the most sensual in the zodiac. The Aquarian mother, on the other hand, sees herself more as communicator than comforter and from the earliest stages of this relationship there can be very different agendas emanating from mother and baby. On the plus side, Aquarius and Taurus are 'fixed' signs. Both, therefore, have an inbuilt dislike of change, a strong attachment to the status quo and a need for consistency. However, the baby Taurus seeks its comfort and security in a highly stable and structured environment and in much physical contact and closeness, all notions that do not come easily to its Aquarian mother, who is much happier in the realm of ideas and prefers to operate within a fairly flexible daily timetable. She is also one of the most gregarious people in the zodiac and sees it as absolutely normal to pass her baby around friends and family so that it is introduced to the social scene and everyone can have a cuddle. To her baby, however, this is a nightmare. The little Taurean is not only very possessive about its mother but also relishes constant attachment. Thus, the mother resents the curtailment of her freedom of action and the baby feels stressed and insecure. She often has to learn the hard way that her baby just needs to be held close, a basic instinct to which its strongly tactile nature best responds. As her baby grows, up the Aquarian will also find that it prefers to make things rather than indulge in chatter, has a love affair with food rather than intellectual ideas and sometimes seems to prefer the conventional to the new. Both signs can also be extremely stubborn and a battle of wills between these two is often a lifelong facet of their relationship. Despite many differences in character, however, mother and child are often very supportive of each other. The Taurean is fascinated by its mother's individuality and the Aquarian respects her child's constancy and quiet application to getting the best out of life.

Taurus Child/Aquarius Father

The Aquarian father can be a wonderful teacher but also a demanding one, and whilst some signs respond brilliantly to that kind of parental guidance, Taurus often finds it quite difficult. By nature the Taurean child tends to take life slowly and surely which is in stark contrast to the Aquarian quick wit and unnerving mixture of rigid thinking and inconsistency. The Aquarian can easily lose patience with what he sees as the rather timid, cautious and even lazy approach of his Taurus child, who equally can feel rattled, unsure and often unappreciated around its father. Both can be incredibly obstinate and there can be a lot of digging in of heels as the child gets older. It is usually the Aquarian who has to make the first move to break the deadlock. Although these two usually have very different interests and outlooks on life, with patience, perseverance and much give and take, a good relationship can be established. Taurus benefits from its father's progressive outlook and humanitarian spirit whilst the Aquarian learns to admire his child's sense of purpose and warm-hearted personality.

Taurus/Aquarius Siblings

Both Aquarius and Taurus like the status quo and routine but in many other ways are very different. Taurus finds it extremely difficult to share and is possessive about everything: to Aquarius, the idea of not being right, or having to apologise, is totally alien to its thinking. Taurus tends to take life rather cautiously and needs a lot of encouragement: Aquarius is trusting and independent. However, both tend to be very friendly and often thrive together on the social scene. They also listen to reason: Aquarius responds to logic and Taurus to the practical side of any requests or rules. So they will usually back each other up in times of difficulty. The Taurean, with its very pragmatic attitude to life, can give a great deal of stability to the more wayward Aquarian and, in return, Aquarius gingers-up the more stolid Taurus and injects a much-needed sense of adventure. If both are made aware of the other's qualities and how much they can gain from each other, they can be lifelong friends and allies. If allowed to retreat into their respective corners, each will possibly grow up feeling totally misunderstood by the other.

Taurus and Pisces

Taurus Child/Pisces Mother

The early days enjoyed by the Pisces mother and her Taurean baby are usually blissful. Both take a very gentle and loving approach to life, and the compassionate Piscean will do everything in her power to make her baby feel it's the centre of her very existence. Unfortunately, probably everything else in the Piscean's life is just as important: focus and organisation are usually singularly lacking in her particular world and once the sometimes chaotic first few weeks after the birth are over, problems can loom large. Taurus craves solid foundations to its life and likes to know exactly what it can and can't do. Pisces happily does things in her own time and at her own pace and finds routine of any kind almost impossible to think about, let alone adhere to. Without the comfort blanket of a set timetable, the baby Bull becomes fractious. Pisces then worries and flaps about even more, creating something akin to panic in her baby, all of which eventually results in a thoroughly unsettled environment for both of them. As a toddler needing firm guidance and sensible boundaries, the Taurus stability and security sometimes feels quite threatened by its mother's rather vague attitude and seemingly total inability to set a course and stick with it. Eventually, through a mixture of stubbornness and winning charm, Taurus runs rings around its mother who loathes getting involved in argument and hassle. The practical little Bull works out early on how to create its own immovable base! Despite this particular glitch in the relationship, these two usually enjoy a close companionship and share many interests. Pisces will never push her Taurean into situations it finds difficult, and her child will love the fact that she's a brilliant storyteller and has such artistic talent. She will admire her child's determination to succeed and its reliability: as it grows up the child frequently becomes the rock around which its mother can happily swim!

Taurus Child/Pisces Father

The Piscean father easily falls into the trap of believing that allowing his child free rein helps develop its potential. With a Taurean child there could be some interesting results. First, the child will become incredibly self-indulgent, and lazy to boot, second it will panic as it feels both insecure and uncomfortable if given neither sense of direction nor a good set of rules and third, its innate determination could turn into pushiness and inconsideration. For Pisces, it will pay enormous dividends to give a lot of attention to his Taurean son or daughter. Making specific times to do things together, teaching it to share and assisting it to develop its naturally warm-hearted and reliable nature will bring great results. The young Taurean loves to help and has common sense in abundance. Many a Pisces father has been taken to task by a three-or four-year-old for going the wrong way, getting timing wrong or forgetting the swimming gear! If Taurus feels neglected during childhood, it can fuel a lasting resentment which leads to estrangement, but much more often love and affection is the hallmark of this relationship.

Taurus/Pisces Siblings

Neither Taurus nor Pisces want to set the world on fire and both thrive in a relatively calm domestic situation. Taurus can become anxious about the Piscean vagueness, convinced that muddle and idealism will get it into trouble, while Pisces chafes against the Bull's over-organised approach and possessive nature. At the same time, Pisces knows full well that Taurus will be its champion and save it from its own worst scrapes, whilst Taurus knows that it can get its own way over anything that really matters. Pisces can also be a great help to Taurus in getting the Bull out of a rut and by making it less fearful of change: the Fish is by far the more adaptable of the two. Equally, Taurus can help to ground Pisces and teach it to stick with situations rather than just swim away at the first sign of difficulty. The little Fish might sometimes feel that its selflessness is being taken advantage of, just as Taurus thinks that Pisces is fickle and unreliable, but generally these two get on extremely well and help each other out for years on end.

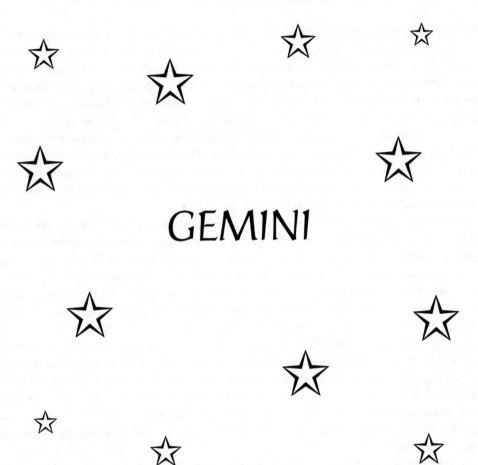

GEMINI

The Gemini Child 0-5 Years

The Gemini baby arrives in the world alert, full of curiosity and desperate to make its views known. Even in the early days, having taken in its immediate surroundings and given its parents the once over, it'll turn its attention to other people and to what's going on in the wider environment. Gemini's inquisitive nature, quick intelligence and genuine interest in the world are obvious from the start, as are its low boredom threshold and inability to concentrate on anyone or anything for any length of time! This is one of the zodiac's liveliest, wittiest and most versatile children, and for those caring for a Gemini it's often as though they are dealing with more than one person. That's quite possible. After all, Gemini is the sign of the Twins and one bundle of energy and chat seems to be everywhere at once, conducting several interesting and simultaneous conversations and planning at least two separate timetables for the next day.

All Gemini children thrive on action and change, which can be thoroughly exhausting for those around them. They do not play quietly and sensibly with a particular toy for more than a few minutes but rarely become possessive about anything either. It's also a given that just as a Gemini seems to become absorbed in something, and perhaps a grateful parent or carer thinks there might be a peaceful hour or so, rest assured the new interest will be discarded and the Geminian quest for novelty starts all over again! With a naturally high activity level, Gemini wants to be on the move and usually learns to crawl and to walk long before the other signs. After all, walking definitely quickens the pace of life and, in the child's eyes, means it doesn't have to wait for the 'old slowcoaches' to carry it around! As for talking, it's been doing that from the moment of birth, but hasn't found itself understood that easily. Learning to communicate is vital to Gemini and it won't need too much encouragement or coaxing for the baby to come out with its first words, and probably a first sentence or two. This is the real Gemini skill and the sooner it can start to chatter, the better.

Even in the nursery Gemini needs intellectual stimulation. Not for this child an over-abundance of hugs and swaddling: it thrives on a general journey of discovery around its own small world as well as being talked to, read to and sung to. Gemini assimilates information very quickly and instinctively knows that reading matter of all kinds is going to be vital in its quest for knowledge. More often than not, it's found asleep in a cot clutching its first cloth book in preference to a favourite teddy or other comforter. Gemini adults tend to read the back of the cereal packet rather than nothing at all, and that habit starts young. If the picky Gemini baby could exist on a diet of air and words it would: getting it interested in food can be a trying business and it's often more comfortable with the little and often routine and grazing than with the three meals a day option.

Parents waiting for their little Gemini to utter those magic first words 'Mummy' and 'Daddy' are often disappointed. It usually finds 'why?' 'who?' 'what?' 'where?' and 'when?' much more to its liking and is the start of a lifelong fascination with facts and part and parcel of its need to know about everything. Gemini is never likely to go in for great intellectual discussion and is rarely interested in looking at issues in depth but this is a child who will turn up at the school gates with an amazing knowledge of the world and of life generally and will come out with some very perceptive comments, not all of them particularly charitable. From a very young age, Gemini becomes the master of the witty one-liner. Logical and rational, the Gemini child truly understands anything that clearly makes sense, which is why it usually responds best to appeals to its intelligence. This is not a sign that easily cooperates with the 'do as I say because I say so' scenario!

Whilst it is thoroughly enchanting for a parent to see its Gemini child taking such an interest in everything and putting so much verve into each and every day, it is also a bit of worry. Just as Aries' boundless sense of adventure has gently to be reined in, so does the Gemini inconsistency and tendency to scatter its energies. Gemini boys and girls are the zodiac's natural multi-taskers and having to concentrate on one thing at a time never brings out the best in them; but without learning to finish tasks, to stick with situations it finds difficult and to do more than skim the surface of subjects, Gemini can find the routine of nursery classes and the new disciplines of the first year at school extremely taxing. At worst it's always in trouble: at best it feels frustrated and angry at having its whirlwind intelligence dampened down. As one of the children in the class with probably most, if not all, the answers, it can also become irritated at having its intelligence seemingly ignored when, hand constantly up, it's not always the pupil picked to give the other three-, four- or five-year-olds the benefit of its knowledge and opinions. Understanding about taking turns, and that other people may have something to say, is not easy for a Gemini child, who always finds it far easier to talk than to listen.

Gemini's natural linguistic skills also mean that it finds learning languages very easy and with its gift of the gab Gemini also knows exactly how to bluff its way through testing questions and out of extremely tight corners. Many a parent has had the wind very firmly taken out of its sails by Gemini's utterly plausible and confident statements, which, on reflection, they realise bear little relation to the truth! Whilst not in the realms of Pisces escapist fantasies, the Gemini eloquence and very quick thinking get them out of a lot of trouble, but equally set them up for much hassle when they are found out! Their legendary ability to sell starts early, whether it's their own innocence or half a dozen pencils they have 'borrowed' from home or the classroom! With a natural manual dexterity, Gemini children are often brilliant at magic too and, whilst probably not operating the three card trick in the nursery class, will more than likely be brilliant at snap and any other game that requires good hand and eye coordination.

Gemini and Virgo are both ruled by the same planet: Mercury. In myth, Mercury was the winged messenger of the gods who zipped hither and thither and frequently interfered where he wasn't wanted. Virgo is well known for its perfectionist tendencies and Gemini is not far behind when it comes to criticism. Usually, because the damning remark is delivered with a considerable amount of unconscious wit, the little Gemini thinks its comments don't hurt more delicate souls. As no Gemini is truly at home with its emotions, this child has to be taught about feelings and how straight talking and barbed comments can upset people. Just as some signs have to learn to be rational, Gemini has to learn about sensitivity and empathy.

With both physical and mental action the prime motivation for a young Gemini it is not surprising that it tends to fidget. Sitting still for any great length of time is not part of its life plan any more than spending time on its own and, pushed into doing something that is so alien to its nature, often results in a lot of stress. Gemini likes to be constantly on the go and positively relishes the challenge of a totally hectic timetable. Being one of the most adaptable members of the zodiac it has no problems whatsoever in switching from one situation to the next. By two or three years old they have probably also mastered the remote control and the phone and frequently decide for themselves exactly what they are going to watch or listen to, or who they are going to call! This constant round of challenge and change can, however, result in over-excitement and nervous tension. Every Gemini child should be encouraged to spend a short time every day just resting, if only to gather its thoughts and to calm itself down. In fact, a quiet twenty minutes with a roomful of books or notepad and pencil keeps most Geminians very happy.

The Gemini child is a delightful, chatty and lively companion who is more than likely to be ahead of the rest in the talking stakes but perhaps finding it less easy on the artistic side or the practicalities. That is not to say that the young Gemini lacks a creative side or can't cope with the mundane necessities of life. It's just that he or she usually hasn't the patience to produce a detailed masterpiece and simply isn't interested in organising routines or getting things ship shape. It'll be one of the friendliest children at the school gate and after its first day in the classroom will know exactly who is who and who said what to whom. Of course, even more important is what the little Gemini said to everyone else – particularly if he or she was able to impart some nugget of knowledge to the teacher. Although life with a Gemini child will sometimes be a puzzle – the changeability and superficiality interspersed with the humour, intelligence and wonderful spontaneity – it will never be dull. This youngster knows how to entertain and how to keep its family, and the world at large, on its toes.

Gemini and Aries

Gemini Child/Aries Mother

In order to thrive fire needs air and Gemini knows how to fan the Aries flames. The cool Gemini air will also be pleasantly warmed by Aries, thus setting the scene for what is usually one of the most stimulating and fun relationships in the zodiac. At birth, the baby Gemini is noticeably alert and interested in its new world and isn't in any way alarmed by the excitement and bustle surrounding its mother, nor her apparently 'try it and see' attitude to child-rearing. Aries immediately feels totally accepted for what she is: a good mother who will nurture her baby's talents, especially when it comes to communication skills, and giving it plenty of scope for exploration. The action-packed Aries day suits Gemini perfectly. This baby is naturally curious and inquisitive, with an attention span that makes the Aries impatience look more like stoic perseverance! Mother and baby will thoroughly enjoy a frantic social life, outings and anything to do with teaching and learning. Possible problems can arise if Aries finds the endless questions from her little Gemini too demanding: answers become curt or the child's queries dismissed. After all, Aries does like to put her own interests first and a gossip on the phone often takes priority over the intellectual demands of her baby. But she has forgotten the Gemini cunning: one way or another her baby will get her attention. This is one of the most logical children in the zodiac and it quickly works out just how things can and should be done! Because both mother and child are naturally good communicators, their relationship is marked by endless chatter, often peppered with unusually witty remarks from the Gemini. Very often, however, mother and baby talk *at* each other, so real understanding can be lacking, and, as neither sign is particularly attuned to its emotions, the relationship is happily conducted more on the surface than in depth. Gemini will always keep its mother young at heart whilst Aries will encourage, inspire and applaud her child's every action.

Gemini Child/Aries Father

The potential for a good relationship between an Aries father and Gemini child is excellent. Both enjoy a fairly frantic pace to life and love to be out and about. Although they talk endlessly, whether they ever really communicate is a moot point as neither is a particularly good listener. Gemini can become quite frustrated if it doesn't get its father's full attention, just as Aries feels his own leadership skills and ambitions for his child are not really appreciated. In trying to enforce his will, Aries often suffers being flattened by his child's perceptive remarks or, worse, finds Gemini resorting to lies and subterfuge to get out of the way of its father's assertive attitude. The Aries temper can also be fuelled by Gemini's ability to ignore instructions and airily dismiss its father's rapidly diminishing short fuse! Gemini, equally, can exasperate Aries by its lack of real application to projects of any kind. Aries, however, will always have a sneaking regard for his child's gift with words and Gemini will respect its father's need to get on in life. A good sense of humour also sustains them and their lively approach to life never fades.

Gemini/Aries Siblings

Gemini/Aries siblings can be quite exhausting for the rest of the household. They exist in a whirlwind of activity, noise and much chatter but whether they really ever understand each other in any sort of depth is debatable. Neither wants to get into the realms of deep emotions nor into the state of each other's soul, so their communication is usually on a fairly superficial level. They are both extremely sociable and, when small, are mutually supportive when it comes to new places and people. Gemini is an absolute rock when it comes to bailing Aries out of one of its foot-in-mouth situations, whilst Aries helps Gemini gain a bit of staying power when its inclination is to bail out before having fully tested the waters. These two are often genuine friends, are amused by the same things and find it easy to settle their differences. The cool, rational Gemini approach defuses much of the Aries temper and impatience, while Aries injects a bit of passion and fire into its more inconsistent sibling. Crucially, the Aries ego cuts no ice at all with Gemini!

Gemini and Taurus

Gemini Child/Taurus Mother

Being next-door signs in the zodiac Gemini and Taurus are very different. Gemini is cool air, extremely versatile and lively in the extreme. Taurus is fixed earth, determined and placid. From the start this mother and baby are coming at life from totally different angles. The Taurean looks to give her baby a thoroughly settled and stable environment and can get quite possessive. Gemini has the opposite agenda: the more people it can meet and communicate with and the livelier and busier the daily routine, the better. Without constant stimulation from the outside world the baby becomes fractious and the mother ever more protective and sheltering, which in turn increases Gemini's tension. And so it goes on. Taurus needs to realise that her baby is not rejecting her just because it wants to socialise and doesn't appear to be utterly dependent on its mother. A more delicate problem for this duo arises around food. Taurus is the zodiac's natural gourmet and usually an excellent cook. For Taurus to find her best culinary efforts dismissed and her baby showing a seeming disdain for the three good meals a day culture, can be a huge disappointment. A Gemini baby is often quite picky over food and prefers either to graze or take smaller meals and more of them. The pragmatic Taurean also likes to define boundaries and to give firm orders. To Gemini that's cause for rebellion, and the more the mother tries to instil discipline, the more her toddler will play up. A plea to Gemini's intelligence and a rational explanation works wonders: Taurus will get what it wants and stalemate will be averted. At worst, these two can go through years of misunderstandings, with Gemini feeling held back at every turn and Taurus nonplussed by a child who deals with the problems by becoming ever more cunning. At best, Gemini learns to appreciate its mother's constancy and loyalty, while Taurus revels in her child's wit and infinite variety.

Gemini Child/Taurus Father

The Taurean inflexibility is often triggered to new heights by a Gemini child, who, in its father's eyes, seems to have no common sense, no ability to concentrate for any length of time and not a reliable bone in its body! In an effort to control what he sees as a rather wayward child, the Taurean's attitude and opinions become more and more rigid. The lively Gemini spirit is quickly crushed in the face of its father's obdurate behaviour and, by the same token, Taurus feels thwarted when his son or daughter resorts to slightly underhand tactics to get its own way. Like all next-door signs, Taurus and Gemini are often poles apart, but with a little bit of tolerance and effort these two can jog along nicely. Taurus can always be a fount of practical advice and patience in the face of his Gemini child's rather haphazard route through life and invariably provides a loving safety net when difficulties arise. He can also teach Gemini a thing or two about persistence as well as learn a lot from his child about venturing into new pastures. A shared interest is often a wonderful balm – neither is particularly competitive and they will just thoroughly enjoy being involved.

Gemini/Taurus Siblings

These siblings often thrive best when they are not forced too much into one another's company. Whilst this relationship can often be very trying in the early years, once they are in different classes in school and involved in their own particular activities, they tend to be more appreciative of each other's qualities. Gemini is thankful for Taurus' common sense and ability to talk it out of the next madcap scheme, while Taurus relies on its sibling's assured approach to life outside the domestic scene. Taurus can also be both patient and understanding when Gemini gets itself into a thoroughly stressed state and at the same time is thankful for Gemini's ability to ignore the Taurean resentment and jealousy. Their differences, however, don't go away. Taurus will feel that Gemini is superficial and uncaring and Gemini will see Taurus as self-indulgent and intractable. But the Taurean charm and Gemini wit are often a binding force and they frequently manage to maintain a long and happy friendship.

Gemini and Gemini

Gemini Child/Gemini Mother

Whenever two people of the same Sun sign get together, there is the possibility of an overload to the system, and with two airy Geminis the gentle breeze soon turns into a gale if not a whirlwind. This mother and child relationship will certainly be lively, their lifestyle action-packed and their days filled with communication in all its forms, whether it's conversation, travel or bargain-hunting at the market! From the start, the baby Gemini feels thoroughly comfortable with its Gemini mother who innately understands that it needs to socialise and has better things to do than cope with set timetables and a list of dos and don'ts. However, with neither mother nor baby setting any kind of order to the day, life for both can become totally disorganised, with both Geminis becoming stressed and tense. It won't take long for the mother to realise that she has to initiate a bit of calm during the day if chaos is not to ensue. With a Gemini mother, the baby will never be short of intellectual stimulation and will receive endless praise at its every new step. She'll also use her communication skills to encourage her baby to learn: with her at its side, this particular Gemini child will probably be reading long before its contemporaries. Where this relationship can stall is in the inability of both Geminis to listen. They will talk endlessly, but whether either ever really hears what the other is saying is questionable. With no real understanding of the other's feelings these two can blunder into unknown territory and unwittingly cause great hurt and angst. The Gemini child can come out with jaw-dropping, insensitive comments, and the mother can shatter her child's happy demeanour with a throwaway thoughtless remark. Despite this potential problem these two usually have a great relationship, united by their enquiring minds and love of a good social life, to say nothing of their quick wit. Later in life they are like two kids at play and have no intention of growing up!

Gemini Child/Gemini Father

For many a Gemini child with a Gemini father, it's often a case of ships passing in the night. Both are so busy and lead such wonderfully disorganised lives that their opportunities for doing something together are severely limited. To start with, of course, the father will be enthralled by this bright and lively baby and will take enormous pleasure in taking his inquisitive youngster out and about. Here is someone to whom he can act as mentor and teacher and, for the moment, can't answer back! He'll encourage debate, won't spend too long anywhere (after all his attention span is not that long either) and will make his child's life one of endless variety and new opportunities. If the Gemini father takes the trouble to really appreciate and understand his Gemini child, he'll be making an amusing companion for life. If, on the other hand, he takes only a superficial interest, thereby encouraging the same lack of commitment to their relationship in his child, or becomes too critical, he could well find that he never truly knows his offspring, despite the fact they talk about everything and yet communicate not at all.

Gemini Siblings

This is usually a thoroughly noisy, happy and livewire relationship where each benefits enormously from the other's rational and logical approach to life, versatility and witty repartee. They are each other's strongest support when it comes to getting out of tight corners and both know only too well how to talk the other around to its way of thinking. Clearly there will be much good communication between two Geminis but there can also be a lot of carping and criticism to say nothing of frustration at the other's inconsistencies and sometimes superficial attitude. They also know, only too well, that the other cannot always be relied upon to deliver: after all, both have busy lives and loyalty isn't always their strongest suit. Geminis tend to know something about everything. Both tend to skim the surface of subjects and relationships, including the sibling one, and an understanding of how the other really ticks is often absent. That, however, doesn't stop these two from having many interests in common and developing a wonderful friendship.

Gemini and Cancer

Gemini Child/Cancer Mother

As with all next-door astrological signs, Cancer and Gemini are radically different, and this is often evident from the start. The Cancerian mother who has ideas of a close one to one relationship with her baby can have her illusions rudely dashed by an alert Gemini son or daughter who is full of curiosity about life and who seems to need its mother only as a source of food! The Gemini baby appears not to hold as sacrosanct the values of its mother: a safe, womb-like environment, much physical contact and a quiet routine. The Gemini baby not only loves the sound of the human voice, needing to be talked to as another little adult, but also delights in seeing new faces and places. This is one of the zodiac's social butterflies, born to a mother who simply adores being at home. So, any ideas the Cancerian mum might have about singing lullabies or just humming or gently crooning to her Gemini baby should be forgotten: discuss the latest news items instead. All those questions posed to the newborn will elicit all sorts of interested expressions, smiles and probably puzzled frowns: for a baby with a low boredom threshold (just like Aries), this will be music indeed. Cancer likes to take life slowly and surely: Gemini thinks and moves at a rate of knots. For the Cancerian mother, therefore, who rarely wants her child to grow up quickly, it comes as a shock to realise that her Gemini intends to get this baby business over as fast as possible. For this relationship to blossom, the mother has to face the fact that her child's affections will probably be shown in words rather than hugs: Geminis are coolly rational and logical, not emotional. She also has to appreciate that no Gemini is likely to tune in to her abundance of feelings and even her own child will be oblivious to her sensitivities. In the long term, and if handled well from the start, both can be of enormous help to each other. Cancer can teach Gemini about being more considerate and Gemini can help Cancer to climb out of her emotionally deep waters. Like all opposites, this mother/child relationship has the possibility of working brilliantly or foundering in a welter of misunderstandings.

Gemini Child/Cancer Father

With a Gemini child it is often very difficult to win an argument, let alone assert one's authority, and this can be particularly annoying for the Cancerian father who takes his role as head of the family extremely seriously. Gemini, even as a child, always debates from a very logical point of view, and from all sides of the argument to boot, and frequently comes off best when up against a Cancerian, whose emotions usually get in the way of rational thinking. The Cancer father does not laugh off this sort of situation and is quite capable of resorting to sulks and silence, a mode of behaviour that is totally alien to his Gemini offspring. Thus are sown the beginnings of a possible lack of communication between father and child. Potential problems also loom when the Cancer father fails to understand why his Gemini child does not relish being cosseted, indulged and protected, just as he did when young, and sees the Gemini curiosity about life outside the home as some kind of personal rejection. This relationship, particularly between Cancer father and Gemini son, can become quite tense, but with compromise on both sides, each can learn to appreciate the other's attributes and to tolerate the differences.

Gemini/Cancer Siblings

Despite being very different and in many ways quite incompatible, Cancer/Gemini siblings often get on extremely well. Because they look at life from radically different perspectives neither feels in competition with the other and they often end up being mutually supportive. Gemini is at his or her best on the social scene and in making friends and can be a huge help to the more diffident Cancerian as it copes with anything that takes it away from its domestic security. Cancer, in turn, will always be there to welcome home the wandering Gemini and to calm its over-active mind. Both have a tendency to fabricate and it will often be Cancer who gets the blame as Gemini finds it easier to mask its feelings. Cancer, however, will have the last laugh because, like the tortoise and the hare, it won't be the nifty, quick-thinking Gemini who eventually wins in the end. If these two can enjoy and appreciate their differences, this can be a very productive and happy sibling relationship.

Gemini and Leo

Gemini Child/Leo Mother

The Leo mother will find her Gemini baby to be just perfect. For a start it is more than happy to be handed around from one admirer to the next, absolutely lapping up every new experience. Its Leo mother, always happy in the limelight, will love showing off her intelligent and alert newborn and will probably be sure to tell everyone that her baby is the brightest and the best! As one of the best organised people in the zodiac, Leo will run an extremely efficient domestic operation but without some of the more rigid timetables laid down by, perhaps, Taurus or Capricorn. Hence, her baby finds just what it needs: a good routine but with opportunities for flexibility and a total absence of chaos. At the same time, however, Leo does not like to be crossed or questioned and her little Gemini will soon query her every remark and test every boundary. With mother taking the attitude that she knows best, and possibly becoming a bit bossy, and her child very keen to exercise its innate curiosity about all aspects of life, there is definitely the possibility for a few disagreements. Thwarted, especially if it's without rational explanation, a Gemini can become quite cunning and sometimes Leo feels her child is running rings around her. She has to tone down the dogmatism as much as Gemini has to learn that there are some things that are not to be questioned. Leo is generally a very warm and loving mother and sometimes finds it difficult to relate to the much cooler Gemini demeanour, just as much as Gemini needs space to move and doesn't always relish its mother's over-the-top attention. The child, however, can always be sure of its mother's praise and affection, just as she will relish its aptitude for learning and these two will love being out on the social scene. Rarely does this relationship hit the rocks. If it does it's usually because Leo tries to interfere too much for Gemini's liking or the Gemini superficiality tries Leo's patience just once too often.

Gemini Child/Leo Father

Leo is ambitious and usually expects to see that same characteristic in his child. Gemini, on the whole, doesn't have a great yen to be top dog and can feel quite pressurised by its Leo father's constant chivvying about where it's going in life. His son or daughter, intent on exploring as many roads as possible, often becomes very stressed when denied room to manoeuvre. Seeing his wishes ignored, Leo can then become dogmatic and stubborn, refusing to help his child if it won't go down his preferred route. At best, however, Leo soon recognises his child's quick wit and innate ability to learn, to say nothing of its interest in the world, and he realises that Gemini responds well to a reasonable challenge. He'll also be enthusiastic about his child's every new venture, although privately worrying that it'll end up nowhere! Leo makes an excellent teacher and these two invariably love going around museums and anywhere else where the father can help to expand his child's knowledge. Both are usually good at word games, although Leo does like to win! More often than not Leo has good reason to be proud of his child and Gemini receives much love and enthusiasm in return.

Gemini/Leo Siblings

These two usually have a lot of fun together. Neither is a loner by nature and both revel in plenty of company. Leo, however, is more fixed in its attitude than its sibling and can sometimes become irritated by the Gemini inconsistency, just as Gemini hates Leo's bossiness and general 'I know best' attitude. As Gemini can talk the hind legs off a donkey and is very versatile, it often manages to get the better of its sibling short term, but Leo definitely has the staying power and beats Gemini hands down when it comes to persistence. Gemini benefits greatly from the Leo enthusiasm and generous nature, whilst Leo is never allowed to get too pompous (Gemini very swiftly pricks that particular bubble) and learns a lot about quick thinking from its brother or sister. Leo can sometimes feel it's been left to carry the can when Gemini's over-ambitious plans fall to pieces, just as Gemini thinks it does nothing but coax Leo out of its stubborn moods, but these are generally blips in a relationship defined by a great sense of humour and much mutual love and respect.

Gemini and Virgo

Gemini Child/Virgo Mother

Gemini and Virgo are ruled by Mercury, the planet astrologically associated with communication, and both have good minds and a rational approach to life. In their own ways, they are also both highly strung: Virgo fusses and worries while Gemini lives on its nerves. To begin with, the Virgo mother is thoroughly delighted with her Gemini child: she immediately recognises her own lively interest in life beaming out from her baby and is thrilled to see its natural curiosity and clear efforts to make itself understood. Gemini, likewise, sees in its mother not only a diligent, safe and practical pair of hands but also a good teacher and someone who will talk as well as listen. So, all should be set fair for a good relationship and certainly on the surface this mother and child often do get along very well. Virgo takes great pleasure in educating her child, giving it a stable environment and being a thoroughly reliable parent. Gemini feels it's in exactly the right environment to develop its myriad interests and communication skills. Problems arise when Virgo starts to realise that her Gemini child has neither her meticulous approach nor her sense of order. She becomes stressed and anxious about her baby who seems to be in a state of perpetual motion and cannot seem to concentrate on anything for more than a few minutes at a time. Gemini can't cope with its mother's perfectionist tendencies, her endless need to organise and her well-meaning remarks which, to her child, sound like criticism. Both Virgo and Gemini can be verbally cutting and even in the pre-school years Gemini can come up with some startling home truths to which Virgo feels honour bound to respond. Gemini is also one of life's adventurers, especially on the social scene, and will talk to anyone while Virgo is more circumspect and fearful and often unwittingly holds her child back. If this relationship fails it's because of a real lack of communication and a refusal to appreciate each other's qualities.

Gemini Child/Virgo Father

Although not particularly ambitious himself, just happy to do a good job and be appreciated for it, the Virgo father often has very different ideas for his child and becomes impatient with the same lack of ambition shown by his Gemini son or daughter. He can also fail to appreciate his child's versatility and lack of application, let alone its complete inability to deal with anything practical. On the plus side, these two usually enjoy lively conversations and anything in which the father can play the role of educator. Virgo appreciates Gemini's alert and keen interest in everything and its endless questions, to which the child knows he or she will get very detailed answers. However, the Gemini tendency to flit from one subject to the next and to live on its wits can unnerve Virgo who is much more comfortable with a more analytical approach to life. When difficulties arise between these two, the father tends to resort to criticism and Gemini to lies and cutting comments. This relationship often works well on a slightly superficial level. Neither is comfortable dealing with emotions and both function best when nothing gets too personal.

Gemini/Virgo Siblings

Virgo likes its own space and its own company: Gemini dislikes both. This fundamental difference in these Mercury-ruled siblings can cause problems. Virgo becomes exasperated at the constant interruptions from Gemini and its sibling's complete disregard for its painstaking work while Gemini fumes at the cold water Virgo throws on its plans and its refusal to 'come out and play'. Although both are great talkers, each can be critical and carping: stony silences usually result. All is not lost, however, as these two can be a mighty combination: the Gemini wit and quick thinking together with Virgo's practical touch makes them able to tackle most situations, and certainly Gemini can be brilliant at bringing Virgo out of its shell, especially on the social scene. Virgo is just as good at saving Gemini from its own worst catastrophes: it soon works out whether the latest Gemini scheme will succeed or fail. As far as each child's nervous tension is concerned, Virgo is the better listener and the more practical while Gemini the more inventive at finding solutions.

Gemini and Libra

Gemini Child/Libra Mother

The Libran mother just wants to be loved and liked by her Gemini baby, who, in turn, really needs someone to dance to its tune and to listen to its every utterance. These two are made for each other and often enjoy an utterly blissful relationship. Libra is kind, loving and gentle and, from the start, puts very few demands on her little Gemini. She is simply keen to accommodate its every need and wish and to make life as pleasant as possible for her baby, something Gemini fully appreciates as it doesn't like being constrained by too much routine nor adrift with too much flexibility. As with any relationship, it's not without one or two problems and, before too long, the quick-witted Gemini realises that its mother can be a bit of a pushover because she'll prefer to give in rather lay down the law and risk a scene. The Gemini tendency to argue every point and to be inconsistent and restless is thoroughly distracting to the mother who can do little to calm the more highly strung Gemini because of her Libran inability to take decisions and make a stand. Once she realises that Gemini responds well to rational argument and to the logic of a situation, she's in easier territory, but her fear of being out of favour with her toddler usually means she'll do whatever is necessary for a quiet life! She can also be embarrassed by Gemini's ability to bluff and its very straightforward remarks, which cause her to put her diplomatic skills and innate tact to good use. Having learned the hard way about her own gullibility in believing her child's every word/lie, she'll eventually be brilliant, however, at bailing her child out of those difficult situations when its gift of the gab has got slightly out of control! Despite their slightly changeable natures, neither tends to brood or sulk nor take problems too much to heart. They will always discuss everything: Libra will be an excellent listener and Gemini will feel that its mother, after much prevaricating, always comes up with the right answers.

Gemini Child/Libra Father

The Gemini youngster, who probably has plans to follow three different careers as well as write a bestseller, is often thankful to have a Libran father who certainly won't put his child under pressure to make firm decisions, let alone go through the unpleasantness of rows and tantrums. He'll usually back away fast if trouble is brewing! The innate Gemini intelligence, which is so evident from the very beginning, is beguiling to Libra who will probably spend much time and money providing his child with books, crayons, videos, DVDs, and anything else to develop those talents. He'll probably also fall for the Gemini sales pitch: the Libran father will, at times, be foolishly generous! These two usually go through life exuding charm, chatter and easy sociability, though the father can often be run ragged by his young Gemini son or daughter who seems, at two years old, to have a formidable amount of both mental and physical energy. The young Gemini can become very frustrated with Libra if he wants to take life easy, but invariably gets its own way. Libra, as ever, just doesn't want to face a scene and gives in about that trip to the playground, the toy shop and then out to lunch!

Gemini/Libra Siblings

These two can be formidable allies. Gemini's eloquence and quick thinking can get its sibling out of many a problem and diplomatic Libra is usually delegated by Gemini to smooth out the Twin's difficulties, whether it's at home, at school or on the social scene. Libra often falls in with its sibling's plans, frequently against its better judgment and to avoid hassle, and then gets furious when it all goes wrong. Gemini, who thrives on a manically busy lifestyle, becomes exasperated by Libra's laid-back attitude, idealism and self-indulgence. Nevertheless, this relationship will be characterised by a lot of chatter and laughter as well as much indecision, as Libra can be changeable and Gemini inconsistent and superficial. Gemini also tends to get impatient with the Libran love of luxury (evident from a very early age) and the very relaxed Libran never understands Gemini's habit of getting itself worked up into a state of nervous tension. It's rare for these two to fall out over anything major: they can talk things through and truly value each other's qualities.

Gemini and Scorpio

Gemini Child/Scorpio Mother

A mixture of air (Gemini) and water (Scorpio) results in a lot of fizz which ultimately goes rather flat and this is frequently what happens in this astrological relationship. Fundamentally these two are very different: Gemini is rational and logical and comes from the head, and Scorpio is emotional and intuitive and leads from the heart. The Scorpio mother, delighted with her Gemini baby who already has such a keen interest in the world, is certain that her disciplined lifestyle will be just what her Gemini ordered. Gemini, who needs constant stimulation and has a very low boredom threshold, feels stifled by too much routine and caution and quickly becomes fretful. The baby sees its mother as lacking in adventure and Scorpio thinks Gemini is never satisfied. With her plans seemingly thwarted, Scorpio introduces more organisation when less is needed, or starts a power game to ensure that her wishes will prevail. The Scorpio determination will eventually come up against the Gemini cunning and sometimes this relationship can develop into a war of manipulation that starts when Gemini is no more than a toddler. On the plus side, Scorpio will always show enormous loyalty to her Gemini baby, however much it tries her patience, and once she relaxes her grip on the reins, Gemini will realise that it has a wonderfully exciting mother whose passion for life is almost intoxicating. Scorpio, however, will never be able fully to control her Gemini child: it'll be verbally quicker than her and mentally three jumps ahead. She also finds it difficult to accept that Gemini is friendly to all and a gift to the social scene and although proud, is often jealous of her child's popularity. At worst, Scorpio thinks Gemini is shallow and feckless and Gemini hates the obsessive Scorpio nature and they keep out of each other's way. At best, Gemini learns about perseverance and appreciates the Scorpio depth of character while Scorpio learns about adaptability and adores Gemini's wit and lively way of life.

Gemini Child/Scorpio Father

As with all Gemini/Scorpio relationships, this can be an all or nothing situation. The Scorpio father usually has fixed ideas about what he wants for his son or daughter. Gemini changes its mind about everything at least twice a day and Scorpio finds it very difficult to understand his child's unfocused attitude. Gemini, in turn, becomes rebellious in the face of its father's somewhat didactic views. Because he sees his Gemini child as inconsistent and possibly rather shallow, Scorpio is convinced that it'll go right off the rails, and finds it very difficult either to trust Gemini or to surrender control whether his child is five, fifteen or thirty-five. Scorpio also craves security and hates change and forgets that Gemini is adaptable and loves to experiment with the new. If neither father nor child takes the trouble to look at the other's way of thinking, this relationship can founder in a sea of resentment and disdain. With some work on both sides, however, Gemini has a loyal friend and powerful ally and Scorpio an engaging and lively companion who will make its father very proud – even if that success has nothing whatsoever to do with Scorpio's plans!

Gemini/Scorpio Siblings

On good days Scorpio finds Gemini to be vastly entertaining and an energetic and witty brother or sister, while Gemini revels in Scorpio's powerful personality and benefits from its loyalty and determination not to give up on what it sees as a slightly unreliable sibling! At more difficult times, Scorpio just wants to sulk in private and hates Gemini buzzing around in such an irritating fashion, while Gemini becomes frustrated and angry at Scorpio's inflexibility and manipulation. Scorpio is one of the most resourceful signs in the zodiac and loves to plot and plan but, because it is not adaptable and versatile like Gemini, tends to fall victim to its sibling's quicker thinking and ability to bluff its way out of problems. On the other hand, when it comes to staying power and all good things coming to those who wait, Scorpio wins hands down! These two often lead quite separate lives and enjoy totally different interests, which, ultimately, saves the relationship. Forced too much into one another's company, their differences and antagonism become very apparent.

Gemini and Sagittarius

Gemini Child/Sagittarius Mother

A Gemini baby arrives in the world alert, inquisitive and with a low boredom threshold. His or her delighted Sagittarian mother will be absolutely thrilled to see that natural curiosity and bright intelligence she longs to foster. Neither rates the 'baby business' too highly. Gemini is keen to find out about the world, which invariably makes it a knowledgeable and interesting companion long before many of its contemporaries, and the innate teacher in the Sagittarian happily responds to her lively child's intellect. More to the point, the mother frequently has the energy, both mental and physical, to keep up with one of the zodiac's most 'on the go' signs! Routine and order aren't high on the list of priorities for either mother or baby, as both prefer a rather happy-go-lucky and impromptu approach to life, but communication is absolutely vital to both. The Gemini baby will be soothed much more by the sound of its mother's voice chatting about the latest gossip and what's been on TV, than any number of snacks or the company of people who find cuddling and cooing preferable to having a good chat and a laugh! The Sagittarian mother instinctively knows what appeals to her Gemini. These two will enjoy a busy life together as both thrive on lots of activity and many plans, both practical and 'in your dreams'! Gemini needs lots of mental stimulation and in its Sagittarian mother has found exactly the right parent to encourage its interests and to engage in endless conversation. Both mother and child will tend to be quite restless and both have a problem with getting on with chores that have to be done. Sagittarius procrastinates and Gemini ignores the issue! At worst, these two can rush through life together in a total state of chaos, with the Gemini child given neither structure in its life nor taught about a sense of commitment to either people or situations. At best, however, this is a relationship that revels in good communication, plenty of laughter and a deep affection that comes from mutual understanding.

Gemini Child/Sagittarius Father

The relationship between a Sagittarian father and a Gemini child usually improves with age, which is not to say that the father will fail his Gemini son or daughter in the early years. Far from it: his myriad interests and flexible approach to life will be a major factor in awakening his offspring's own curiosity and encouraging its hobbies, and no father could be more assiduous in educating his child. Where these two can come unstuck is in their very different approaches to learning. Gemini skims subjects and is concerned with quantity rather than quality. Sagittarius, on the other hand, is more intellectual and always has an eye to future professional or academic goals. The Sagittarian father can become exasperated with his Gemini child's seeming lack of focus and inability to see the bigger picture. Discipline is also often an issue between these two: both argue the point endlessly and both try to have the final word. There are also likely to be clashes between the father's lifestyle and the needs of the child and the Gemini often feels a lack of sustained attention from the father. However, these two generally have much in common, frequently behaving like over-excited kids all through adult life.

Gemini/Sagittarius Siblings

This is a sibling relationship that will never be dull. Both enjoy a busy, challenging and probably rather noisy lifestyle and whilst not likely to engage in physical rough and tumble, will certainly indulge in verbal fisticuffs at every given opportunity! In fact, the arguments between these two can be thoroughly wearing to everyone around but are meat and drink to the siblings, who usually think of a quarrel as an intellectual exercise rather than a volley of personal abuse. Neither sulks and they are well able to sort out their differences. Both Sagittarius and Gemini thrive on physical and mental activity and a frenetic social life. They are therefore quite happy to be ferried around from one class to another and equally content to be allowed to stay at home surrounded by books, the internet, TV and, more often than not, a large circle of friends and acquaintances. Sagittarius and Gemini usually remain life-long friends, with the exchange of ideas their personal key to sibling unity.

Gemini and Capricorn

Gemini Child/Capricorn Mother

A wonderful intelligence and keen curiosity shines out of the eyes of the newborn Gemini. Its delighted Capricorn mother immediately sees a willing pupil who'll be a joy to teach, whilst the baby takes in a haven of security and stability within which it will be able to run rings around its mother! From its earliest days, the Gemini baby is extremely sociable and interested in everything. Once it starts to walk and talk, it wants to be everywhere at once and never stops chattering, more especially asking questions. For the Capricorn mother, who thrives in a stable routine and an orderly environment, the arrival of this whirlwind of a Gemini can be thoroughly unsettling. It seems to run to its own timetable and doesn't sit still for a moment and, whilst her child is definitely a keen student, she has to conduct lessons on the hoof rather than at the more settled times she'd prefer. She also quickly finds out that Gemini does not appreciate being told to 'do as I say': he or she will ask 'why?' and expect a proper answer. An intellectual battle of wills often exists between the Capricorn mother and Gemini child, leaving the mother flustered and the child either feeling crushed or ignored. Often Capricorn sees her child as superficial and scatterbrained, whilst Gemini rates its mother as too conventional and exacting. Asking a Gemini child to fit in with a disciplined Capricorn routine is just as impossible as hoping that the mother will understand her child's spontaneity. However, after many misunderstandings during the early years, they often come to admire each other's qualities. Capricorn certainly appreciates the defusing power of the Gemini wit (obvious at a very early age) and Gemini truly respects the firm foundations laid by its mother. Both tend to steer clear of the emotional arena and the meeting of minds improves with age. As with other incompatible zodiac signs, distance helps this relationship to flourish in later years.

Gemini Child/Capricorn Father

For the Capricorn father, who has his sights fixed firmly on the top job and a certain standing in the community, the attitude of a Gemini child can be perplexing in the extreme. Everything he believes in seems to be of no consequence whatsoever to his offspring. Capricorn values tradition and anything that has stood the test of time. His Gemini child focuses on the future. The father trusts in order and routine, an attitude viewed by Gemini as inflexible and over-conventional. The child is adaptable, spontaneous and changeable, qualities the Capricorn usually interprets as inconsistent, restless and two-faced. The father's authoritarian attitude is rarely taken seriously by the logical Gemini. However, it's often the case that opposites attract and certainly the father will love his child's inquisitive nature and wonder at its social confidence and quick wit. Equally, Gemini will come to respect its father's reliability and determination to do his best for his child. These two will probably never be really close, but after what are often very stressful teenage years, the relationship can settle into one of loving, but sometimes grudging, admiration.

Gemini/Capricorn Siblings

Whatever their position in the family, this is invariably a relationship between the sensible older statesman (Capricorn) and the eternally young Peter Pan (Gemini). At best, Capricorn lends a steady, guiding hand to its restless sibling and Gemini can ginger Capricorn out of its entrenched views and pessimistic attitude. For the most part, however, this relationship is frequently dogged by misunderstandings. Gemini sees Capricorn as throwing cold water all over its most exciting (and improbable) plans whilst the Capricorn sibling views Gemini as irresponsible and scatty. Gemini also resents the fact that Capricorn always puts work and duty first, whilst, to Capricorn, Gemini's 'flying by the seat of your pants' attitude and its obsession with being out and about is incomprehensible. A shared sense of humour, as shown by the Capricorn dry wit and the Gemini's starring role as king or queen of the amusing one-liners, often keeps this sibling relationship from going totally off the rails, as does the certain knowledge that each is able to come to the other's rescue when the need arises.

Gemini and Aquarius

Gemini Child/Aquarius Mother

The intelligent and inquisitive gaze emanating from the eyes of her newborn Gemini is often the biggest thrill for the Aquarian mother who immediately recognises a kindred spirit. Both mother and baby are air signs, totally comfortable in the realms of communication and fully understanding of each other's less than effusive emotional manner. From the earliest days Aquarius will chatter to her baby just as though she is talking to another adult, and the little Gemini will seemingly take it all in and, as soon as possible, try to respond. Neither mother nor baby sees the parent/child relationship as one of tactile bonding although it's very important for a Gemini to see the mother's face when she is talking and, of course, both need to hold and be held to a certain extent. What they really respond to is the teacher/pupil role: the mother is an excellent educator and her baby is more than keen to acquire knowledge and they will have much fun together exploring the baby's new world. These two will be out and about almost from day one. Both like to socialise and have a fairly low boredom threshold: the little Gemini will thrive on the constant activity and new ventures planned by its mother, the least of which will be her determination that her child will have a large group of friends. As in all relationships, there can be a few pitfalls. Gemini is far more versatile than Aquarius and less perverse and during the teenage years Gemini can become annoyed with its mother's intransigence and rather rigid opinions. Equally, the Aquarian mother can find the Gemini tendency to bluff its way through situations and its slightly scatterbrained approach to life thoroughly irksome. The Aquarian, who is truly humanitarian and places great value on friendship, can also become irritated by Gemini's rather superficial attitude to friends and family. Gemini, on the other hand, gets impatient at its mother's loyalty to people who really don't deserve her kindness. Despite these niggles, these two generally enjoy a deep and lasting friendship and find much happiness in each other's company.

Gemini Child/Aquarius Father

The excellent communication that usually exists between Aquarius and Gemini sometimes breaks down between the Aquarian father and his Gemini child. Gemini is naturally curious and inherently argumentative, seeing debate as part and parcel of the learning curve of life. The Aquarian father, who likes to think he has the correct handle on most things in life (if not all!) doesn't take kindly to what he sees as an attitude that questions his authority. He can also become both confused and irritated by his Gemini offspring's verbal dexterity and short attention span. In turn, his Gemini child finds it difficult to cope with the Aquarian father's rather autocratic approach. On the plus side, these two will have a great time visiting museums, playing chess, discussing books and enjoying a good social life. Laughter and wit will also be a big part of their life together. A lot will depend on the maturity of the Aquarian (and his ability to revise his opinions) as to whether this father/child relationship blossoms or struggles to survive. On the whole these two resolve their difficulties as neither sulks nor harbours resentment.

Gemini/Aquarius Siblings

This is potentially one of the best sibling relationships in the zodiac. It is invariably characterised by happy times, activity and endless chatter, which swings between intelligent debate and caustic disagreement at a moment's notice. Both signs tend to be quick-witted (Gemini in particular being adept at the pertinent one-liner) and are keen to have the last word, though neither broods about imagined slights or lost arguments. These two enjoy a full social life and lots of friendships and thrive in a busy environment. Neither is particularly adventurous but that doesn't stop them from coming up with grand plans of all kinds and from egging each other on in anything from harmless scams to idealistic notions for a glorious future! Aquarius gains a lot from the Gemini versatility and adaptability and, in turn, teaches its Gemini sibling about loyalty and perseverance. If this relationship is going to turn sour, it's usually because of the Aquarian contrariness and the Gemini inconsistency, but these two normally remain eternal children, eloquent, witty and lively to the end.

Gemini and Pisces

Gemini Child/Pisces Mother

At first, the Pisces mother thinks her bright, alert baby is utterly adorable and Gemini revels in its mother's gentleness and sensitivity. What neither realises, of course, is that they are both at their best in a world without boundaries and, if possible, with little sense of order. In the early days and weeks their ability to function in a rather haphazard way is perfectly acceptable to both. Therefore, they usually enjoy a very close relationship because each seems to understand the other's way of going about things. Problems tend to arise once Gemini is walking, and even more so when it is talking. Pisces finds it very difficult to instil timetables or discipline and Gemini quickly works out that once its mother has had her day or two of taking control, it can once again call the shots. She becomes frustrated with what she sees as a wayward youngster and retreats, either into her imagination, her creativity or into something where no one is going to answer back! Equally Gemini, who thrives on doing three things at once and needs a lot of attention plus fair, firm and gentle guidance, feels ignored. Suddenly these two are dashing around in separate circles, Pisces swimming well away from the noisy demands of her child and Gemini getting into all sorts of mischief, usually through boredom. The Piscean vagueness and Gemini inconsistency are often a recipe for many misunderstandings, not helped either by Gemini's pertinent and, sometimes, unthinking remarks which cause deep wounds to the emotional Pisces. Spending time with her Gemini will bring the Pisces mother huge rewards, but her patience is often tried by her child's rather limited attention span and Gemini just senses that its mother really has better things to do. At worst, these two just meander down totally different paths completely mystified by each other. At best, Gemini learns much about compassion from Pisces who in turn enjoys her child's wit and rational wisdom.

Gemini Child/Pisces Father

To the Pisces father, a Gemini child can seem demanding in the extreme. His son or daughter dances around him, constantly seeking his attention. The endless Gemini chatter is just not his style: he wants to drift gently through life, quietly indulge his child and be allowed his own space. Neither father nor child has much in the way of staying power and it only takes a few rebuffs from the father and one too many tries at testing the boundaries from the child for this relationship to get into difficulties. The father, who is one of the most sensitive and intuitive men in the zodiac, is also appalled at his child's lack of feeling, but does admire Gemini's way with words. For the Pisces father and Gemini child relationship to develop well, both have to learn a lot about tolerance and making time for each other. This relationship tends to work better between a Gemini daughter and Pisces father. In a father/son relationship, Gemini loses patience with what it sees as an unreliable and weak-willed father. However, as both are adaptable and neither holds grudges, even the most difficult situation can be redeemed.

Gemini/Pisces Siblings

The dreamy Pisces and the overactive Gemini often get on better than expected. Both love living in a fairly disordered environment, so there'll be no trashing the other's neat and tidy room, and both are adaptable and versatile and never get stuck in a rut. Gemini takes heart and gains much from Pisces' vivid imagination and creative abilities, whilst Pisces is happy to be drawn into Gemini's latest scheme or three. However, in times of crisis neither can be totally relied upon and when it comes to facing down parental demands or coping with a less than appealing chore only one is left to face the music. The other is nowhere to be seen, despite having sworn sibling vows to stick together! The Piscean sensitivity is also difficult for Gemini to cope with and the Fish certainly doesn't understand why Gemini has to indulge in cunning ploys to get its own way. At best, these two recognise their differences but make the most of each other's qualities. At worst, they see each other as untrustworthy and never take each other that seriously.

CANCER

The Cancer Child 0-5 Years

The Crab possesses a hard, protective shell within which it hides its very soft and vulnerable flesh and the Cancer child is exactly the same, concealing its vulnerabilities beneath a strong defensive shield. This young member of the zodiac needs very careful nurturing in the early stages if it is to gain either any measure of self-confidence, or to develop that marvellous tenacity, shrewdness and emotional resourcefulness that will be such an asset as it goes through life. Cancer is not a self-starter: it needs plenty of encouragement, support and understanding, to say nothing of parents who are blessed with both patience and fortitude. The early years with such a changeable and sometimes rather fearful little soul are not always easy, although the love and affection emanating from the Cancerian will more than make up for any frustrations and difficulties.

Cancer comes into the world with its intuition fully operational and quickly picks up on atmospheres around the home and any personal tensions. It makes its feelings known immediately: smiles turn to tears for no seemingly obvious reason. This baby, more than any other, is susceptible to a change in the tone of voice, its mother's state of mind, general upsets and any kind of domestic discord. Its shaky grasp on security seems easily threatened. That intuition, however, shouldn't be ignored as it gets out of babyhood. Very often Cancer's feelings about people and situations are totally, but inexplicably, right.

Its emotional state is also very closely linked with its stomach. An unhappy little Crab often can't, or won't, eat and invariably complains of an upset tummy. Most Cancerians do not enjoy big meals at any stage of life. The 'Crablet' is usually a two hour feeder when tiny and even when it's developed a more civilised timetable, invariably prefers little and often. It usually possesses a delicate digestive system and often uses that as an excuse for becoming faddy about food. Making a drama of mealtimes is never going to help any member of this sign, but a lot can be achieved by gentle persuasion. Appealing to a Cancer's emotions is the only way to go as it's invariably immune to rational argument and logical thinking. Cancer is also one of the zodiac's great worriers (coming close to Virgo at the top of the league!). Even the smallest Crab frets about all sorts of things, its fears usually totally unfounded, and time taken to talk over its anxieties is never wasted. The Cancerian child also tends to suffer from pangs of guilt, whether it's telling tales on a sibling or the fact that's it's snowing and the car won't start, something over which it has no control at all.

That, however, is but one half of the Cancer story as this is also one of the most ambitious signs of the zodiac and, far from being wimpish or unable to cope, it has its own definite game plan. All Cancer children have a goal in life but, crab-like, they tend to zigzag, or toddle sideways to get there. It's very easy to forget that under that veneer of wails and angst, there lies a very determined little character. The fact that this determination is coupled with a wonderfully sympathetic and loving attitude makes the Cancerian's need to get to the top seem so much less aggressive than, say, Aries or Leo. The Cancerian tenacity is also much to be admired. Even the youngest doesn't give up on things quickly and its extraordinary staying power means it's still ready to make a grab when others gave up long ago.

Cancer has been labelled 'moody' and this changeability is obvious in the sudden smiles and tears of babyhood and equally evident in the amenable Cancerian child who, for no apparent reason, turns into a stubborn, self-pitying and extremely touchy little Crab. This sign has also cornered the market in its ability to sulk. In a good mood, the Cancerian child will be open to education in all its forms and will also be friendly and helpful. In its more negative moments a fraught parent will be dealing with a snappy temper, a thoroughly pessimistic attitude to everything and a mountain of stress that nothing will seem to ease. The 'terrible twos' for this sign is usually more about tears than tantrums, which are frequently much more effective in getting attention than drumming heels, shouting and red-faced anger. For the Cancerian's parents, it's very much a matter of timing and making good use of the positive phases when the child will be a real delight. Trying to force Cancer into anything when it's effectively gone into its shell and has retreated from life, is a complete waste of time and can build up all sorts of resentment in the child who never forgets anything! All Cancerians have a phenomenal memory and the child will take great pleasure in reminding his or her parents of their every mistake and misunderstanding, what was done in the heat of the moment and, worse, who said what to whom – verbatim! More difficult to deal with, however, is the Cancer child's tendency to be economical with the truth! Wide-eyed innocence and a totally plausible story often cover up its own bad behaviour and land someone else right in it! A sceptical approach often saves a parent from charging down the wrong path and reading from the wrong script!

A young Cancerian child thrives best in the home, whether it's his or her own domestic environment or that of a much-loved grandparent or childminder. Unlike its next-door neighbours, Gemini and Leo, who just love being one of a crowd and get a real buzz from other people and social situations, Cancer tends to be shy and takes more time to hone its social skills. Primarily it needs to develop a very strong relationship with one particular person. That person will be able gently to introduce the rather diffident Cancerian into the larger world without making it feel insecure or nervous as it comes out of its protected environment. Thrown into a social mélée in the expectation that it can cope will, in fact, probably make the child feel that becoming a hermit is a pretty good option. If it's not to develop a very clingy approach, which is often a Cancer trademark, it needs to be lovingly tended like a delicate hothouse flower. If a softly, softly approach is adopted, by the time it goes to school it will be just as confident as a Sagittarian or Aquarian and ready to become a kind and stalwart friend to all and sundry. The young Cancerian is also, by nature, very protective of others and loves to take people (old and young) under its wing.

Many adult Cancerians are avid collectors. This need to accumulate anything from soft toys to family photographs or stamps starts at a very early age and can be used most effectively in helping Cancer to count or to read. The natural domesticity of Cancer also makes it both an avid spectator and keen participant in the kitchen as well as a budding little gardener. It's often very green-fingered and takes real pride in seeing cress grow on the blotting paper or the new shoots pushing their way up in the window box. The pre-school Cancerian usually learns most and responds best in a situation that makes it feel 'at home', whether it's his or her own home or in a small group. In its good mood, of course, Cancer is a model pupil in any pre-school environment: on a bad day, it whinges, whines and carps and become extremely tiresome!

With this natural collector of the zodiac, sorting out the toy box and clearing out anything that has run its useful life will generate a battle royal. Cancer is a hoarder, and an untidy one at that, and teaching it to clear up and clean is never easy. Acute distress is also often occasioned when what is effectively rubbish is destined for the wastepaper basket! Getting rid of anything that has at any time been dear to a Cancerian takes much time and diplomacy.

Cancer is ruled by the Moon and is the most feminine sign in the zodiac (just as Aries is the most masculine). Baby boy Cancerians adore their mother from birth and despite what more macho types might think, these youngsters are not a lost cause and are certainly not tied to the maternal apron strings. It's all too easy to become irritated at the young boy's sensitivity and often over-emotional behaviour. A Cancer man who is all bluster, bravado and on the defensive is usually one who, as a child, had his finer feelings knocked for six and learned early on to hide his lovable and gentle nature. A fine balance has to be drawn between developing a little boy's sensitivity and intuition and teaching it to stand on its own two feet.

The Cancer child is hugely affectionate and very easily hurt. Time spent in the first five years developing its sense of security and understanding its sometimes hypersensitive nature will never be wasted. Like anything that has been carefully looked after, it will bring huge rewards as it blossoms. The Cancer child will also feel safe in the knowledge that at home it has a true and protective champion who will ensure that this sympathetic, affable and thoughtful individual not only conquers many of its irrational fears, but also achieves its ambitions (often in a caring field) and finds true contentment in life. Slowly and surely, and sometimes sideways, the Cancer child makes its happy and successful way in the world.

Cancer and Aries

Cancer Child/Aries Mother

The Cancerian baby arrives in the world ready to be quietly soothed and instinctively understood. It also requires much demonstrative affection, to say nothing of its mother's devoted and full-time attention. A busy Aries mother is not quite what the little Crab had bargained for and, equally, she can feel completely ill-equipped to deal with her baby's shyness and sensitivities, let alone its inability to let go of her hand. The Aries can-do attitude and full social life is often totally lost on her Cancer child who just craves stability and a meeting of souls rather than of minds or new friends. The Aries mother, despite her slightly fragile ego, always gets on with life and shows a brave face. Her Cancer child, on the other hand, doesn't have that natural fortitude, preferring to make its fears abundantly clear and, in its moments of crisis, retreating firmly into its shell. And the more Cancer retreats, the more Aries pushes! It normally takes Aries some time to realise that she has to deal very gently with her child's need to move slowly and surely through life, giving comfort and reassurance at every stage. Throw a Cancerian into the deep-end in any situation and Aries will be coping with a clingy and petulant baby. Cancer is 'changeable' and, from day one, the utterly straightforward Aries mother is faced with the little Crab's mood swings. Aries quickly loses patience with this unpredictable behaviour, in turn making her child even more prone to sulks and shilly-shallying. As the child grows up there is a danger that Cancer will resent its mother's pushy approach and lack of finer feelings, just as Aries is at a loss to understand her child's insecurities. At worst, these two founder in a state of mutual incomprehension. With significant effort, however, this relationship can bring rewards to both. Each respects the other's ambitious nature and Aries will be in awe of her child's tenacity and shrewd attitude to life, just as much as her child will worship its mother, knowing that, in her, it has a true champion.

Cancer Child/Aries Father

The 'what you see is what you get' Aries father is often completely mystified by his enigmatic and complex Cancerian child. The father/son relationship can prove particularly difficult as Aries frequently fails to understand his retiring, gentle and cautious child. He thinks his Cancerian son is a bit of a wimp until he finds that his seemingly diffident child has a will of its own and a determination second to none. With a daughter, Aries feels thoroughly protective and indulges all his 'knight in shining armour' tendencies. However, the changeable Cancerian personality and tendency to whinge can exasperate him: his straightforward manner, too, sometimes does more damage to the Cancerian sensibilities than he realises. If Aries can learn to appreciate his child's more caring approach and Cancer admire its father's get up and go attitude and his basic need to get the best from himself and from others, this relationship has a chance to prosper. Without a great deal of tolerance on both sides, however, this father and child can drift apart, each baffled by the other and frequently nursing emotional bruises as well.

Cancer/Aries Siblings

The confident Aries, who rushes into things without a forward glance or strategy, is frequently annoyed by Cancer's negativity, seeing its brother or sister as pouring cold water on all its plans. Worse still, Cancer usually feels duty-bound to inform a parent of what's going on, causing Aries to distrust its sibling and to see it as a tell-tale. Cancer, in turn, thinks Aries does nothing but get everyone into trouble and trample heavily all over Cancer's finer feelings. The bossy Aries approach also grates with Cancer. On the plus side, of course, Aries can be absolutely marvellous at dragging Cancer out its moods, boosting its self-confidence and helping it along on the social scene. Equally, Cancer is not only a wonderful shoulder for Aries to cry on, but is also pretty good at providing its sibling with alibis. A Cancer child can be wonderfully vague about the actualité! As with all Cancer/Aries relationships this one will bring great dividends if both take the trouble to make it work.

Cancer and Taurus

Cancer Child/Taurus Mother

From the moment of birth, a Cancerian baby feels totally safe in the arms of its Taurean mother whose prime concerns are stability, security and the building of firm foundations in life. Here is a mother who can soothe away all her baby's worries and will never push it into situations where its mettle is tested. Both signs are also extremely tactile and will happily spend hours snuggled up together in what Cancer sees as a wonderfully cosy nest. The baby Crab will also thrive in the Taurean's well-regulated domesticity and, although there may be a few niggles about the food (Taurus loves its food and may find the Cancerian's slightly picky attitude a bit annoying), these two will rub along together in what others might see as somewhat self-satisfied harmony. They often have much in common: both love being in and around the home (where Cancer prefers to learn its social skills), are eminently hospitable and tend to be talented where it comes to making things. Taurus also copes well with the Cancerian moodiness, instinctively understanding that her child responds best to the softly-softly approach. A gentle push rather than a hefty shove gets the right results. However, Taurus can also be stubborn in the extreme and, pitted against her Cancerian's determination, can easily make a three act drama out of a three minute sketch. Both then retreat into a stony silence! From an early age, Cancer fears impending poverty and squirrels its pocket money away. Taurus enjoys shopping at the luxury end of the market. Cancer can learn a lot from its mother about the pleasure of giving and of enjoying its cash reserves while the tut-tutting little Crab can often save Taurus from its worst financial excesses! Taurus will always be a fount of dependability and practical help to her Cancerian child and, in turn, will receive much loving gratitude, sympathy and emotional support. This relationship only gets into difficulties if Cancer is allowed to cling too tightly or Taurus becomes over-protective or possessive.

Cancer Child/Taurus Father

The Taurean father is very conscious of his position in the world and needs to be seen as caring, loving and able to provide the best for his child. It also matters that his son or daughter is perceived as happy and well-behaved, giving him cause to glow with parental pride. A Cancer baby, known as much for its smiles as its petulance can give Taurus some difficult moments. He'll never know, when taking his little Crab out and about, whether laughter or sulks are going to be on his child's agenda. He's also often at a loss when dealing with Cancer's sensitivity and vivid imagination, preferring as he does the pragmatic and sensible approach to life. However, the Taurean father is patient and thoroughly reliable, qualities that are highly valued by his Cancer child, who will always feel safe and protected in his care. The Crab's moody emotionalism, tears and frequent determination to do things the hard way may well irritate and baffle Taurus, but at the same time he admires and respects his child's sympathetic and loving approach to the world at large and, more particularly, its quietly resolute attitude to getting on in life. This relationship usually starts well and gets better by the year.

Cancer/Taurus Siblings

Cancer and Taurus children thrive best in the home where they value domestic security, a good routine and entertaining their friends: both are much happier if the social scene comes to them rather than having to be ferried here, there and everywhere. They are invariably mutually supportive in stressful situations and often come to each other's rescue when the going gets tough. On the whole this is generally a sibling relationship that works extremely well. Taurus provides Cancer with a wonderfully strong and sensible shoulder to cry on and, as well as proving steadfast in times of trouble, is excellent at dealing with Cancer's endless worries. Cancer, in turn, is a wonderfully sympathetic listener, shows immense sensitivity and is very protective of its sibling. Sometimes Taurus comes up against Cancer's slightly unforgiving nature just as much as the Crab has to cope with the Taurean obstinacy. Whilst never understanding Cancer's intuition, Taurus learns eventually to trust it.

Cancer and Gemini

Cancer Child/Gemini Mother

The Cancerian baby exudes love and devotion but at the same time senses that its mother has both a limited attention span and low boredom threshold. Cancer's intuition is spot-on and sooner rather than later it has to cope with a haphazard routine, much socialising and being handed around Gemini's legion of friends and acquaintances. Gemini's ability to overcrowd the day does not stop with the arrival of her baby: Cancer just has to fit in as best it can. Small wonder then that the already over-committed Gemini mother is faced with a scratchy and temperamental baby who craves a safe and quiet existence, as well as a slower pace of life, and whose vulnerabilities and worries are being magnified at every turn. Logical Gemini versus emotional Cancer has the potential for life-long misunderstandings unless, to begin with, Gemini takes time to tune in to her baby's sometimes clinging, touchy and sensitive nature. Her little Cancerian is not anti-social, but needs a steadying hand, much demonstrative affection and a gentle approach to anything that takes it away from its mother, or into an unknown environment. It doesn't have Gemini's innate confidence and panache nor her innate curiosity about life. Both mother and child can be changeable: Gemini has to put up with Cancer's moods and sulks whilst her child has to cope with a mother who does nothing but change her mind and her plans at least three times daily. With this seemingly difficult Cancerian baby to deal with, Gemini often fails to recognise her baby's sheer determination, ambition, shrewdness and loving sympathy. At worst, this mother and child struggle to fathom each other's way of thinking and operating. At best, Gemini learns to appreciate her adoring, kind and tenacious child, while Cancer benefits from Gemini's wit, versatility, logic and encouragement in all areas of life. Most of all Gemini has to learn to mind read and to listen. It takes much patient detective work to get to the root of a Cancerian child's problems.

Cancer Child/Gemini Father

The Gemini father, who is not, on the whole, one of the zodiac's most ambitious men, often fails to appreciate his Cancerian child's determination to get to the top. He is often slow, therefore, to encourage his child's talents and can become particularly mystified by a Cancerian son who seems to be over-sensitive and prefers hanging around the home to being out and about. Gemini never does anything at half pace, whether it's walking or talking, and finds it difficult to cope with a Cancerian who, mentally or physically, rarely seems to get into top gear. Equally, Cancer becomes distressed at its father's busy lifestyle, which leads to broken promises. When irritated, the Gemini father will come up with some very sharp remarks, which his Cancer child will, firstly, not forget and, secondly, retaliate with its own set of home truths. On the plus side, Cancer benefits greatly from its father's logic and sense of fun whilst Gemini secretly admires his child's tenacity and kind, protective attitude to those it loves. At worst, these two can drift apart later in life, each finding the other impossible to deal with.

Cancer/Gemini Siblings

These two often get on very well as there is no sense of competition and both rule their own particular roosts, Cancer in the home and Gemini in the wider world. Cancer is always on hand to soothe away Gemini's stress (even the youngest member of this sign lives on its nerves) and is often protective of its sibling, whilst Gemini lends a helping hand to Cancer who is so much more diffident about trying anything new. Gemini is also good at laughing away Cancer's imaginary worries and generally lifting the Crab out of its darker moods. Both, however, can be changeable and both have a knack of coming out with tactless, pointed or downright hurtful remarks. Arguments can blow up out of nowhere, particularly when Cancer chooses to remind Gemini of a previous discussion. Money can also become an issue: the financially cautious Cancerian will be forever bailing out the more cavalier Gemini with the contents of the piggy bank. These two usually develop a life-long friendship, especially if they are not forced too much into each other's territory.

Cancer and Cancer

Cancer Child/Cancer Mother

On the face of it this relationship should be absolute bliss for both mother and child, since both are emotionally needy, crave a stable domestic scene and a strong sense of security and need lots of demonstrative affection. In practice, however, both seem to pick up on the other's worries and insecurities, leading to a stressed mother and fractious baby who then goes off its food, causing the mother even more worry – and so it goes on. These two either exist in a state of tranquil ecstasy or in an emotional whirlpool in which both of them are drowning in a mass of hypersensitivity and contradictory moods. The difficulties inherent in this relationship can sometimes start very early on but most only become apparent as the child gets older. The Cancerian child needs lots of encouragement and praise: basically it is not a self-starter and needs to be chivvied to attempt anything that it sees as some kind of challenge (whether it's learning to walk, talk, feed itself or go to a birthday party). Because the Cancerian mother tends to be over-protective, she is unlikely to push her child into this unknown territory (after all, she knows how awful she felt when she was faced with anything new), which ultimately leads to frustration for both. Equally, in true Cancerian style, both mother and child can be subject to mood swings and tearful sulks when neither is able to understand the other and both their imaginations run riot. Misunderstandings develop out of nowhere and, because neither is adept at verbalising feelings, resentments tend to fester and ultimately run deep. On the plus side, both mother and child will probably gain much pleasure from the domestic scene and will happily indulge their habit of hoarding. Collections of anything and everything will fill the home. This is very much an all or nothing relationship, which, for most Cancer mothers and children, works out well, but certainly can't be taken for granted just because they are the same sign.

Cancer Child/Cancer Father

For the Cancerian father the very idea of having a child of the same sign brings a sense of deep contentment. If he has a daughter, she will definitely be the 'princess' he'll be able to protect. If he has a son he'll have an ally in another man who truly understands his sensitive nature. That is one scenario which, with luck, could well materialise. However, there is another side to the story. Sometimes the protective instincts of the father can seem almost smothering to the child, especially if the daughter has ambitions in life which have little to do with home and family. Cancer tends to approach everything in an extremely roundabout way. For Cancerian children, therefore, who look for strong guidance and plenty of constructive advice, a father of the same sign can sometimes be a disappointment. There is also the problem of too many emotions careering around the family, made more troublesome if the father hides his own feelings behind bluster and bravado. The child then disappears into his or her own shell and communication is in danger of breaking down completely. Long term, however, the Cancer father/Cancer child relationship can become a pleasure to both, although it usually takes the self-knowledge of the child to initiate a better rapport.

Cancer Siblings

With two Cancerian children the initial battles are for the attention of the parents, particularly the mother. As babies and young children that attention can be sought through charm on the one hand and major dramas at mealtimes on the other. Once they get older, both will want to be Mummy's helper. One of the problems with two Cancerian children is that neither is going to be able to jolly the other along, whether it's to get out and about or to snap out of a mood. Both will tend to shut themselves away, brooding on all sorts of negative feelings, rather than talk about what's bothering them. On the positive side, however, family life is often enhanced by two Cancerian children as they truly value the home and everything it represents. At best, Cancer siblings will look after each other and be mutually protective. At worst, they will know exactly how best to destroy each other's very vulnerable nature.

Cancer and Leo

Cancer Child/Leo Mother

Like all astrological next-door neighbours, Leo and Cancer are chalk and cheese. The Leo mother is one of the most capable women in the zodiac and runs her life with a mixture of brilliant organisation and a dash of pzazz. She truly believes that good administration and a hefty dollop of common sense can solve everything. Unfortunately, her Cancerian baby doesn't follow quite the same recipe and finds its mother's self-confidence and often rather showy lifestyle quite perturbing. The generous and loving Leo, who has organised her baby's meals, playtime, social life and sleep with almost precision timing, fails to understand her unhappy baby, who seems uneasy and tearful in the face of her efficiency. Cancer needs its mother's undivided attention and comfort and wants nothing more than to be cuddled and soothed in a pleasantly quiet environment. In the first few months Cancer would really like to set the daily agenda. Leo loves to be out and about and thrives in company: Cancer needs a very careful introduction to the social scene and doesn't take kindly or quickly to being part of a large or noisy group. For many Leo mothers, a Cancer baby can become a drain and an enigma: nothing she does appears to be right. Leo has to put her own needs very firmly in second place in order to establish the bonds that will sustain the mother/child relationship: once Cancer feels utterly secure it will be confident enough to trust its mother and to follow her lead. Leo also tends to be exasperated by the Crab's sulks and negativity. Although she is, in fact, far more sensitive than is generally thought, she finds it very difficult to cope with her child's overactive and often pessimistic imagination and general whingeing. Much give and take is needed to make this relationship work well. At worst, these two can be completely mystified and upset by the other's behaviour and prefer to keep their distance. At best, the Leo mother can be a positive and protective influence in her Cancerian's life and equally learn a lot about thoughtfulness, patience and tenderness.

Cancer Child/Leo Father

The fearless Leo father often finds his more timid Cancer child both irritating and slightly disappointing, until he realises that ambition runs deep in the veins of his son or daughter. Leo is a natural boss – he needs to be at the top of life's ladder – and by the same token enjoys his role as head of the family and making it clear that he knows best! The more diffident Cancer tends to see its Leo father as calling all the shots and failing to understand its vulnerabilities. Feeling it's being pushed around, Cancer either retreats into its shell, or indulges in extreme negativity, carping and thoroughly changeable behaviour. With a little bit of understanding on Leo's side, he can make a wonderful relationship with his little Crab. Leo is a naturally good teacher, can make outings and simple, everyday matters seem both interesting and exciting and can also be very protective towards his more sensitive child. Once Leo realises that Cancer blossoms when nurtured kindly and slowly and that there is a very shrewd and determined little soul underneath the clinging and touchy persona, he can be a great source of strength and encouragement to Cancer who in turn will adore its wonderfully showy, positive and loyal father.

Cancer/Leo Siblings

Cancer/Leo siblings can be mutually very supportive. Cancer is a wonderful listener and will probably spend hours hearing about Leo's latest over-the-top drama and its rather dodgy outcome, while Leo will be first rate at jolting Cancer out of its constant and pessimistic 'what if?' scenario and encouraging it to be a little more daring. Cancer is also one of the few signs that will recognise and understand Leo's innate sensitivity and Leo will feel comfortable in letting Cancer see beneath the bombast. This relationship often works better if Leo is the elder child. In this case, Cancer will probably worship its rather glamorous sibling, countering Leo's more bossy attitude with slightly underhand behaviour! If Cancer is the elder, then it will take on the role of parent to Leo, dragging it back into line after every misdemeanour! At worst, these two can come to grief because Cancer is always telling tales about Leo, whilst Leo interferes in all aspects of Cancer's life.

Cancer and Virgo

Cancer Child/Virgo Mother

Virgo and Cancer often make a wonderful duo. At birth Cancer immediately feels safe in the arms of its Virgo mother, having intuitively picked up on her common sense, practicality and ordered existence. She, in turn, is ready to accommodate her sometimes snappy but utterly devoted Crablet and to smooth away its anxieties. What the baby hasn't yet sussed is that its Virgo mother tends to stress and worry just as much as any Cancerian. Virgo sets herself extremely high standards for motherhood and often frets and fusses over every detail. Her Cancerian immediately picks up on the tension, gets itself into a bit of a tizzy, and, before very long, mother and baby are both upset and probably in tears. A slight relaxation of the Virgo routine, a reassuring word from a friend or relative and the realisation that spending time with her baby is perhaps more important than clearing and cleaning, can quickly transform the situation. Her Cancerian needs much demonstrative and loving attention and Virgo, although not particularly tactile, is well able to give it. As her baby grows up, Virgo gives Cancer a thoroughly stable and well-ordered environment in which to develop and mother and baby often enjoy many of the same interests. Virgo is also a wonderful fount of wisdom and pragmatism in the face of her child's overactive imagination and, equally, Cancer can demonstrate a very mature understanding of its mother from an early age, often showing empathy and sympathy when she's not having a particularly good day. Arguments over tidying up and the state of the bedroom invariably occur between these two, as Virgo tends towards the minimalist look and Cancer, who loathes throwing anything out, favours clutter. Virgo also deals extremely well with Cancer's moods, rarely moved to peaks and troughs by either the smiles or tears, and encourages her child to find some kind of sensible middle road. These two usually develop a close and loving bond and telephone bills, later on, can become exorbitant!

Cancer Child/Virgo Father

The Virgo father is something of a perfectionist and tends to be both demanding and quite critical of his children. His Cancer child, whose confidence can be fragile at the best of times, finds this really difficult to cope with and rather than put up a fight or prove it can do better, often retreats and gives up, throwing in some stinging remarks and a few sulks for good measure. At the same time, Virgo is irritated by his little Crab's emotionalism and sensitivity, finding it impossible to understand how anyone can be so impractical and moody. However, these two are invariably united in their tendency to worry and stress (and in their frequent bouts of stomach problems) and in their determination not to rock the boat. The Virgo father will make it his business to get involved with Cancer's interests, show his son or daughter how things are done or made and act as an excellent mentor. He will also be thankful that his child is home-loving and has such an affectionate nature. Virgo's workaholic tendencies, however, can be quite unsettling to his Cancer child, who needs its father to be a big part of a harmonious domestic scene. In the teenage years this relationship can be fraught: neither is prepared to discuss anything and both sit and brood.

Cancer/Virgo Siblings

As with the other Cancer/Virgo relationships, the siblings tend to get on well although it's not always sweetness and light. Virgo prizes routine and order and Cancer takes a far more slapdash approach. Invariably they bicker about Virgo's nitpicking attitude, Cancer's tendency to whinge (and sometimes to sneak!) and just how amazingly quickly the Crab can scuttle away when it comes to clearing up and putting the toys away. As both tend to get themselves in a lather about all sorts of unnecessary and imaginary worries, they can often wind each other up quite unwittingly. It's often Cancer who is the first to put his or her worries aside in order to listen to its Virgo sibling, but it's usually Virgo who eventually comes up with the sensible answers to problems. Both enjoy the comforts of home and, whatever hassle they might have with each other, will quickly put up a united front when trouble looms. These two tend to trust and to rely on each other well into adulthood.

Cancer and Libra

Cancer Child/Libra Mother

The gentle, charming Libran and the emotional, loving Cancerian should be a relationship that is blessed by the gods. The Libran will be utterly entranced by her needy little Cancerian who will see its mother as the epitome of calm. So what could go wrong? 'Changeable' is a word that applies to both signs: Libra is indecisive and Cancer's emotions go up and down like a yo-yo. Whilst Libra will probably provide the prettiest nursery for her child, her ability to give her little Cancerian a firm foundation on which to set out its stall of touchiness and fears is quite another story. Equally, even the smallest Cancerian can easily manipulate Libra: she'll be reluctant to upset anyone, least of all her new baby (who can turn on instant tears at will) and usually gives in rather than hold the line. Cancer, however, is often very unsettled at never being given firm boundaries. Mother and child frequently misunderstand each other and communication in the early years is often on a road to nowhere. Cancer finds it difficult to rationalise, which is the Libran strength, and Libra to fathom the deep emotions of her child, especially when it decides to clam up for fear of being hurt. On the party scene, which Libra cultivates assiduously and of which her baby Crab is more fearful, she will ensure that she eases her child into the most harmonious elements of her social circle. Both Libra and Cancer are achievers but reach their goals by different routes. Libra will never lose patience with the Crab's rather slow, firm and yet sideways approach to life, and Cancer will never cease to admire its mother's diplomacy, charm and people skills when it comes to getting her own way. If no effort is made, particularly by the mother, to put a stop to any hurt silences and to seek some kind of understanding, then these two can drift apart, but generally this twosome is very loving and very giving. Neither really wants to cause upset and both will forgive and forget much in order to maintain harmony.

Cancer Child/Libra Father

The Libran father, adept at working a room, often becomes frustrated at his Cancerian child's lack of social ease and grace, while Cancer cringes at being pushed forward or shown off by its father. With neither father nor child ever wanting a showdown, Libra gets further annoyed when his child retreats into sulks and a generally defensive attitude (usually spiced up with perceptive and painfully accurate comments). Cancer is equally puzzled at its father's inability to realise that its deep feelings cannot just be brushed aside or rationalised. Real empathy and deep communication rarely exist between this father and child, but on the surface they generally get on famously. Libra will love taking his Cancer son or daughter to all the best places, encouraging an interest in the arts and understanding his child's need to get on in the world. His natural optimism and breezy confidence will also be a wonderful antidote to his child's endless anxieties. Sometimes Cancer would like firmer guidelines from its father, and finds it all too easy to take advantage of Libra's need to please, but genuine affection is usually the hallmark of this relationship.

Cancer/Libra Siblings

Libra hates upsets and quarrels and Cancer prizes domestic harmony, so this sibling duo has an excellent starting point in their relationship. However, with Libra bending over backwards to accommodate Cancer and Cancer determined not to upset its parents, and particularly its mother, both can then brood intensely about injustices or imagined slights rather than discuss the issues. Libra will often see its Cancer sibling as prone to crying over absolutely everything, while Cancer despairs of Libra ever coming to a decision about anything and often resents having to take responsibility for its sibling's every action. On the plus side, of course, Libra is brilliant at getting Cancer to come out of its shell, especially outside the family unit, whilst Cancer is a fount of sympathy, intuitive guidance and support to the dithering Libran. As they get older, Libra often despairs of Cancer's moods and inability to move on whilst Cancer frets at Libra's liberal spending habits and whinges about always being the one who works to maintain the relationship.

Cancer and Scorpio

Cancer Child/Scorpio Mother

The Scorpio mother and her Cancer baby are intuitively united not at birth but at conception. The natural instincts of Cancer to worship its mother and of Scorpio to be passionate about her child find an excellent home in this relationship. Both function at a deeply emotional level and genuinely understand each other's feelings and vulnerabilities. Scorpio provides a secure environment and sensible routines for her nervous little Crab and is attuned to her baby's every whim. In turn, Cancer is comforted by the strong Scorpio presence and definite ground rules. However, it's not all plain sailing. Both mother and child can tend to be secretive, finding it difficult to verbalise their feelings. Rather than struggle on, Scorpio shuts down and Cancer retreats into its shell leaving issues unresolved. Before this breakdown of communication, Scorpio will have no doubt made some blisteringly hurtful statements and Cancer a few sharply barbed comments! It is also easy for the young Cancerian to feel totally overwhelmed by the Scorpionic obstinacy and for Scorpio to feel stymied by her baby's calculating attitude. Deep down, however, both truly understand the other's dilemma and even as a toddler, Cancer will try to make its Scorpio mother feel better after any upsets (usually by offering a small gift) and she will be extremely tactile with her baby by way of apology. Neither sign ever gives in verbally! Scorpio craves being at the top of life's ladder and will soon suss out her baby Crab's ambitious nature and encourage it to get ahead in the world. Whether it's the swimming pool (both are water signs), reading or playing games, a competitive element will never be far away and Scorpio will exert just the right pressure on her little Cancerian. She knows this baby has to be carefully nurtured. Usually this relationship develops into a strong and life-long bond but if the Scorpio loyalty is tried once too often or the Cancer feelings betrayed, both might choose to back away from any kind of friendship.

Cancer Child/Scorpio Father

A Scorpio father has a particularly strong affinity with a Cancerian child although it often takes many years before he fully appreciates his offspring's strength of character. With a daughter he is very protective, but where a son is concerned he often has problems identifying with its very sensitive nature. A lot will depend on how Scorpio deals with his own emotional vortex. If he tries to cover up his vulnerabilities with rather autocratic behaviour he'll push his Cancerian into the deep end of life, hoping it'll swim. It will, and well away from him! If he is more comfortable with his feelings, then he becomes a wonderful father, gently encouraging his little Crab and giving it a huge amount of support. He will invest much time and effort in his offspring (and probably want a good return!) and will be delighted to see Cancer's ambitious streak emerging, albeit slowly and cautiously! Stubbornness and wilfulness can sometimes blight this relationship, especially if the father tries to exert too much power and control and both father and child can put up impenetrable barriers when hurt or defeated. Despite pitching into choppy waters from time to time, the Scorpio father and Cancer child usually emerge stronger over the years.

Cancer/Scorpio Siblings

On the one hand Cancer/Scorpio siblings fight for their mother's attention, frequently behaving in a thoroughly underhand and manipulative manner. Far more likely, though, is a deep appreciation of the other's loyalty to home and family, and a true understanding that both operate from the heart and feelings. Scorpio is good at encouraging the Crab to venture outside its protective shell. In turn, Cancer helps Scorpio to tone down its rather forthright approach and to learn to share. The Scorpio loyalty and sense of honour comes as a real revelation to Cancer, whose own greatest attribute will be its ability to fuss over, protect and lend a sympathetic ear to its dynamic sibling. In the bleakest scenario, these two will sulk and brood in silence over imagined slights and words said in the heat of the moment and allow communication to break down. Cancer/Scorpio siblings usually become very close as they get older. They are definitely the keepers of each other's secrets.

Cancer and Sagittarius

Cancer Child/Sagittarius Mother

The Sagittarian/Cancer mother and child relationship can be somewhat unnerving for both and it can take a great deal of time for these two to develop anything remotely approaching a real understanding. From the moment the Cancer baby arrives, its emotions are on tenterhooks and he or she is highly sensitive to atmosphere. Born to a mother whose intuition and emotional antennae are not highly developed, the baby Crab frequently feels adrift on a rather inhospitable shore. Cancer needs to be made to feel safe and secure and, as a baby, needs a great deal of attention and cuddling within the confines of its own protective home. This is not the Sagittarian forté. She is happiest chatting to her baby, taking it around on her busy social schedule and leaving it for an hour or two with grandparents, child-minder, next-door-neighbour, anyone in fact she feels will be good with, and for, her child. This frantic pace and constant change of venue and people are thoroughly frightening to her Cancer baby who, through insecurity, wails interminably. Feeding then becomes a problem and the Cancer child is adept at creating mealtime dramas. Tensions, therefore, between mother and baby can easily arise as both have totally different needs and ways of going about life. For the Sagittarian, her rewards for giving her baby that much more personal attention will be numerous. Once the Cancer baby feels secure in the affections of its mother, then that love will be doubly returned and the baby will move heaven and earth to please the Sagittarian, which can be a blessing once Cancer takes its first tentative steps into the outside world. The Sagittarian mother needs endless patience (not a trait associated with the Archer!) with her more socially diffident child. At worst, these two go through life saying 'I just don't understand you', but at best they learn a lot from each other: Sagittarius develops sensitivity and Cancer confidence.

Cancer Child/Sagittarius Father

A Sagittarian father will have little difficulty with a Cancerian daughter: he will be charmed by her natural shyness, compassion and kindness. It is often far more difficult for the adaptable, optimistic and outgoing Sagittarian to develop a good understanding with his far more sensitive and vulnerable Cancerian son. Any Cancer child will certainly see its Sagittarian father as fun to be with and will rely on him for wisdom and sound guidance. The problems arise from the Cancerian attachment to the home, which fly in the face of the Sagittarian need to see life as a glorious challenge. There's nothing worse for Cancer than daunting adventures! Cancer also likes to take life at a relatively slow pace, which can irritate the father who relishes life in the fast lane. The best Sagittarian father nurtures his Cancerian child's caring qualities, boosts its self-esteem and self-confidence and gently encourages its ambitions. In turn, Cancer learns a lot from its father about good judgment, taking calculated risks and enjoying life. Both have to work at this relationship, but the potential rewards for father and child can be enormous.

Cancer/Sagittarius Siblings

The Sagittarius/Cancer siblings tend to love or loathe each other: indifference rarely comes into the equation! However, neither emotion is set in stone and the love/hate situation tends to chop and change all through childhood. As young siblings, however, it can be a relationship fraught with problems. Cancer is all tears, machinations and running to a parent, which the more open, honest and independent Sagittarian finds not only unfair but also thoroughly underhand. Sagittarius, in turn, tramples tactlessly all over Cancer's finer feelings, verbally knocks Cancer for six with its intellectual arguments and can be patronising and boisterous in the extreme. On their good days, of course, Sagittarius finds Cancer a kind and considerate listener and is able to coax the Crab out of its shell. This relationship probably works best with a Sagittarian brother and Cancerian sister but, whatever the situation, these two take time to appreciate each other's qualities and to cope with their differences.

Cancer and Capricorn

Cancer Child/Capricorn Mother

Capricorn and Cancer are opposite signs in the zodiac. In each other, both signs can find a sense of wholeness. The vulnerable, sensitive and highly emotional little Cancerian is born to a mother who wants nothing more than to provide her baby with security, stability and a well-organised life. In turn the Capricorn mother sees the loving trust in her baby's eyes and initially responds well to its rather needy nature. Problems soon arise, however, because Capricorn and Cancer function on very different emotional levels. From the moment of birth, Cancer is susceptible to atmosphere and needs plenty of reassurance. Capricorn is a pragmatist (and certainly keeps her feelings under wraps) and as far as she's concerned, if the baby is fed, warm, loved and in a good routine, everything's OK. The Cancerian baby instinctively knows that its mother is focusing on other things and then feels insecure. Insecurity leads to crying, and usually loss of appetite, and its poor mother is absolutely oblivious to the cause of her baby's distress. The Cancer baby needs much cuddling and lots of affection, which is in no way beyond its Capricorn mother's abilities. It's just that she's got so much else to do and she can't see that all this attention is really necessary. Despite this slight blip, Capricorn makes the most wonderful mother for the Cancer baby. Capricorn truly understands her child's fears about going out into the world and is patient when it becomes a bit clinging. She will never rush her child into changes. She is also captivated by its kind and compassionate nature, and Cancer in turn thrives with such a reliable and patient parent. During the teenage years, an emotional impasse is quite possible: Cancer becomes particularly moody and touchy and Capricorn retreats behind a veil of authority and discipline. Generally, however, there is much love between these two and a genuine appreciation of each other's qualities.

Cancer Child/Capricorn Father

The Capricorn father/Cancer son relationship is usually very different from Capricorn's relationship with his Cancer daughter. In the latter case, he is the protective, (sometimes over-protective) reliable and successful father to his usually very feminine daughter who charmingly winds him around her little finger. She normally feels thoroughly secure with her father around and he delights in showing off his daughter. These two often pursue joint hobbies such as music and collecting antiques. The Capricorn father's relationship with a Cancerian son is potentially much more difficult. All young Cancerian boys have a very strong relationship with their mother, are frequently very gentle by nature and are often seen by the Capricorn father as being a bit 'soft'. Once the Cancer son suspects his father's disapproval he retreats into his shell, thus alienating the Capricorn even further. Capricorn, however, has much to offer his son in the form of practical guidance, an understanding of his ambitions and a rock around which the little Crab can test the waters of life. By steering Cancer's many attributes down productive channels he'll receive much love and appreciation from his son.

Cancer/Capricorn Siblings

The most important factor that unites these siblings is home and family. Both place a high value on a secure and stable domestic scene within which they can flourish. Neither takes a devil-may-care attitude to life – in fact they could be seen to be ultra cautious about everything – and they need much pushing and shoving to get involved in social activities. Within the family, however, there can be much jostling for position as both will want the undivided attention of either father or mother. Rivalry between these two is not uncommon: both want to succeed in life and a sense of competition often makes both do well at school. However, exasperation is usually not far from the surface. Capricorn thrives on order, is self-contained and reliable and can't cope with Cancer's moods. Cancer exists in chaos, is emotional and changeable and frequently resents Capricorn's rigid approach. The things that unite them are, however, far greater than those that divide them and neither is interested in rocking the sibling or larger family boat.

Cancer and Aquarius

Cancer Child/Aquarius Mother

Mix together air (Aquarius) and water (Cancer) and to start with there is the most glorious effervescence. Later it all goes flat. This is often the scenario for this mother/baby relationship, which brings together two incompatible signs of the zodiac. In the excitement of giving birth the Aquarian enjoys all the fizz of a close relationship with her baby. In a short time, however, the differences between the two elements become obvious and both mother and baby can feel deflated. The Aquarian, with her innate confidence and rather cool emotional responses, is mother to a baby who is needy, vulnerable, worried and insecure. The Cancer baby needs constant reassurance, cuddles and a generally tactile approach from its mother and, preferably, only its mother. Aquarius, on the other hand, is absolutely delighted to pass her baby around her friends and family, chat endlessly to it about her thoughts on various aspects of life and to whizz around at a fairly frantic pace. All this is thoroughly unsettling to her little Cancerian who is looking for a quiet and secure environment and lots of close contact with its mother. Thus the scenario develops of a fractious baby and a stressed mother and all because they have differing needs from the mother/baby relationship. Frequently, an Aquarian mother has to go through a major re-think about bringing up her child if she is to avoid the Cancerian sulks and moods that come from misunderstandings. More importantly, an insecure Cancerian tends to cling and nothing is more at odds with the Aquarian independence. Sole attention to her baby will give it confidence and a sense of safety, as will easing it into new company, whether a grandparent, best friend, nursery group or the wider social scene. The hard work the Aquarian puts in to establish a strong and viable relationship in the early years will be rewarded later when she has a wonderfully loving child who will be eternally grateful to its mother for her wisdom, her encouragement and her kindness.

Cancer Child/Aquarius Father

It can take all the Aquarian father's rational intellect to work out how to cope with his Cancerian child. These two have a totally different outlook on life and the Aquarian finds it very difficult to understand the Cancer insecurity. Aquarius usually rates friends way above family and to be faced with a child, particularly a son, who seems more than happy within the domestic unit, is puzzling in the extreme. In his inability to comprehend his child, the Aquarian father often becomes both impatient and didactic, making a sensitive situation even worse. Cancer views his or her father as a bit of a bully and Aquarius sees the child as over-emotional. With a bit of patience and perception, Aquarius will realise that his child is, in fact, ambitious, shrewd and very loving. Given the right encouragement Cancer will blossom under his wisdom, guidance and friendship. Aquarius can often learn a lot (particularly from a Cancerian daughter) about the importance of showing feelings. This is never going to be one of the easiest relationships, but a genuine sense of loyalty and love can be fostered between the two if the Aquarian is prepared to take on the challenge of the early years.

Cancer/Aquarius Siblings

Either these siblings grow up extremely close to each other, on the basis that opposites attract, or they go through childhood totally perplexed by the other's behaviour. In theory, Cancer should be delighted by the Aquarian wit and inventiveness, just as Aquarius should prosper from the Cancerian kindness and imaginative approach to life. In reality, Aquarius becomes exasperated by the touchy emotionalism of the Cancerian whilst Cancer finds it difficult to cope with the Aquarian contrariness and emotional coolness. Aquarius also tends to trample over Cancer's finer feelings just as much as Cancer scoffs at the Aquarian's radical ideas. Within the family, however, these two have totally different agendas. Cancer thrives within the domestic scene, while the Aquarian sibling wants nothing more than to be out and about: so neither treads on the other's patch and each can be helpful to the other. Aquarius fosters social confidence in the Cancerian, and Cancer can smooth troubled family waters, especially when Aquarius threatens rebellion.

Cancer and Pisces

Cancer Child/Pisces Mother

Cancer and Pisces are water signs and, from the start, this mother and baby are totally in tune with each other. Each functions at a high level of intuition and both tend to express their deepest emotions with tears. The Cancer baby will know it's come to a mother who truly understands its worries and rather changeable personality, to say nothing of its sometimes overactive imagination. In turn, the Piscean mother will be enchanted with her little Crablet, immediately sensing its compassionate and loving nature. These two usually swim happily along together, enjoying many of the same interests (whether it's art, music, water sports, collecting seashells or anything else that takes their fancy at a particular time) and pouring their hearts out to each other, knowing the other will be a very good listener. There are, of course, a few blots on this particularly happy landscape, the main one being that Cancer is a much stronger personality than Pisces. Whilst no Cancerian child ever wants to upset its mother, it will soon realise that it can run rings around Pisces who, with her escapist tendencies and unworldly approach to life, sometimes takes her eye off the ball and is certainly not consistent in setting boundaries and routines. This is thoroughly unsettling to the Crab, who, denied a fairly ordered environment, shows its nervousness by being clinging and tearful. Pisces quickly loses patience and tends to drift further away from her needy Cancerian, who, in turn, senses that its mother isn't quite as committed to the relationship as it would like her to be. Rational communication between these two can also be a problem because both are quite secretive. Tears from mother and child usually hide much deeper feelings which remain hidden and unspoken. Thus all sorts of resentments can build up which, usually, have no basis in fact whatsoever. Generally, however, these two develop a close and loving relationship, with the Cancer child taking on a more parental role as it gets older.

Cancer Child/Pisces Father

For a Cancer child who craves a secure and stable domestic environment, it can be quite unnerving to have a Piscean father who seems to come and go at will, has no set routines and seems unable to take a firm stand on anything! On the other hand, when Pisces *is* around he'll be a wonderfully hands-on parent, getting fully involved in his child's life and certainly appreciating Cancer's ambitious nature. He, of course, usually just dreams – the grass very definitely being greener somewhere else in the world – and is therefore delighted to think that his very determined child will make the most of its potential. The Piscean father is very loving and extremely easy-going and, because he can't be bothered with moods, whinging and all the other Cancerian tricks, it's very easy for his child to rule the roost. With exaggerated imaginations (sometimes leading to downright lies on both sides), no defined boundaries and too much sensitivity, these two often swim along in a bit of a muddle but are rarely disposed to blistering arguments or total indifference. Both will show much demonstrative affection and emotionally they will always be on the same wavelength.

Cancer/Pisces Siblings

Cancer/Pisces siblings can get on famously, each appreciating the other's highly sensitive nature and both having many interests in common. Swimming, photography, art, music and creating collections can usually keep this duo happily occupied for hours and, as both tend to thrive amidst a great deal of clutter and mess, neither will be stressed about tidying up. Both signs, however, can be economical with the truth when it suits them and highly manipulative. They also have wonderfully vivid imaginations, putting a spin on situations that would leave the politicians gasping. With Cancer more determined and tenacious, and perhaps slightly better at putting on the wide-eyed innocence, it's often the Crab that wins – then feels guilty about getting Pisces into trouble. Both siblings can retreat into hurt and seething silence from time to time as neither is particularly good at discussing anything calmly and rationally. Despite some difficult times in the relationship, Cancer and Pisces siblings are usually there for the long haul. They understand each other all too well.

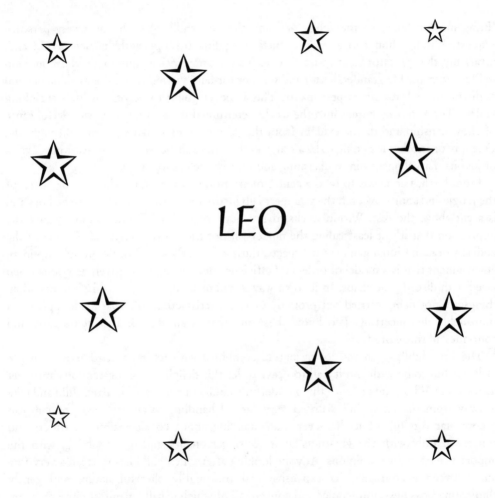

The Leo Child 0-5 Years

'Bring me sunshine', so the song goes, and the Leo child takes this as a very personal request. Watch a lion cub at play or just struggling to cope with its new world and, invariably, the spectator can't resist a smile. It's the same with a young Leo whose mission in life is to make life grander, better and warmer for family, friends and the world in general with the sheer force of its personality. This is never going to be one of life's shrinking violets. The Leo baby comes into the world determined to be noticed, its wonderful sense of showmanship and drama evident from the very beginning of its journey through life. One way or another it's going to be a star, whether through clever attention-seeking devices or just its marvellously sunny, charming and utterly enchanting disposition.

From birth, Leo needs to be the centre of attention. After all, it's the king or queen of the jungle and somehow even the youngest cub instinctively knows it's born to be boss and is a cut above the rest. Within weeks, if not days, of its birth it will definitely give the impression that it's at least ruling the nursery, if not the entire household. As one of the zodiac's organisational geniuses it expects, during the early years, to be brought up in an environment that is a model of order and efficiency and becomes positively fractious when faced with disorder or chaos. In its own way it will make it very clear to its parents when things are not being carried out properly or to its satisfaction: the roar of disapproval is thoroughly disconcerting. Leo knows best and that is an attitude that starts early and continues all through life.

The Leo child's open and loving nature combined with its innate enthusiasm for life makes it fun to be with and it's all too easy to let this delightful youngster constantly get its own way. Who wants to curb this wonderfully ebullient and warm-hearted child and take it away from the limelight? Without very careful handling at an early age the cub can become far too full of itself, never understanding about consideration for others and concerned only with the greatness of its own personality and, once talking, with the importance of its own opinions. Anyone looking after a Leo child has to tread a very fine line between encouraging its expansive and thoroughly cheerful nature and gently eliminating bossiness, intolerance and conceit, all of which usually manifest quite early on.

Crushing the little Leo's spirit with massive amounts of disapproval, however, is probably not going to get the best results. Leos of all ages are far more sensitive than is realised. They usually mask this vulnerable side of their nature with a lot of noise and much shrugging of shoulders, but the Leo flair and optimism is easily deflated and it can take a long time for the cub to recover from being cut down to size. Gently encouraging Leo to listen to what others have to say should also be on the agenda if it's not going to grow up in the belief that its views are all important and not to be questioned. Leo responds best to affection and a sense of humour and any criticism of this child should be conducted with a measure of both.

Like the other fire signs, Aries and Sagittarius, Leo children display dash and verve, are always on the go and love to be appreciated. For the most part they take centre stage for all the right reasons, but once they feel they've been consigned to the wings, make it their business to regain attention. The Leo hiding behind the sofa or making mischief in the next room is just as much taking the lead role as the one showing off its skills to admiring friends and relations. All Leos have a pronounced flair for drama and from an early age little Leo girls are attracted to jewellery, glitz and anything that spells glamour (and, after all, gold is the Leo metal) while the Leo boys tend towards the macho and the expensive. Whether born with hair or not, Leos usually end up with a very fine mane, and girls in particular are often drawn to hair accessories. The Leo style is not necessarily about toys and possessions in abundance: they are far more appreciative of things that are special in some way and like to be ahead of the pack when it comes to the latest 'must have' item. From babyhood, Leo instinctively knows about the right labels and feels thoroughly comfortable with the best in life!

It won't take long for the toddling Leo to take on the role of organising friends and siblings and once at nursery or with a carer will want to be in charge of all and sundry. Whilst its flair for sorting out everyone else's seemingly disordered life is second to none, it is often charged with being bossy and, at worst, bullying. Not everyone wants to do things Leo's way. However, Leo is neither aggressive nor manipulative and is often deeply upset to think that what it sees as its kindness in bringing order out of chaos is misinterpreted. The cub just needs its energies redirected: sorting out the toy box or rearranging the book shelf could be just what's needed to save Leo's face and to put its efforts to positive use. Just when tears and a dose of the short, sharp Leo temper is expected, the cub can astound everyone with a wonderful show of generosity, both of spirit and of cash. Even the youngest will give up its pocket money to someone in greater need. The Leo magnanimity is also legendary: at an early age it recognises other's achievements and is quick to show its pleasure at a friend's good fortune or someone else's happiness.

Where Leo probably needs a lot of help is in coping with life's more mundane tasks and the situations that take it behind the scenes. Whilst the Virgos and Cancers of this world need help in coming out to the front, Leo needs to understand the importance of occasionally being the back-up crew. It's also not always brilliant at doing the groundwork of any project, preferring to stick on the final star, shell, leaf or piece of pasta and take the credit for the whole picture. Learning that others sometimes rightly win the applause is often a hard lesson for little Lions. The creative streak in all Leos should be fostered, however, whether it's music, art, cooking, gardening or producing and starring in a three-act play.

Despite the Leo tendency always to know best, and even the youngest can be quite dogmatic, it can also be extremely kind and thoughtful. Many a small Leo has been known to enquire solicitously about the health of its friend's granny, whether that nice lady in the shop has had her baby and if there's something it can do to help Mummy or Daddy if either is a bit stressed. Encouraging this loving and thoughtful side of its nature is never a wasted effort. Whilst Leo is never going to be in the Virgo league of 'Mummy's little helper' it will certainly help out with much drama and panache and bask in the praise.

Well before Leo reaches the school gates it will have taken on the role of leader in whatever environment it finds itself, but at the same time Leo is not that comfortable with change and rather relishes the status quo. It certainly doesn't have the Sagittarian versatility or the Gemini adaptability. Flung into new situations without careful preparation can leave a Leo child both extremely uneasy and uncertain. The feeling of floundering in different circumstances and suddenly having to cope with totally new surroundings is often covered up magnificently by a loud show of power and bossiness, which then adds to the problems by alienating the little cub from those he most wants to like and impress. Leo needs to be

142

gently briefed for any new start in its life, from the arrival of a sibling (whose life it will be organising from day one!) to its first day at school. On the plus side, of course, Leo is extremely sociable and thrives in company, especially if it's entertaining in its own home. Time taken in the early years to make Leo feel totally confident about meeting new people in new places will stand it in extremely good stead for later on.

Every member of this zodiacal sign is at its best as a glorious Lion rather than a downtrodden domestic moggy and it takes much patience and understanding for that Leo baby to develop into a magnanimous King of the Jungle. Dealing with the young cub's ego, its need for centre stage and its often interfering and rather bossy manner can drive most parents to distraction, but this child's warmth, affection, eagerness to please, kindness and faithfulness is reward indeed for all the efforts made to encourage its attributes and to gently moderate its less attractive characteristics. On its first day at school, Leo will probably have everyone organised, will be radiating warm enthusiasm and a great sense of humour and will doubtless already be holding court as the leader of the pack. This child will surely bring a ray of sunshine into everyone's life.

Leo and Aries

Leo Child/Aries Mother

Colour, warmth and a great deal of energy are synonymous with the Leo and Aries fire and this duo is often be a force to be reckoned with. Both are optimists, thrive in the limelight and have an enormous enthusiasm for life, as well as generally going about their business in an extremely bullish manner. Neither relishes having too much time to stand and stare! Leo will just love its mother's action-packed day and the way in which she encourages her little cub to get involved with anything and everything. Both tend to be uneasy in emotional territory and it's this area that frequently brings an initial difficulty to the relationship. The Leo youngster is far more sensitive than would appear and its innate confidence can be quickly crushed by the forthright Aries manner. Far from dusting itself down and starting all over again, as would Aries, her child can quickly give up and become irrationally stubborn. Aries and Leo also relish being top dog and there's usually a lot of ego involved between these two. Leo will do anything, from temper tantrums to hiding, in order to draw attention to itself: it needs to hold centre stage. Aries, by rights, thinks it is the boss, likes to give orders and to be obeyed. Even with a small Leo involved, this jostling for position as number one is never far from the surface. The Aries 'leap before you look' and general 'can do' approach to life is also very often lost on Leo, who is much more averse to sudden change. New ventures, however exciting, need to be introduced slowly if Leo is not to feel thoroughly unsettled. The Leo inflexibility is often triggered by a sense of uncertainty. Despite the fact that this relationship can, from time to time, be characterised by highly dramatic arguments and much flouncing and slamming doors, these two are usually friends for life. Leo admires the Aries courage and leadership just as much as Aries loves her child's showmanship and generosity of spirit. They particularly enjoy their spending sprees!

Leo Child/Aries Father

The Aries father sets a fast pace, not only for himself but also for his child, and an extroverted little Leo will probably love his or her Aries father's energy, action plans for the weekends and rather grand strategy for life. At the same time, however, Leo is far less gung-ho than its father and, although loving to be the centre of attention, it likes to ensure that it's setting its own agenda, not dancing to Aries' tune. A stand-off between the impatient Aries and the intransigent young Leo often features in this relationship. Little Lions also tend to be quite full of themselves, something which Aries admires on the one hand as it denotes a huge amount of self-belief, but finds irritating on the other as he tries to cope with his child's 'I know best' attitude. At worst, Aries crushes Leo's wonderful optimism and confidence. At best, he expertly recognises and encourages his child's organisational skills and understands that his child's bossiness is probably a cover-up for certain sensitivities. Generally these two usually have much fun together but if big egos get in the way, they can drift apart later on, each frustrated by the other's inability to listen or to care.

Leo/Aries Siblings

The bossy Leo and the adventurous Aries make a formidable sibling duo and usually enjoy a relationship that is characterised by a lot of noise, laughter and general warmth towards each other. Because, however, both are natural leaders, each wants to call the shots and amidst the bonhomie there's invariably a lot of arguing and attention seeking. Leo has the more dramatic flair and quickly turns a spat into a three-ringed circus but Aries gains points with its wit and ability to forget quarrels and to change the subject. Rarely do these two seethe with anger, bear grudges or refuse to resolve their differences. Leo is particularly good at helping Aries to develop sensible plans, rather than ideas flung together and not thought through, whilst Aries can jolt its Leo sibling out of its fixed views. At worst, Aries can crush Leo's splendid spirit with well-chosen, unkind remarks and Leo can be dogmatic and patronising towards Aries. At best a shared sense of humour sees them through any difficulties and later on in life they understand each other's extravagance!

Leo and Taurus

Leo Child/Taurus Mother

Leo and Taurus are both fixed signs which means that they share an inbuilt dislike of change and are inflexible. The Leo baby born to a Taurean mother instinctively recognises its mother's steadfastness and reliability and knows that it's not going to be thrust into uncertain and choppy waters. In turn, Taurus is delighted with her little Leo who seems to be determined to be the centre of attention and in whose eyes she can see both love and loyalty. Taurus, however, can be very possessive of her baby, which goes totally against the grain with Leo, whose mission statement is to bring sunshine to everyone's life! She, therefore, surrounds her child with often unnecessary routines and regulations which, as well as cramping the Lion's social style, also crushes its enterprising spirit. Taurus is far more cautious than Leo and can sometimes feel inadequate in the face of her child's overweening confidence and self-belief. The inherent rigidity of both Taurus and Leo means that there can be some spectacular deadlocked situations, with mother and child entrenched and obstinate. Luckily Taurus is patient and pragmatic and, after having given Leo time to cool off and re-think, invariably finds some way out of the problem. As both signs tend to love the luxury end of the market, an outing with the credit card usually helps enormously! She will be delighted that her young Leo is already picking out the most desirable labels, the shiniest jewels and the best places for juice and biscuits. This relationship prospers when Taurus allows Leo to develop its showy, sociable nature as well as its leadership skills and creative flair. She also has to know exactly when to rein her child back (with much kindness and understanding) and equally when to allow it to move confidently ahead. Without much initial work from the mother this relationship can founder in a great deal of resentment but, at best, Taurus sticks with her cub through thick and thin and Leo appreciates its strong-willed and affectionate mother.

Leo Child/Taurus Father

The Taurean male is never backward at coming forward with his opinions and, with a confident, positive and slightly know-it-all Leo youngster around, he can soon feel thoroughly discomfited. Whilst Taurus will do everything in his power to provide the best for his son or daughter, he usually expects a return on his investment and frequently fails to realise that a Leo child has its own very firm ideas on what constitutes success and achievement. With neither father nor child being particularly strong in the adaptability stakes and both intent on having their own way, there can be some dramatic rows and upsets before any kind of truce is reached. Early on, of course, Taurus delights in his sunny-natured, affectionate child who is clearly in its element being shown off and indulged. Leo also revels in its father's loving and demonstrative nature and both signs are also very creative. A lot of give and take is needed if this relationship is to run smoothly: very often they respect each other a great deal but fail to warm to each other, especially once Leo becomes just as intolerant as its father.

Leo/Taurus Siblings

Leo and Taurus children are resistant to change, very sociable, appreciate the finer things in life and are innately generous (although Taurus will be far more possessive about its toys and treasures than Leo). However, they tend to have fixed views about everything. The Leo bossiness is up against the Taurean obstinacy in every area of life and, without some early lessons in how to back down gracefully if losing a skirmish or an argument, these two can exist in a climate of intolerance and utter frustration. Leo usually shows a great deal more flair than the steadier Taurus, and often gets away with more than its placid sibling, but relies on down-to-earth Taurus to sort out its latest over the top misadventure. Taurus is equally dependent on Leo to jolly it out of resentment and negativity and to inject a bit of originality and enthusiasm. Taurus can also tame Leo's pomposity! While many Leo/Taurus siblings often enjoy a lasting friendship, there are some that cannot see beyond each other's dogmatism, interference and self-indulgence.

Leo and Gemini

Leo Child/Gemini Mother

Gemini is enchanted by the adoration that emanates from her Leo baby while her little cub is fascinated by its lively, witty and talkative mother who makes life so interesting and exciting. As a baby who thrives in the limelight, Leo will just love being handed around Gemini's friends and family, and Gemini will be thankful that her baby doesn't seem to be at all clinging but just radiates sunshine and a thoroughly happy demeanour. She'll also make it her mission to add to her already numerous commitments as she enrols her toddler into swimming lessons, music groups, Mums & Tots sessions or anything else that is going on in the neighbourhood. Leo is in its element in this whole big social scene and soon becomes leader of every little activity. The sky, however, is not totally cloudless in this relationship. Gemini is one of the most adaptable people in the zodiac, but is also emotionally rather cool, while her child is inflexible, bossy and needs much warm and demonstrative affection. Leo, who needs firm boundaries and a routine, can also become perplexed and uncertain when the Gemini whirl becomes something akin to chaos. Leo's fears then manifest in tantrums, stubbornness, sulking or anything else to get attention. Gemini gets further frustrated when she realises that it's virtually impossible to debate anything with her child: Leo doesn't listen, has made up its mind and no one will change it. Hugs and cuddles usually help convince Leo that it might be wrong over certain issues but Gemini is usually more comfortable in the intellectual rather than the physical realm. Subtly Leo can start to rule the roost! At worst, Leo sees its mother as changeable and living on her nerves whilst Gemini thinks Leo is rigid and pompous. On the plus side, and much more likely to be the long-term picture in this relationship, Leo learns much from its mother about versatility and about being open to new ideas while Gemini admires Leo's grand plans, staying power and loving generosity.

Leo Child/Gemini Father

This relationship is usually characterised by much talking although whether there is any real communication is probably questionable. Gemini is not a brilliant listener at the best of times, whilst even the youngest Leo is firmly convinced of the rightness of its opinions. Unfortunately, therefore, Leo is never likely to be stimulated by its father's love of argument and debate but will gain enormously from his interest in books. These two invariably have a lot of fun together, enjoy a busy timetable and admire each other's wit and enthusiasm for life. The Gemini father will do much to foster anything his child sets its mind to, fascinated by Leo's creativity and uncanny ability to take centre stage. Gemini is also frequently in awe of his offspring's flair for the dramatic, if rather less tolerant of Leo's sulking when it doesn't get its own way. In addition, he rarely understands his child's fierce ambitions and also resents its rather bossy attitude, whilst Leo can become frustrated at its father's inconsistency and lack of staying power. If Gemini's rather cool approach isn't seen as rejection by the more emotionally effusive Leo, this is usually a relationship that flourishes over many years.

Leo/Gemini Siblings

As long as Gemini allows Leo (even if it is a much younger sibling) to be the boss, this relationship will be wonderful, as both will then be in the winning position. Leo is comfortable taking the leading role, while Gemini knows that it is quite capable of running rings around its sibling and getting its own way! This is usually a very loving and happy relationship as both enjoy company, a fairly hectic pace and endless chatter. Gemini's plans are sometimes a bit too haphazard for the more organised Leo, who can become thoroughly irritated by its sibling's inability to be on time for anything, let alone in the right place. Leo's flair for the dramatic and its insistence on interfering in everything equally irk Gemini who cannot understand how anyone can get so worked up about things. Although, at times, Leo feels it constantly has to keep Gemini in line and Gemini resents jollying Leo out of its sulks this is rarely anything but a mutually supportive relationship.

Leo and Cancer

Leo Child/Cancer Mother

Leos are full of grandeur, as befits the sign associated with the King of the Jungle, and the Lion cub makes sure it's hogging the limelight as soon as it arrives. It's here to be noticed, to be admired and to rule by the sheer force of its personality! For the Cancerian mother, who generally goes about life in a much quieter fashion, this can all be rather overwhelming. She feels she's being bossed about by an attention-seeking son or daughter who expects to be the very heart of family life and who is also setting the domestic agenda and routine. If things don't go to plan, the Lion's short, sharp temper erupts, quickly followed by huge smiles and happy gurgles. He or she has shown who's in charge! Rather like the other fire signs (Aries and Sagittarius), the Leo baby can easily dent the Cancer mother's fragile self-confidence and convince her she just hasn't got a clue. Like any relationship that, astrologically, is quite challenging, there are some potentially big problems. It can be easy for the Cancerian to criticise because she just doesn't understand her child's enterprising attitude to life, nor it's innate self-confidence, and holding her child back can be her way of coping with the problem. Unfortunately this tends to crush Leo's natural enthusiasm, which can then emerge in its negative manifestation of bullying. Leo, in turn, can make Cancer feel inadequate, fussy and dull. However, on the positive side of this relationship, mother and child can both benefit hugely from the other. The Cancerian mother, because she cares about the welfare of the whole family, will be able to teach her little cub that it's not the only child in the world – a valuable lesson for any Leo! At the same time she can also provide a secure base in which her child's spirit can both flourish and be carefully guided. Her Leo child, who is more sensitive than is realised, has the ability to inspire and enchant her and to understand her fears and feelings.

Leo Child/Cancer Father

From time to time, life can seem to be nothing short of a battle royal between a Cancer father, who prizes his role as head of the family, and a Leo child who is born to rule. The elder is full of passive resistance and the younger awash in rather dogmatic self-confidence and determination to get its own way. Both are ambitious and there's often an element of competition between them which, for the most part, is quite subtle but sometimes (particularly with a Leo son) can become overt and far too keen for family harmony. The Cancerian father's tendency to hide from situations it either doesn't like, or can't cope with, also brings it into conflict with a Leo child who usually fears nothing and has the initiative and enterprise to tackle issues head on. Financial matters often become a bone of contention too, as these two personify the 'save versus spend' lifestyles. It takes time for the Cancer father and Leo child to appreciate that their differences can be mutually beneficial: Leo learns a lot about respecting people's feelings from the father, whilst at the same time smoothing the Cancerian's naturally worried brow and helping him to enjoy life.

Leo/Cancer Siblings

With these two zodiacal neighbours, it tends to be either a very close relationship, each gaining enormously from the other's qualities, or a situation where communication and mutual understanding seem totally non-existent. Cancer frequently feels completely overawed by the grand and pushy Leo, and gets its own back through rather devious means. Leo forgets, at its peril, that although Cancer appears very vulnerable and sometimes rather weak, it has a very tough shell within which it can plot, plan and get itself out of trouble. At worst, Leo comes over as a bully and Cancer as tied to its mother's apron strings. Both siblings will want to make their mark in life and can gain much by taking a leaf out of the other's book. Cancer is patient and sympathetic; Leo is generous (both financially and in spirit) and has excellent organisational skills. If both are astute enough to recognise and acknowledge the other's innate gifts and to laugh at each other's more negative traits, this can be a very supportive and loving relationship, based as much on respect as on family loyalties.

Leo and Leo

Leo Child/Leo Mother

Same sign relationships are never dull. At best each showcases the other's finer points and does much to cover up the less attractive traits but, at worst, each thinks it is outshone by the other and resents seeing a mirror image of its failings. With a Leo mother and child, even at birth, there will be a great sense that they are going to have a marvellous time together. The baby will know that it has come into a well-organised domestic scene and to a mother who will be all too keen to make sure her little Leo is the king (or queen) pin around the home – and anywhere else for that matter. She will also encourage her child's innate creative tendencies and broad-minded thinking. The Leo mother, however, is also queen of her domain and problems soon arise when the baby starts, as do all Leos, to assert its claims to the throne, usually while still in the highchair. Before very long there is a clash of egos and wills, both determined to be centre stage and in control and both thinking they know best. A toddling Leo with very fixed ideas can be formidable indeed! It is not at all surprising that this relationship is frequently characterised by clashes of temperament and stubborn impasses, followed by a silent, and sometimes bitter, retreat while both mother and child re-think tactics. Luckily the Leo mother is the first to appreciate her child's well-hidden sensitivity and understands how important it is not to crush her youngster's enthusiasm and self-confidence. She is also aware that the Leo child's bossiness must be gently curbed. Mother and child can both be dogmatic and intolerant but at the same time are extremely loyal to each other and wonderfully generous and warm-hearted. She will do her utmost to push her child to the top and to help it achieve its ambitions and will be the first to revel in its ultimate success. The good things in life will always keep these two together and, with maturity, each will recognise the other's need to be boss and, from time to time, the importance of basking in the other's limelight.

Leo Child/Leo Father

There's likely to be an excellent understanding between the Leo father and child. Both want the same things from life and both exude a sense of power, magnanimity and showmanship. As they are also both naturally demonstrative and loving, there is a lot of warmth and generosity as well as a certain straightforwardness in the relationship. However, there can also be a lot of jostling for position, especially as the Leo youngster starts to develop a mind of its own. The Leo father will certainly do everything he can to help and encourage his child in whatever field his son or daughter chooses. Whilst his child will be thrilled at the enthusiasm emanating from its father, it doesn't take long for the little Leo to work out that it's perhaps fulfilling its father's dreams rather than its own. The Leo cub's refusal to toe its father's line and the alpha male's insistence on knowing what's best for his child often causes a major stalemate with resentment high on both sides. Despite worrying that his Leo child is going to usurp his throne, the father usually takes enormous pride in his son or daughter and, if both remember their station in life, this can be a mutually beneficial relationship.

Leo Siblings

All Leos like to be the boss and within this sibling relationship there can be a lot of pushing and shoving for the leadership role or, in the first place, for the sole attention of a parent. As neither child is likely to acquiesce over anything, there can be a great deal of noisy ordering about and intolerance as well as a total inability to listen to or to understand each other. A competitive edge is also likely to feature in everything – from the sports they enjoy to who made the best jokes and got the biggest laughs. After all, both children are showmen or women of the first order! On the plus side, however, they are likely to be extremely kind and generous to each other (both financially and in spirit), be mutually loyal and faithful in the face of a parental ticking-off or hostility in the playground (neither is prone to grassing up the other) and share a great sense of humour. Their understanding that the best things in life are not free at all, but vastly expensive, also binds these two together. If the relationship fails, it's invariably because a big ego gets in the way of real friendship.

Leo and Virgo

Leo Child/Virgo Mother

The Leo baby, up-front, showy and destined to take centre stage is born to an industrious, conscientious mother who prefers to work behind the scenes. She looks at life's smaller pictures and her Leo child is preparing to paint vast landscapes. At the start of this relationship Leo will certainly feel it's within a well-organised environment, that its every whim is being attended to and that its mother is putting her baby's needs first. It won't take long, however, for the baby to feel it's being quietly thwarted. Virgo worries, fusses and usually becomes thoroughly over-protective of Leo, whose message to life in general is 'bring it on'. Rather than taking her baby out and about, she'll see the slightest sniffle or perhaps a tinge of pink on the cheek as a perfectly good reason to keep her baby swaddled tightly at home. She ends up with a fractious baby, thoroughly frustrated at what it sees as being held back. Virgo then works even harder at mollycoddling her baby Leo and a vicious circle ensues, one which often continues right through childhood. Stress is also invariably inherent in this mother/baby relationship as Virgo prizes neatness and order and Leo really doesn't understand either concept. Much hassle often occurs between these two over the minutiae of life rather than the grand designs, Virgo frequently spending hours rationalising her decisions to a little Leo whose thinking is more expansive and mind a great deal broader than her own. It doesn't take long for Leo to try to rule the roost, organising its mother and becoming quite bossy. On the plus side, of course, Virgo can be a wonderful support to her Leo child, working in the background to ensure it does well at school and in the world generally, while Leo will be brilliant at jollying its mother out of her 'nervy' moments. A wise Virgo mother will know she is the power behind the throne of her successful child and a magnanimous Leo will be the first to acknowledge her role.

Leo Child/Virgo Father

On the one hand Virgo will be a wonderful father to Leo, supporting his child's every new interest. On the other, he'll fail to understand his child's larger than life personality and its need to do things in a grand style: Virgo thinks this is showing off. The perfectionist in Virgo also finds it greatly irritating that his Leo child seems not to care about finishing off projects neatly, tidying away toys or keeping things in any kind of order. Criticism hits Leo very hard. Virgo sees the Leo self-confidence, optimism and enthusiasm and never realises it covers up a personality that can be quickly and easily crushed. Leo, at an early age, can begin to see its Virgo father as a bit of a wet blanket, while Virgo despairs of a child who is becoming bossy and more intolerant of 'guidance' by the minute. Money can also become a bone of contention: Virgo is flabbergasted at how fast Leo spends its pocket money on such flashy goods. It takes much give and take for this relationship to work well, but Virgo is rational and adaptable and Leo generous and faithful and, over time, each usually comes to appreciate the other's qualities.

Leo/Virgo Siblings

These two often get on quite well as both have very different needs from family life. Virgo is happy to be fussed over and revels in being 'Mummy's little helper' while Leo likes a bigger stage and seeks to entertain, charm and lap up the applause. Virgo, of course, frets when Leo mucks up the jigsaw and arranges the books in the wrong order, while Leo fumes about its sibling's nit-picking, hypochondria and constant questioning of orders. Leo can be infuriatingly bossy and organising and hates to lose an argument. When Virgo picks holes in its plans and is proved right over detail, the short, sharp Leo temper erupts. Virgo then retreats, usually complaining of a stomach problem brought on by nervous tension. Gradually, Leo learns to trust Virgo's discernment and frequently better judgment and Virgo puts faith in Leo's ability to bring sunshine and excitement into their lives. At best, these two very different personalities make a great team: at worst, the Leo bombast and Virgo's analytical approach lead them down totally different roads.

Leo and Libra

Leo Child/Libra Mother

The Leo child is eager to please and the Libra mother keen to be liked. In many ways this is a delightful relationship, with both mother and child endowed with an abundance of charm and the easy-going Libran more than ready to cope with, and massage, her baby's ego. From the start Leo will relish Libra's appreciation of the finer things in life and feel thoroughly comfortable in the laid-back and harmonious atmosphere that its mother strives to create. She, in turn, will be both adored and admired by her sunny-natured child, who will do its best to make her feel she's doing an excellent job. The naturally affectionate Libran is instinctively at home with the overtly loving Leo, and mother and child will thrive together on a busy social schedule: they love company, parties and being out and about. In order, however, for Leo to fulfil its potential, it needs to have its more grandiose schemes and its rather organising nature carefully channelled. Libra hates discord of any kind, and it's often difficult for her to be consistent with Leo over boundaries and discipline. She vacillates: one day she's all laissez-faire and the next she's calling the shots, and Leo quickly twigs that she's unpredictable. Sooner rather than later the little cub is running rings around its mother, its smile, jollity and innate self-confidence beguiling Libra into not making a scene. Without occasionally being pulled up for taking over, interfering or lack of patience, Leo is in danger of becoming bullying and intolerant. Libra has to force herself to cope with a truculent and stubborn Leo if she's not to see her child either become unpopular or unpleasantly attention-seeking. If Libra loses control of her cub early on, she can feel pressurised and bossed around by Leo as it grows up but on the whole this relationship prospers. Leo values its mother's cool and rational approach to life and Libra gets a real buzz from watching her child tackle everything with such supreme enthusiasm and flair.

Leo Child/Libra Father

The Libran father loves having a Leo child by his side. Here is someone who instinctively understands the whole business of making the right contacts and spending money on luxuries and who seems to radiate leadership potential. All this when his Leo son or daughter is probably only two! Libra will also be keen to foster Leo's ambitious streak, although he can sometimes get flustered by Leo's pushy and direct approach to getting on in life. His tact and diplomacy often have to be employed after his child has made either pertinent remarks or asked an embarrassing question. Where Libra frequently comes unstuck with Leo is in decision-making and discipline. All too often he opts out, not realising that Leo then sees him as a soft touch. Without firm guidance his Leo youngster can become insufferably pompous, dogmatic and egocentric and the Libran father is frequently baffled as to why his little cub is so difficult when he has been such a model of restraint and kindness! The teenage years are the worst for this combination when power battles usually loom. The good things in life, however, usually unite this father and child and a joint spending spree can do wonders for both.

Leo/Libra Siblings

The easy-going Libra can easily find itself outmanoeuvred and out-gunned by its more assertive Leo sibling who will tend to take charge of this relationship wherever he or she comes in the pecking order. Watching Libra unable to make up its mind, giving in to stronger personalities and then huffing and puffing about being taken advantage of will drive Leo to distraction. The only answer is to get its charming sibling organised and if that means being a bit bossy, then so be it! Libra, however, has its own powers. Leo needs Libra's diplomatic skills to cover up its latest verbal gaffe, to say nothing of the Libran's ability to make those wonderfully quiet and sensible suggestions about some rash action Leo is about to take – usually saving the Lion from making a total fool of itself. Libra will always be enchanted by the loyalty and warmth of its sibling, just as much as Leo will be captivated by Libra's affability. These two enjoy the same lifestyle and respect each other's ambitions. Their friendship rarely comes to grief.

Leo and Scorpio

Leo Child/Scorpio Mother

The attraction, at birth, between this mother and child is enormous. Leo knows its mother is strong, capable and extremely determined to do her best for her child. Scorpio just loves her sunny-natured baby who clearly wants to be the centre of her world and already seems to be showing signs of a show- business career! She will provide a thoroughly stable environment and strict routines in which her little cub will thrive (neither sign is happy with too much chop and change) and will also ensure that her son or daughter is ahead of the pack when it comes to those milestones that define babyhood and early childhood. Leo is keen to please and wants to make its mother happy – up to a point. Both mother and child can be formidably stubborn: neither is prepared to give in and because Scorpio has a staying power that is not in Leo's armoury, she invariably wins. The victory, however, is often short-lived, because in defeating Leo, rather than negotiating and finding a compromise, she finds her youngster less enthusiastic about her plans and less willing to accommodate her wishes. Their mutual obstinacy also leads to each retreating to its own corner amidst much seething and sulking. Leo is one of the most open signs in the zodiac – what you see is what you get – whereas Scorpio is the most private. The young Leo is often mystified by its mother's suspicious nature and seeming inability to discuss anything honestly, just as much as Scorpio wishes her cub didn't make so much noise and brouhaha about everything. This relationship will definitely have its more dramatic moments. The deep Scorpio feelings and passions will be at odds with her Leo child's dogmatism and self-centredness and battles royal will probably break out over any threat to Scorpio's rule. At worst these two complain bitterly about each other and develop a very cool relationship. At best they put their innate loyalty to good use and learn valuable lessons, Leo about perseverance and Scorpio about trust and openness.

Leo Child/Scorpio Father

The Scorpio male and his Leo child are both highly ambitious but Leo would prefer to have its own game plan rather than be forced to fall in with its father's. From an early age, whether it's deciding on a sport to follow, a hobby to take up or perhaps even telling the childminder how to do the job, the Scorpio father likes to control. The young Leo is, at first, thrilled to have such a powerful and forceful father whose organisational skills seem to match its own, but soon becomes despairing and frustrated at having its ideas crushed and plans thwarted. Scorpio, of course, only has his child's best interests at heart but while Leo is waiting for that enlightenment, father and child go through some extremely stressful times. Scorpio sees Leo as bombastic, over-confident and intolerant, whilst Leo, although often mesmerised by its father's energy and magnetism, thinks he's obsessive. A Scorpio father and Leo son can often part company, each seeing the other as impossible to deal with, but a Leo daughter is often much better at dealing with Scorpio's complex nature. However, despite the stalemates, hurt silences and rows, both are immensely faithful and loyal.

Leo/Scorpio Siblings

There are some sibling relationships that fall into the immovable object and irresistible force category and this is one of them. On the one hand, if left to their own devices and not forced too much into one another's company, they will get along famously. On the other, they can be constantly at loggerheads. Leo will complain bitterly about being manipulated by Scorpio who, in turn, will resent its sibling's constant interference and bossiness. Both will want to call the shots, Leo through becoming more and more dogmatic and Scorpio through sheer determination and, frequently, fairly underhand tactics. Leo, however, is better at a more open and longer game and usually wins against a young Scorpio who looks for short-term gain. Scorpio can also become very jealous of its sibling, especially if Leo is doing well at something, which is in stark contrast to Leo's generous magnanimity. Both, however, will show great loyalty and love to the other and it takes much for this duo, hassles notwithstanding, to give up on each other.

Leo and Sagittarius

Leo Child/Sagittarius Mother

Sagittarius and Leo are both fire signs, share an enormous enthusiasm for life and are geared to action, enterprise and initiative. From the start mother and baby have the same outlook, self-confidence and determination to be at the heart of things. Neither is usually found hovering in the shadows. The Sagittarian mother is more than happy to let her Leo baby take centre stage, probably basking in reflected glory as her regal little Lion cub showers all and sundry with magnanimous smiles. She is also adept at dealing with the Leo obstinacy, finding it easy to coax her child into a more adaptable frame of mind. These two will thrive on a busy social life and plenty of drama! Later on they'll no doubt enjoy massive spending sprees together as both take a somewhat cavalier attitude to money. In all relationships, of course, there are potential problems and these two are no exception. Leo develops best in a fairly well-organised environment and this is definitely not the Sagittarian mother's strong point. Sagittarius is extremely versatile and quick to take in anything new, while Leo is much happier with the status quo, and the baby can find the mother's seemingly haphazard approach to life quite unsettling. Her baby will make it very obvious when things are not going to the Leo plan, becoming fractious in the extreme and exhibiting the short, sharp temper that is typical of the sign. Leo is also an extremely self-centred sign and can be a tad bossy from a very early age, something the Sagittarian usually finds irritating once the initial baby charm has worn off. These are relatively minor problems, however, in one of the zodiac's better relationships. More than anything else, these two have a tremendous ability to buoy each other up during life's more trying moments and, with many interests in common, often enjoy a great sense of camaraderie.

Leo Child/Sagittarius Father

With a Leo baby taking its place at the centre of the family and destined from birth to rule the roost, the Sagittarian father can find himself quickly pushed aside by this bundle of charming, but determined, joy! His Leo child will always want its own way and the Sagittarian father will find it difficult to maintain a firm line where discipline is concerned. Being inconsistent merely fuels the baby Lion's sense of being boss, which then infuriates the father who sees his authority as being undermined. The confident Leo child is also good at hiding its more sensitive nature, which makes its relationship with its father slightly more complicated. Sagittarian men are even less able than their female counterparts to tune in to emotional vulnerabilities and the Leo child's ego can be badly bruised – quite unintentionally – by the father's sometimes tactless and thoughtless behaviour. For the most part, however, the Leo child and Sagittarian father get on very well, Leo benefiting from its father's wisdom, encouragement and sense of adventure and Sagittarius thriving in his child's generous, expansive and enthusiastic attitude to life.

Leo/Sagittarius Siblings

Sagittarius and Leo siblings invariably become great allies early on and usually maintain that friendship throughout their lives. They see life and situations in broad strokes and panoramic vistas and possess big hearts and unbounded enthusiasm. Both tend to have many interests, enjoy a busy social life outside the home and share a great sense of humour. From an early age, these two like to do things in style and, whether it's their pocket money or Gran's tenner, just love to spend money. Leo is certainly more competitive and ambitious than Sagittarius and can be a spur to the Sagittarian to make greater efforts. In turn, the Sagittarian sibling can do much to make Leo aware that there are other people who have to be considered in life and to curb both its self-centredness and dogmatism. The Leo sibling will also come to rely on the Sagittarian's philosophical outlook, just as much as Sagittarius will benefit from Leo's excellent organisational skills. Short, sharp temper tantrums apart, these two bask in each other's qualities and have plenty of good times together.

Leo and Capricorn

Leo Child/Capricorn Mother

To the sometimes rather self-contained Capricorn, the arrival of her playful little Lion cub, exuding huge rays of sunshine and clearly loving being the object of great adoration, is an absolute delight. Leo is equally thrilled to find that it has a mother who seems dedicated to making its life run like clockwork and happy to be at its beck and call. It's not long, however, before the Capricorn mother realises that she has something of a bossy show-off on her hands. It also becomes clear that her young child takes a fairly cavalier attitude to money and appears to yo-yo between bouts of rather restless activity and excessive laziness. All this is in stark contrast to the more disciplined, prudent, thrifty and discreet Capricorn approach to life, to say nothing of its hard-working ethos. In her efforts to impose some kind of order and control, she frequently reins in her little cub far too tightly. Although she will be brilliant at curbing her child's rather overbearing approach and at making it see that other people have to be considered, she also has a tendency to crush its open-hearted, generous and happy spirit. Leo is far more sensitive than Capricorn appreciates, and has a great dignity: it is not difficult for the mother to ignore both, whereupon her child either comes back on the attack, and very noisily to boot, or retreats in a sulk and makes a battle plan. Leo can therefore see its mother as someone who both cramps its style and hasn't a clue about either its sensibilities or the good things in life. It usually takes a lot of effort for these two to develop a close relationship. If Capricorn is open to her child's more adventurous mind-set and Leo picks up on its mother's perseverance and determination, they can both benefit. More importantly, both want to get to the top of life's ladder. In a love of material success and status, they have much in common and later in life this often becomes the mainstay of an affectionate bond.

Leo Child/Capricorn Father

The Capricorn father definitely sees himself as head of the family and takes his parental responsibilities very seriously. His Leo baby comes into the world with the clear idea that it's king or queen of the castle and destined to rule. The potential for a power struggle at some stage is obvious. Initially, Capricorn loves the idea that his Lion cub is popular, high-spirited and enthusiastic about everything. Like everyone else associated with a little Leo, he basks in the sunshine that just radiates from his child. Equally, Leo appreciates its father's dry wit, encouragement to do well and the sense of security he engenders in the family. However, the sometimes flashy and spontaneous Leo nature, to say nothing of the way it spends its pocket money, starts to irk its Capricorn father who sees his child as thoughtless, extravagant and even rather reckless. In turn, Leo thinks of Capricorn as repressed, rigid and pessimistic and, more to the point, totally unappreciative of its natural leadership skills. During the teenage years, as much with a daughter as with a son, these two usually have a fairly traumatic time, but the long-term prognosis can be good, especially if Leo is successful in life.

Leo/Capricorn Siblings

With these two there can be much jockeying for position in the family. Leo naturally thinks it is boss, whilst Capricorn needs to be in control of both situations and its sibling. Frequently they waste a lot of time squabbling and in attention-seeking ploys, which give one of them short-lived satisfaction. Leo also tends to see Capricorn as a bit of a killjoy, whilst Capricorn views Leo as conceited and spendthrift. As with all astrological relationships that are inherently incompatible, it takes time and effort for each to appreciate the other's qualities. Leo can do much to jolly along the more cautious Capricorn, especially on the social scene, while Capricorn can help Leo with its grand plans – especially if it means injecting some common sense or looking at more practical ideas. Neither is particularly emotional but, in time, both come to understand the other's hidden sensitivities. The Leo enthusiasm is also a good antidote to the Capricorn pessimism and laughter is definitely their best medicine.

Leo and Aquarius

Leo Child/Aquarius Mother

The Leo baby arrives in the world with one thing on its mind: to be the centre of attention and the sunshine in everyone's life. This suits his or her Aquarian mother admirably. She belongs to one of the most sociable signs and expects her child to be exactly the same. Therefore, she basks in her baby's limelight as he or she is adored by all and sundry and makes its presence felt. Aquarius and Leo are opposite signs in the zodiac and both feel complemented by the other: that is not to say, however, that the relationship is going to be straightforward and comfortable. The Leo ego is on display right from the start and this can be quite disconcerting for the Aquarian mother who is much more at ease with a wider humanitarian outlook. Her child's attention-seeking nature can also be a source of contention: she prefers to make her point coolly and intellectually and finds it difficult to understand the roar, fire and temper of her ebullient cub. Both Aquarius and Leo can be very stubborn and this relationship tends to experience great clashes of will, the first of which often occurs well before the 'terrible twos'. It is also often forgotten that Leo is far more sensitive (particularly to criticism) than it ever appears and it is not difficult to crush the enthusiastic and sunny Leo disposition with a few well-chosen, and wrong, words. The Aquarian mother frequently falls into this trap as her emotional detachment can blind her to her Leo baby's sensibilities. Her child's confidence and bombast are often nothing but a thin veneer. However, on the plus side, the Aquarian mother will encourage her child's interests and social aspirations and give plenty of wise guidance. These two will also have a lot of fun together. In return for her lively and inventive attitude to motherhood, her Leo child will bring her huge delight and a warmth and generosity of spirit (and wallet) that is truly humbling.

Leo Child/Aquarius Father

From an early age Leo wants to be the King of the Jungle, and in an Aquarian father comes up against someone who is reluctant to give up his crown. Power struggles between father and child (and just as much with a daughter as a son) often occur sooner rather than later, and an innate wilfulness from both parties results in a reluctance to find any middle ground. However, there is also much warmth and affection between the Aquarian father and Leo child and often many shared interests, (including the joy of good living!) although the wise Leo child steers away from the same line of work as its Aquarian father. It can be very difficult for Leo to come out of the Aquarius shadow! In order for the relationship to flourish, Aquarius has to encourage his Leo child's need for the limelight and must also offer much praise and sensible guidance. He also needs to understand the fiery Leo emotional nature that he tends to find slightly threatening, so different is it from his own more detached feelings. Leo, in turn, should appreciate its father's loyalty and friendship which will always stand the test of time, even when Leo has eventually won the crown!

Leo/Aquarius Siblings

Like all fire signs, Leo thrives on action, initiative and enterprise. Aquarius, by contrast, takes a much more detached and intellectual approach to life but is inventive and willing. Together these two can make a formidable duo, Leo giving Aquarius a much-needed push to put ideas into action, and Aquarius perhaps putting the brakes on Leo's sometimes grandiose plans. Unfortunately, both signs can be obstinate and far from making the most of each other's talents and learning from each other's strengths, they frequently bring out the worst in each other. Leo tends to become bossy and patronising, whilst Aquarius revels in being contrary and unpredictable. However, this sibling situation rarely reaches a total impasse. Their mutual love of the social scene, their natural charm and their innate understanding of each other (whether it's admitted or not!) usually bring a close friendship, although not one where they live in each other's pockets. This relationship needs space if it is to prosper and the dynamics often work best when Leo is the older sibling.

Leo and Pisces

Leo Child/Pisces Mother

The dramatic, ebullient Leo baby, whose raison d'être is to brighten up the world and to take charge of each and every facet of life, is born to the most gentle, compassionate and unworldly mother in the zodiac. Pisces happily swims in her own deep pools and quietly muddles through, hoping that the mundane and distinctly unglamorous parts of her day will be taken care of (or preferably just go away). Leo needs routine, a certain amount of discipline, to know where the boundaries are and, most important of all, to feel that it's in a totally organised environment. Sensing a certain amount of chaos around at an early age, the baby can become singularly fractious, fuelling the Piscean's escapist tendencies, whether it's an extra glass of wine in the evening or taking on additional commitments outside the home. Once toddling and showing a bit of independence, Leo starts to call all the shots, making the already insecure Pisces feel even more vulnerable. Reluctant to enforce rules and quickly giving up on unequal struggles she then wonders why her child starts to become bossy and, at worst, rather bullying. Leo likes to be centre stage and quickly voices its displeasure at its mother's rather vague and piecemeal attitude to its achievements. Despite the potential problems, this relationship will never be lacking in love. Leo invariably shows utter devotion and Pisces selflessly and happily indulges her child. She also understands the more sensitive side of Leo's character and intuitively picks up the worries hidden by her child's intolerance and bombast. Both mother and child are also highly creative, the Piscean imagination blending wonderfully with the Leo showmanship and sense of drama. This relationship works well if Pisces can instigate an element of order and discipline and devote much time to her cub. Without a lot of effort, however, these two remain an enigma to each other, Leo seeing Pisces as weak and vague and the mother thinking her child is pompous and opinionated.

Leo Child/Pisces Father

Most Piscean fathers are devoted to their children and wouldn't dream of letting them down, but to a Leo child who can be demanding at the best of times and needs much praise and encouragement, its father always seems to have something better to do. The fact that he is not making Leo the centre of his life 24/7 is enough to make his child feel that he is an absent parent! Far from it. Pisces will do much to encourage everything his cub takes on, will be extremely supportive and understanding in times of trouble and is likely to be instrumental in guiding Leo towards the arts. He'll also be entranced by his cub's warmth and generosity even though, at times, he'll feel he's being pushed from pillar to post by a stronger personality. Leo desperately needs Pisces to take a strong lead and gets utterly frustrated at its father's general vagueness. This relationship often works better with a Leo daughter, who will just adore her gentle father. A Leo son can quickly lose patience with what it sees as weakness but is frequently amazed at his father's perception and insight – and grateful for it as well.

Leo/Pisces Siblings

To Leo, Pisces is a mystery, whose tearful dramas have to be soothed and idealistic notions brought firmly down to earth while Pisces thinks Leo is a bossy show-off and intolerant to boot. Leo frequently becomes exasperated at the chaotic state of its Pisces sibling's existence just as much as the Fish resents being organised by Leo and having to listen to its entrenched views. Despite these difficulties, and this is never going to be one of the easiest sibling relationships, there can be some wonderful rays of sunshine. The Piscean ability to pick up on its sibling's hidden concerns is an enormous help to Leo, who finds the Fish to be a sympathetic listener and full of good intuitive advice. Leo is excellent at injecting a sense of purpose into Pisces, helping it make the most of its talents, and saving the Fish from its own worst follies. Of course, Leo can lead the gullible Pisces down all sorts of unsuitable roads, but is frequently left to face any music alone while Pisces protests innocence and swims quickly away. If opposites attract, then these two will remain friends for life but sometimes this relationship just fades away.

VIRGO

The Virgo Child 0-5 Years

Usually very amenable, thoroughly likeable and seldom prone to tantrums or obstinacy, a Virgo baby is one of life's little joys. Just like the adult members of this sign, the smaller version is practical, hard working and reliable, as well as fussy and perfectionist. Unlike its astrological cousins Aries and Leo, however, Virgo will never noisily crave the limelight. Its modest demeanour, quiet intelligence and generally retiring nature are charming enough to make it the darling of its parents, siblings, wider family unit and numerous friends.

From the start, Virgo babies know that cleanliness is next to godliness. Nappies need to be changed on a very regular basis, highchairs kept particularly clean, clothes spotless and toys in meticulous order. An out-of-sorts Virgo baby is probably complaining bitterly about what it sees as untidiness, discomfort, lack of routine or something else that its poor parent is not carrying out in quite the preferred manner. This is a sign that tends to like things 'just so' and the perfectionist tendencies show themselves very early on. It's no good thinking that the baby or youngster won't notice when things are wrong. This is a child that very definitely has a mind of its own and, when in an environment that doesn't quite come up to scratch, he or she can be extremely determined about not joining in or not accommodating anyone's wishes. There'll be no grand display of histrionics – just a lovely smile and a quiet insistence on getting its own way.

As well as being quite fastidious in its general lifestyle requirements, the Virgo baby also tends to have a fascination with food, although totally different from the Taurean's sheer enjoyment of mealtimes and general glory in eating. Virgos are born with an innate sense of what is healthy and good for them and seem to know exactly what they should or should not put into their system. Whether turning down apple purée, but relishing spinach, or dismissing pasta in sauce and craving avocado, the Virgo baby shows its discriminating approach to food as soon as the weaning process begins. The breast-feeding mother of a Virgo baby also finds that she has to be very aware of her own diet: this is an infant whose delicate digestive system is easily upset and whose equally sensitive nervous system becomes quickly stressed when something is not to its liking. This is one of the zodiac's natural worriers, second only perhaps to Cancer, and is the sign that gets even more stressed when there is nothing to fret over! Calming the little Virgoan's imaginary or real fears can be a regular feature of its upbringing. It is not naturally blessed with an abundance of self-confidence and, without constant reassurance, it can easily become withdrawn. Hugging cares and woes to itself and being concerned about all sorts of hypothetical problems, the young Virgo can easily become prone to illness.

'Mummy's little helper' is a favourite epithet to describe this willing and practical member of the zodiac. The Virgo youngster is thoroughly at home helping out in the kitchen or garden, in the supermarket or looking after the needs of a sibling. At three years old it almost relishes the responsibility of finding its favourite yoghurt or its father's preferred cereal, weighing out an ingredient, planting bulbs or fetching and carrying equipment needed for a baby brother or sister. Virgo is also brilliant with pets and, more than most, is utterly reliable in looking after them. It thrives on being useful: this is not a child who wants to indulge flights of fancy, plan grand adventures or be a leading member of the social scene (although Virgo children are usually extremely popular). Tidying away toys, keeping its room spick and span and making sure its clothes are stored in an orderly fashion are also Virgo hallmarks, although this potential neatness is not always obvious. Sometimes its space can seem crowded and even chaotic, but somewhere in the room a shelf, a drawer, a cupboard or a box of crayons will be meticulously arranged!

On the whole, the Virgo child quickly understands the logistics of building blocks, plastic bricks, construction kits and anything else that has to be put together. After all, these are the future DIY experts and conquerors of the flat pack. He or she has a wonderfully enquiring mind, likes to be kept busy and wants to find out how things work. At an early age, too, Virgo starts collecting: stamps, shells, pressed flowers, stickers, anything, in fact, to which it can give its detailed attention. However, in its obsession with both detail and getting things absolutely right, Virgo can seem both slow and pedantic. It needs to be encouraged to widen its perspective at times and, whilst never asked to abandon its high standards, reminded that it's quite human to make the occasional mistake! Virgo's quest for knowledge is also paramount. It usually loves books, wants to learn to read and to write and will be very appreciative of visits to museums, historic houses and anywhere else where its intellect is both fed and challenged. Virgo is not overtly ambitious and is usually happier as second in command or, more likely, the power behind the throne. In the playground or at nursery, the little Virgo is often Leo's bag-carrier and strategy maestro and absolutely indispensable!

Virgo is honest and straightforward and, more often than not, a wonderful mimic. It therefore has a huge talent to amuse and to embarrass! There is nothing malicious about Virgo: if something needs to be said, and especially if the child thinks it's for someone else's good, then it is sure to come out with statements that leave everyone open-mouthed. Although it can be frighteningly astute and critical from the moment it learns to talk, it finds criticism and teasing difficult to take. Much diplomacy is often needed around a small Virgo but it's equally important not to crush its genuinely open nature. A charming diffidence rather than optimism and ego is one of Virgo's inherent traits and, without encouragement to develop a more outgoing side, it can become retiring and unsure: even worse, it ties itself to its mother's apron strings and takes years to undo the knots. Virgo is often seen as something of a loner, which is not the case at all: it's extremely self-sufficient. It greatly values its friendships but does not feel the need to socialise simply for its own sake. No Virgo child ever sits and twiddles its thumbs: he or she always has some important project to get on with.

Like the other earth signs (Taurus and Capricorn), Virgo thrives in a settled routine and a stable environment although it is definitely more adaptable than the others. Whilst it will get itself into a right old lather if anything akin to chaos looms over the horizon, let alone gets into the home, it is certainly able to cope with minor changes and different systems. In fact, getting a Virgo child involved in anything new around the home is very important. For a start he or she will love the feeling of being part of what is going on and, even more, will probably be more organised than some other members of the family!

Despite its often quiet and cool demeanour, the Virgo baby needs lots of demonstrative affection. Because it's not naturally effusive it's all too easy to forget that this is an extremely tactile child and, without encouragement, its wonderful sense of touch can easily wither, leading to possible emotional problems when it is older. It usually responds best to quiet and gentle discipline. Harshness, noise and strict rules and regulations lead to fear rather than respect, to say nothing of all that pent-up worry.

This is one of the most winning, willing, unassuming and delightful children in the zodiac and one of the most underestimated. Because it goes about life in a quiet way, gets on with what it enjoys and never goes out of its way to cause trouble, it is very easily overlooked. However, it's the tortoise and hare syndrome and very often the Virgo child comes first through sheer diligence and application as well as its genuine desire to be helpful. It is also naturally discriminating and discerning and rarely does a young Virgoan make a mistake in its friendships or actions: this is not a four-year-old who is taken in by a showy nature or hollow promises. In fact, glitz and glamour are never likely to be part of the Virgo lifestyle. Even the youngest favours the sensible over the silly or the impractical!

Rather like Sagittarius, the Virgo child is often wise beyond its years and can seem much older than many of its contemporaries when it reaches the school gates around its fifth birthday. Although nervous about this big change in its life it will, in all likelihood, immediately take an even less certain pupil under its wing, sorting out his or her coat, books and chair and probably acting as protector in the playground. This youngster is kindness and gentleness personified who, in its own quiet way, knows exactly where it is going and how to get there.

Virgo and Aries

Virgo Child/Aries Mother

In many ways Aries and Virgo are astrological misfits and, as with all inherently difficult relationships, there is both the potential for great success and an equal possibility of complete failure. The Virgo baby will be in absolutely no doubt about its mother's genuine pleasure at the arrival of her newborn. Aries does nothing quietly or by halves and will immediately be arranging a busy social life for herself and her baby, needing to fit in as much as possible into their day. Sitting in peaceful contemplation is never her style. Unfortunately her Virgo baby thrives in a settled routine and a less harassed and much more tranquil environment. Although not a baby who normally clings to its mother's apron strings and who is certainly very sociable and interested in the world around, Virgo often finds the hectic pace and general uncertainty highly stressful. Its rather pernickety approach to food and its fastidiousness (all too evident in the smallest Virgo) can be confusing and irritating to Aries who doesn't see why her baby can't just go with the flow. It takes a lot of patience to get the best from a Virgo child. He or she likes to take life slowly and cautiously, putting great effort into doing everything perfectly and, like Gemini, is full of questions about anything and everything. This is not the Aries forté: she wants everything accomplished now, and preferably five minutes ago, doesn't enjoy stopping for any length of time to explain things to a three-year-old and cannot understand the fussy and analytical approach to life that seems to preoccupy her child. Virgo thus feels unappreciated and starts to lack confidence, whilst Aries believes her child to be pedantic and potentially rather negative about life. However, if the early years can be successfully negotiated, then Virgo gains a great deal from its enthusiastic and go-ahead mother, whilst Aries benefits from her child's more discerning manner and perceptive comments! At worst, these two end up in a state of mutual apathy: Virgo feels trampled on and Aries crumbles under a volley of criticism.

Virgo Child/Aries Father

The Aries father is frequently baffled by a Virgo child. His natural optimism and can-do attitude are invariably lost on his son or daughter, who in no way wants to go out and conquer the world. His child's rather charming reticence is, to him, completely incomprehensible and he usually becomes irritated at the Virgo fussiness and obsession with the safe route. Stress and nervous tension then make the child even more worried about doing the wrong thing, causing Aries to believe that only more autocratic parenting will sort out the problem. This father/child relationship tends to be easier with a daughter, as Aries will be naturally protective and find the modesty enchanting rather than exasperating. With a son the dynamics are much more difficult as Virgo is never likely to possess his father's ego and energy, and Aries will frequently feel that his son is going nowhere. With patience and a little bit of understanding Aries can make an inspirational father to Virgo, encouraging its meticulous approach and practical talents. In return, Virgo will be confident enough to show its father just how clued-up it can be as well as proving, later on, to be a very safe pair of hands.

Virgo/Aries Siblings

This sibling relationship frequently works quite well. Neither feels threatened by the other as each has its own agenda for life and place within the family. Aries loves the social scene, has a general sense of adventure and is constantly making grand plans for the future. Virgo, although good in company, often prefers a quieter life, is brilliant at being the power behind its sibling's throne and provides a very useful and necessary brake when the Arian's ideas go way over the top! Virgo is also often employed as the negotiator when the going gets tough: Aries may have the bluster but it's Virgo who can string an argument together and put it across. However, Virgo can often become stressed by Aries' constant need for action and its inconsiderate attitude whilst Aries frequently sees its Virgo sibling as a wet blanket and tell-tale. At best, these two appreciate and make the most of each other's skills. At worst, they go through life permanently arguing or in a state of complete indifference.

Virgo and Taurus

Virgo Child/Taurus Mother

Taurus and Virgo are both earth signs and share the same need for security, stability and certainty. From the beginning the Virgo baby will feel thoroughly cosseted and safe with its Taurean mother, whose routines and down-to-earth approach will soothe and comfort her child and ensure that its delicate nervous and digestive systems aren't shaken up in any way. Taurus will equally feel thoroughly appreciated, delighting in her amenable and quietly sociable little baby who takes such a bright-eyed interest in everything. The innate Virgo intelligence invariably shines through when in a stress-free environment. Mother and baby are both very practical and, early on, Virgo will love helping in the kitchen, garden, nursery – anywhere in fact where it can both learn and be useful – and a Taurean mother will know exactly how to make her Virgo feel as though her day has been made by her young child's helpfulness! Neither will be desperate to cut a dash on the social scene but as both are inherently hospitable, they are likely to do much entertaining at home and, with its mother's encouragement, Virgo will soon be the star host or hostess. No relationship is totally perfect and with this duo problems tend to arise because Virgo is much more adaptable than Taurus and often feels held back, especially in early childhood, by its more cautious mother. Taurus can become inflexible and obstinate when faced with new steps her child wants to take and greatly fears its desire for any kind of independence, whether it's about making its own decisions or taking on new ideas. Virgo loves to acquire knowledge but Taurus knows best and a clash somewhere along the way is inevitable. Food can also be a battleground for these two: Taurus just loves to eat and Virgo can be very picky, something the mother sometimes sees as rejection of the first order. These problems, however, are rarely enough to stop this relationship from flourishing over the years.

Virgo Child/Taurus Father

The Taurus father finds his Virgo child's modesty, discernment and diligent approach to life an absolute joy. In turn, Virgo sees its father as patient, affectionate and gentle, a fount of practical knowledge and a very stable personality. Both tend to be very practical and his youngster will be the first to offer to assist with the toolbox, a DIY project or cleaning the car, while Taurus will encourage, and spend money on, anything Virgo wants to collect and will probably spend hours helping with his child's construction kits, sandcastles and artistic endeavours. However, the Taurean father can be stubborn and didactic and hates to have his authority questioned. This comes as a shock to his more flexible offspring who likes to look at all sides of an argument and to analyse situations. Frequently Virgo feels it is pushed into situations against both its will and its better judgment, sliding into real or imagined illness as a way of getting out of difficulties. The older Virgo child will resort to criticism, which in turn can bring on a bout of the father's earth-shaking temper! Despite these small blips, this is usually a very sound relationship which tends to improve with the years.

Virgo/Taurus Siblings

On the whole there is much more to unite these siblings than to divide them. Both love domestic security, have a very practical and common-sense approach to life and neither is overtly ambitious, although both like to feel that they can take on responsibilities of some kind from a relatively early age. Problems arise when Virgo feels it's being taken advantage of by its Taurean sibling. Taurus can be excessively self-indulgent, but immensely charming too, and it doesn't take long for the little Bull to be sitting back dishing out the orders and watching its Virgo sibling doing all the work. Taurus loves luxury and the easy life: Virgo is naturally industrious and feels it has to earn everything, from pocket money to appreciation, something Taurus quickly realises! Virgo, in turn, can be critical, fussy and permanently worried about everything, which riles the laid-back Taurean. However, Taurus is invariably able to calm its sibling's fears, just as the analytical Virgo mind comes up with plenty of answers when Taurus has dug itself into an opinionated hole.

Virgo and Gemini

Virgo Child/Gemini Mother

As Virgo and Gemini are both ruled by Mercury, astrologically symbolic of communication in all its forms, there will never be any lack of learning, chatter and activity in this relationship. At birth there is likely to be an immediate recognition of each other's intellect and their mutual quest for knowledge. After that, the differences between the two signs will start to emerge. Gemini likes to take life at a gallop: routine and order are rarely found in this mother's vocabulary and she takes pride in what she manages to cram into each and every day. Her Virgo baby, who prefers an ordered and quieter environment, becomes quite stressed at all this uncertainty and dashing about, firstly dissolving into worried wails and tears and secondly, going completely off its food or suddenly becoming thoroughly changeable in its general likes and dislikes. Virgo is also very self-sufficient and never craves company for its own sake. Its Gemini mother doesn't take too kindly to being on her own and likes to surround herself with people. Her baby can easily feel abandoned when it thinks its mother isn't giving it the required attention, and many a Virgo child has been known to toddle away from a social gathering. Once walking and talking, Virgo finds there are a few more hurdles to overcome. The baby likes to learn slowly and in depth, as opposed to Gemini's butterfly approach. Gemini finds it really difficult to give her child, or anyone else for that matter, her concentrated attention, thereby frustrating Virgo who feels ignored or useless. Later on this relationship can degenerate into criticism, cruel wit and barbed comments, with a mother and child who talk a lot but communicate little. Gemini will be maddened by Virgo's sometimes prissy attitude, just as her own inconsistency will irritate her child. At best, however, Virgo learns social confidence from its mother while Gemini comes to appreciate her child's practicality and hard-working ethos.

Virgo Child/Gemini Father

For the Virgo child who seeks a reliable and conscientious father figure, Gemini can sometimes be a bit of a disappointment, certainly in the early years. His own social and business life keeps him extremely busy and it's usually a case of his child having to fit in with him, not the other way around. The Gemini father can also think his Virgo son or daughter is a bit unadventurous and will find it very difficult to relate to his child's modesty and shyness. However, Gemini is a talented educator and his little Virgo usually benefits greatly from any time he devotes to teaching. This, naturally, improves once his child is on the move and starts to talk: Gemini will love giving his youngster the benefit of his numerous opinions, discussing anything from the weather to learning the alphabet and making time to do things together. The sharp Gemini wit (which is not always charitable) and the Virgo tendency to criticise can drive a wedge between these two later on, as can the Gemini inconsistency and Virgo's obsession with convention, but communication rarely dies completely.

Virgo/Gemini Siblings

The Virgo/Gemini sibling relationship is often complex, usually noisy, sometimes silent, but never dull. Both are good mimics and have a wonderful way with words, so laughter frequently enhances the good times and acts as a release of tension in the more stressful. That verbal dexterity, however, can also be a thorn in both their sides as the Virgo sibling can be extremely critical and Gemini sharp and devastatingly accurate. Gemini, who takes a very carefree and 'make it up as you go' attitude to life, tends to become irritated with Virgo's slow and perfectionist ways, and generally there is often a lot of impatience simmering between the two. One of Gemini's major gripes with this particular sibling is how often Virgo uses 'illness', either to gain sympathy or to get out of a difficult situation, whilst Virgo can't believe how cunning Gemini can be and how easily it can tell absolute whoppers! On the plus side, of course, Virgo usually comes up with practical solutions to any Gemini problem, while Gemini eases Virgo out of its comfort zone, making life a lot more exciting.

Virgo and Cancer

Virgo Child/Cancer Mother

A baby Virgo born to a Cancer mother, who takes the whole maternal business extremely seriously, will think it's found a seventh heaven. The baby's every need will be attended to and he or she will just love the sense of security it gets from such a devoted parent. In return, the Virgo offspring will quickly make the Cancer mother feel more than adequate at the job she finds so fulfilling, thus creating a strong and affectionate bond between the two. As the child grows up, it will be very keen to help around the home and to provide practical solutions to problems. The Cancerian feels she has a wonderfully understanding companion and can quickly come to rely on the Virgoan's talents, and the Virgo child instinctively feels comfortable with its Cancerian mother. But it isn't all sweetness and light. Even as a baby, Virgo can be quite demanding and becomes easily stressed when faced with mess or disorder. Although the Cancer mother's nurturing qualities would not be faulted by any other sign, the Virgo baby will fret over a nappy that isn't immediately changed (and not put on in exactly the right way!), the face that isn't cleaned and surroundings that are cluttered or chaotic. With the Cancerian's tendency to hoard and to live in a 'homely' environment, the Virgo baby can find the sheer business of day-to-day living quite exhausting! All Virgos take an interest in diet and, even for the very youngest, food fads can quickly develop. Cancer, however, often sees problems over food as something akin to personal rejection. This baby also has a very enquiring mind and needs a great deal of mental stimulation and intellectual challenge which is not always the Cancer mother's first priority. She's invariably happier with the physical closeness and emotional tenderness than with a meeting of minds. Despite these potential difficulties, most Cancer mothers and Virgo children get on famously, although both sometimes need a shove to get out into the world and to cope with the challenges of life.

Virgo Child/Cancer Father

The Cancer father, who will always respond brilliantly to a child who values security, loves its mother and shows a practical bent, tends to have a great relationship with a Virgo son or daughter. With a daughter in particular, he is thrilled to have someone who appreciates everything feminine as he's never at his best with the ladette culture. Where Cancer and Virgo tend to diverge is over ambition. Cancer wants to be up there at the top of the ladder, having chosen a rather meandering but ultimately fairly safe route to get there. Virgo, although a workaholic, is far less ambitious and often doesn't achieve its true potential but at least is usually very happy with its choice of job. Clashes can be frequent between a Cancer father and a Virgo child over this differing attitude to career advancement. The Cancer father can also be too cautious for the adaptable and versatile Virgo, whose plans are often frustrated by a parent who is wary of change. The milestones of growing up are never easy for a Virgo child with a Cancer father, who is reluctant to see his offspring attain independence, whether it's a night with a grandparent or going off to University. Generally, however, there is more to cement this relationship than tear it apart.

Virgo/Cancer Siblings

Any Virgo/Cancer relationship is going to be beset with worries, and the sibling situation is no different. Cancer feels guilty about everything and its mind goes into overdrive about imaginary disasters while Virgo becomes stressed and anxious. At worst, these two younger members of the family can spend hours in a state of nervous tension, Virgo getting more and more tetchy and Cancer more emotional and irrational. At best, however, Cancer is able to soothe the thoroughly agitated Virgo, who, in turn, can give its over-sensitive sibling plenty of practical advice and help. If there are going to be problems, they will surface from Cancer's rather touchy response to any Virgoan criticism, and the Virgo need for routine, neatness and order against the Cancerian's erratic attitude to getting things done or helping out. Nevertheless, both signs enjoy the comfort and security of the domestic scene and within the family these two will often stick together tenaciously when trouble looms.

Virgo and Leo

Virgo Child/Leo Mother

Leo and Virgo, like all zodiacal neighbours, are complete opposites but luckily for the Virgo baby, who prizes routine and order, Leo is a wonderful organiser and she will certainly make her newborn feel that she has the domestic agenda under control. She is also the most tactile of the fire signs, which comes as a relief to Virgo, who needs to feel very secure and thrives on being comforted. However, Leo likes to live in a big world and will soon be taking her baby out and about, inviting all her acquaintances in for coffee and expecting Virgo to feel at ease within such a busy scene. Unfortunately, Virgo quickly becomes rattled, fretful and goes off its food, and, as childhood progresses, suffers more than its fair share of stomach problems when under any kind of nervous strain. The Leo mother also loves to push her child forward and tensions arise when her baby fails to 'perform': this showing off scenario is just not Virgo's ball game. Leo, of course, takes her baby's non-compliance as personal rejection, but certainly doesn't give up and a battle royal develops. Once her child gives in, it will wonder why it didn't do so earlier: the effusive Leo praise is definitely worth the inconvenience or the blow to the Virgo pride! Many of her child's qualities are lost on Leo, who doesn't go a bundle on discernment, modesty or diligence, and the more adaptable Virgo usually fails to understand why its mother is so obstinate and fearful of change. Once able to talk, Virgo can be both perceptive and critical but Leo knows she is always right, doesn't listen and often fails to appreciate her child's intelligence. Leo, however, is a good teacher and Virgo a willing pupil and these two often enjoy reading and learning together, although the mother has to be incredibly patient with her child's slow and painstaking approach. This relationship, at worst, leaves each baffled by the other and unable to find any meeting point later in life. At best they recognise their differences and resolve to make use of each other's talents.

Virgo Child/Leo Father

The Leo father likes to feel that his cub is as ebullient, showy and confident as he is and is often mystified by a Virgo child who is modest, meticulous and rather shy. At best, Virgo brings out Leo's protective instincts and certainly with a Virgo daughter he can be utterly charmed by her quiet demeanour, even being extremely gentle in the way he bosses her about! With a Virgo boy it's more difficult as Leo will have high expectations of his son and fails to understand that Virgo functions best in the background and has no wish to be centre stage. It takes time, but Leo can learn to appreciate his Virgo child's companionship, willingness to help and ability to get things done, although still getting irritated at the pernickety attitude and hypochondriac tendencies of his offspring. His child, in turn, begins to relish its father's enthusiasm for life, magnanimous behaviour and grand plans, even if Leo's impatience, snobbishness and fixed opinions are tough to deal with. It's Virgo who's adaptable and versatile and Leo who ultimately gets stuck in situations of his own making, as can become all too clear in the teenage years.

Virgo/Leo Siblings

The Leo child needs to be a mini King of the Jungle and its Virgo sibling is naturally at home as a second in command, although more often than not the power behind the throne. Although both are naturally sociable, it's Leo who thrives in a busy social whirl and 'loves everyone' with Virgo taking a more discerning attitude to friendships, often preferring the domestic scene and helping out at home. As long as neither is thrown too firmly into the other's territory these two can get along just fine. Leo, however, likes to boss its sibling around, revelling in the sound of its own voice and Virgo loves to correct, criticise and fuss, all of which results in a lot of noisy arguing and plenty of hurt silences. Virgo also tends to get stressed when Leo fails to appreciate its hard work and attention to detail, just as much as the Leo temper ignites at its sibling's petty quibbles and fastidious behaviour. These two never really understand each other at a deep level, but eventually Leo learns to value Virgo's practicality and common sense, while Virgo basks in the Leo sunshine.

Virgo and Virgo

Virgo Child/Virgo Mother

Same sign relationships can be a blessing, a bane or a mixture of both. The mother will certainly understand exactly where her child is coming from just as much as her baby will, from the start, see its mother as the most superb mind reader. Just as likely, though, is the mother's frustration when she sees her less desirable traits shining forth from her child! The Virgo mother and baby begin life together in a perfect little cocoon, within which everything will be wonderfully well organised, neat and tidy. She'll be sensible about having people around, certainly won't crowd her newborn and will take meticulous care over her baby's feeding. After all, she understands the Virgoan digestive system and its tendency to break down at the slightest hint of stress. However, because her natural concerns are immediately picked up by her baby this duo often exists in a state of high anxiety during the early weeks and months, sometimes aggravated by the Virgo mother's insistence on putting household business ahead of her child's needs. The little Virgo quickly senses that quality tactile time is rationed as its mother struggles to abandon duty in favour of what she sees as indulgent playtime. On the plus side, of course, they will thoroughly enjoy the same things, whether it's cooking, gardening, making clothes, decorations, candles or anything else the mother does well and efficiently. She will also be aware of her child's need to learn slowly and thoroughly and will be an enormous help in that area as long as she can keep the well-meaning remarks (criticism) or debate (nit-picking) over issues that aren't really important under wraps! When life is good for the Virgo mother and child it will be brilliant, as there is so much mutual understanding and both thrive in being adaptable, reliable and each other's greatest friend and helper. In more difficult times both exude fussiness, obsessive worry and hypochondria and fail to see any kind of bigger or more positive picture.

Virgo Child/Virgo Father

The Virgo father is one of the most capable in the zodiac: he'll be thoroughly involved in his child's upbringing from the beginning and certainly won't shirk his fair share of nappy changing, a job he probably does to perfection! His Virgo child will be supremely confident in its father's abilities and will possibly choose to ignore his tendency to take over when his equally practical child tries its hand at something new. Both tend to get on with life in a quietly methodical fashion and usually share many interests. They prefer to function in a well-organised routine, but the father's time management is such that plans frequently go haywire. As adaptability is part and parcel of the Virgo make up, they usually gloss over the problem but the child worries, convinced it's not good enough company. Father and child are naturally good communicators and for the Virgo child it's really important to understand the dynamics of any situation. The father's perfectionism meets its match in his Virgo child: both demand the best from each other. This relationship often progresses in fits and starts but deep down the feelings are usually constant.

Virgo Siblings

With Virgo siblings there is likely to be much carping and angst and yet much interesting discussion and a great sense of humour as well as a tremendous ability and willingness to help each other out. It's particularly important for these two to have their own personal space in the home as each values privacy and needs time alone. Homework, hobbies and play will always involve total dedication to the subject, so there is often complete silence in any family with two Virgo children while they tackle the task in hand. However, each thinks it has the better (and only) solution to anything and everything and there is often much unwelcome interference in the other's projects. Their delicate constitutions are also in competition. From an early age two or more Virgo children will be fighting for parental attention to their aches, pains and ailments. Generally these siblings stick together, only too aware of each other's strengths and foibles, but perfectionist demands can sometimes cause them to re-think the relationship.

Virgo and Libra

Virgo Child/Libra Mother

Virgo and Libra are astrological neighbours and very different. Virgo is painstaking and hard-working, Libra easy-going and refined, but always determined to make life good for others, especially her baby. Virgo, therefore, is thrilled to find it's the centre of its Libran mother's world and to realise she is making such superb efforts to ensure her baby's comfort and well-being. Libra is equally enchanted by her modest and seemingly very intelligent baby who quickly shows its appreciation of her every action. Virgo's worries are thus alleviated and most Libran mothers won't have to deal, in the early stages, with the cranky and faddy side of this particular baby. Problems tend to arise in this relationship once the first few months are over and the early demands on the mother's timetable start to ease. Virgo loves routine and order: Libra takes a more laissez-faire approach and can be indecisive and changeable. Her child becomes thoroughly disconcerted and fractious when there are no fixed points and this stress manifests as eating problems, various minor illnesses and a general out-of-sorts demeanour. In an effort to improve matters, Libra decides to let Virgo call the shots. Further stress is therefore put on Virgo who would just love its mother to put some order into the day and set some basic rules! Socially, too, there can be problems between mother and child. Virgo is naturally quite shy and Libra very sociable and confident in company, and she often fails to understand that her youngster needs to be gently coaxed into the outside world. She's frequently at a loss, too, to comprehend Virgo's obsession with detail, its need to get things just right and its strong work ethic. Libra wings it – successfully and with panache! This relationship often works because neither makes a song and dance about their differences. Libra is often grateful to Virgo for its industry and reliability and Virgo appreciates in its mother's idealism, tact and eagerness to please.

Virgo Child/Libra Father

The urbane and laid-back Libran father is often perplexed by his more serious-minded and diligent Virgo child, although delighted at its intelligence and keen interest in learning. In turn, Virgo is fascinated by its father's charm, diplomacy and ability to spend so much money, but often annoyed at his indecisiveness and reluctance to enjoy a really good debate. Very often the no-nonsense and practical Virgo seems far more mature than its ambitious and pleasure-loving Libran father and sometimes Libra resents the old-fashioned looks emanating from his son or daughter. He also becomes irritated by the Virgo fads and fussiness, although does have more time for his child's perfectionism. After all, he is an idealist and can relate to wanting to get things just right. Virgo would love to have its father all to itself occasionally and it would also be good if Libra didn't change his plans so often: the uncertainty does nothing for the Virgo stress levels. Although very different, these two often gain a lot from each other. Libra usually brings a lot of fun into the Virgo world just as his child later turns out to be reliable, practical and a godsend in any crisis.

Virgo/Libra Siblings

The charming, easy-going Libran often runs rings around the modest and conscientious Virgo, getting it to do all the work while glorying in the praise and thanks. Virgo gets its own back through criticism, blaming Libra for all its ills (imaginary or otherwise!) and refusing to bail its sibling out of its next crisis. Virgo also loves its own company and gets extremely irritated with Libra who hates solitude and never respects Virgo's privacy. The rather frivolous Libra loses patience with its more prissy and conscientious sibling although relies on the more practical and quick-thinking Virgo to find solutions to problems. Despite their differences, these two often complement each other and get on well. Libra is excellent at helping its more diffident Virgo sibling on the social scene, whilst Virgo quietly forces Libra into making decisions and sticking with them. The highly strung Virgo is also grateful to Libra for talking through problems and alleviating stress, just as much as Libra depends on Virgo to brush up its rather slapdash work and lend its pocket money. Virgo saves while Libra spends!

Virgo and Scorpio

Virgo Child/Scorpio Mother

A Virgo baby arrives in the world looking for an ordered lifestyle, a good companion and an environment where it can hone its strong work ethic. With a Scorpio mother it has found just that and, in turn, she has a child who will thoroughly appreciate her sense of purpose, discernment and analytical mind. Above all, perhaps, for the intensely private mother, she has a baby who also values its own space and isn't likely to cling. From the start, Scorpio will adopt a very fixed routine for her baby, which will suit Virgo admirably although, being more adaptable than its mother, may find it strange that she is reluctant to adapt the regime to suit her child's changing needs. Scorpio can be intractable in the extreme and has no idea of the meaning of 'go with the flow'! Ambition, too, runs deep in her veins and she'll love her little Virgo's enthusiasm for learning and for taking in everything slowly and surely. This is one mother who will not lose patience with Virgo's diligence and need to get everything just right. She'll also do her utmost to encourage her child's interests and, sometimes, even becomes pushy on Virgo's behalf. Later on, of course, she'll realise that Virgo does not have her drive to get to the top and sometimes that can cause problems in the teenage years. With her own deep and hidden emotions, Scorpio is well placed to understand Virgo's fears and worries. She intuitively picks up the tensions that result in Virgo's aches and pains: another reason why a Virgo child feels supremely comfortable with a Scorpio mother. A potential problem can arise if Virgo starts to criticise: Scorpio can snap back with devastating accuracy, with seething silences as a result. On the whole, however, these two bring out the best in each other: Virgo does nothing to trigger the Scorpio jealousy and the mother makes sure that her child's finicky traits are nipped in the bud. In later years, Virgo is a fount of practical help to its more emotional mother while Scorpio's loyalty sustains Virgo through thick and thin.

Virgo Child/Scorpio Father

The Scorpio father tends to be passionate about anything that really matters to him and he'll particularly show that abundant enthusiasm towards his child. In fact, his amenable and conscientious Virgo son or daughter, who shows practicality and intelligence, is a perfect project for Scorpio. At the beginning, Virgo will love its father's attention and thrive under his encouragement and drive, but the Scorpio male can be autocratic and stubborn, something his child will find really difficult to understand. Although Scorpio sees the analytical Virgo mind and its painstaking approach, he fails to realise that his child is more versatile than he is and is certainly not as rigid in its thinking. Once at school, Virgo can look at its father's attitude in a totally different light, and yet will probably do little to change matters, except withdraw slightly and start to prefer its own company. Scorpio then becomes suspicious and resentful of his child's behaviour and suddenly he is faced with a thoroughly stressed child who retreats from conflict citing a cold, headache or a painful little finger! The general outlook, however, for these two is good: Virgo knows it can always depend on Scorpio who, in turn, admires his child's work ethic and discernment.

Virgo/Scorpio Siblings

On the surface this will never appear to be a relationship of equals. Scorpio loves to exert power and control while Virgo prefers to be second in command. However, in reality, Virgo is often pulling the strings behind the scenes and does much to channel Scorpio's emotions and actions down constructive paths, to say nothing of defusing many of its obsessions. These siblings usually get on very well. Each understands the other's need for privacy, while Virgo is in awe of Scorpio's ambition and perseverance just as much as Scorpio respects Virgo's practical skills and attention to detail. Jealousy can sometimes rear its ugly head if Scorpio thinks Virgo is the family favourite or seems to be getting all the luck. Virgo can be equally unpleasant to Scorpio in its critical and sometimes rather stuffy approach and can become exasperated at Scorpio's rigid thinking and inability to change. These two, however, relate at a deep level and much of their quarrelling and sibling angst is mere surface display.

Virgo and Sagittarius

Virgo Child/Sagittarius Mother

The Sagittarian mother, on giving birth to a Virgo baby, can feel distinctly uneasy. She seems to be undergoing a silent questionnaire from her newborn as to whether she is capable of looking after her rather demanding new arrival. She will notice the studied stare: her baby is already working out the logistics of living with this particular mother! The Sagittarian approach to life tends to be more carefree and haphazard than ordered, and Virgo is precisely the opposite. The baby gains its security from a sense of routine, neat and tidy surroundings and a sometimes exaggerated need for cleanliness. Its mother tends to find all of this alien to her nature and the more her baby frets and fusses, the more distracted she becomes, and any vestige of order and routine she has managed to install quickly goes out of the window. The real bond between these two lies in their mutual quest for knowledge and information and during her baby's early childhood they usually start to enjoy marvellous times together in all sorts of educational pursuits, games and just general chit chat. The communication factor can also ease any difficulties in the first few months. The Virgo baby, just like its Gemini cousin, loves the idea of conversation. The Virgo tendency to worry, however, can grate with the Sagittarian's naturally optimistic approach to life as can its obsession with the minutiae of life. The mother looks at life's big picture and her Virgo child can only see the detail. This is one of those astrological relationships that either succeed brilliantly or fail dismally. At worst, these two are a complete mystery to each other: Virgo thoroughly discomfited and stressed and Sagittarius irritated beyond belief at her picky and over-fastidious child. At best Sagittarius widens Virgo's horizons and injects pace and humour into its life, while Virgo brings its mother down to earth, helps her to face life's realities and becomes a wonderful ally.

Virgo Child/Sagittarius Father

This zodiacal father is no different from others in that he is enchanted by the new arrival, but finds it more difficult than some to cope with the restrictions a new baby puts on his life. The Virgo baby, to him, seems to be incredibly demanding and makes him feel that he is doing nothing right. Whilst this certainly won't dent his self-confidence, it will play havoc with his already limited patience and he'll find other things to do with his time. Age, however, can do wonders for these two, as can the power of speech. The Virgo child will relish having a father who is not only a natural teacher but also a mine of sound advice and inherent wisdom. The Sagittarian's good judgment about situations and people will also marry very well with his Virgo child's discriminating nature. If they enjoy sport, there is an added bonus as both these signs invariably relish the game for its own sake rather than for the acquisition of trophies. Nevertheless, a lot of give and take is needed if this relationship is not to founder in a sea of misunderstandings, usually brought about by Virgo's fear of the grand plan at odds with the ebullient 'can do' attitude of the Sagittarian.

Virgo/Sagittarius Siblings

Sagittarius and Virgo are alike in many ways and totally incompatible in others. The Sagittarian is likely to be much more rumbustious than its Virgo sibling and impatient with the Virgoan's meticulous and ordered existence. It is also likely to see Virgo as prissy or fussy and possibly tied to its mother's apron strings. In turn, Virgo can find its brother or sister's happy-go-lucky and sometimes over-the-top, thoughtless behaviour thoroughly alarming and immature. Both have the ability to be verbally destructive: Virgo through criticism and Sagittarius by a mixture of superiority and supreme lack of tact. Sagittarius also has to learn that Virgo needs privacy. There are some huge advantages, however, to this sibling relationship. Knowledge and the dissemination of information are meat and drink to both signs. They also love debate and are open to new ideas and to reasoned and sensible argument. With careful nurturing these two can learn to appreciate each other's qualities and, with much good humour, to tolerate their differences.

Virgo and Capricorn

Virgo Child/Capricorn Mother

Both the Capricorn mother and Virgo baby think this is a match made in heaven. Her Virgo child wants nothing more than a safe, secure and well-organised environment and that's exactly what its mother is best at providing. She'll understand her baby's need for an orderly existence and certainly not too much drama. At the same time, she's going to be thrilled at her child's thirst for education. Unlike a Gemini, who thrives on a superficial knowledge of anything and everything, her little Virgo will be keen to learn in detail about as much as possible, a frame of mind that suits its Capricorn mother perfectly. From the moment of birth, these two invariably feel a special bond. They understand that life is a serious business, involves hard work and duty and there are no quick fixes. That is not to say this is a dull or boring relationship as these two invariably have a lot of fun together, but they are often very happy with their own company and don't feel the need for a frantic social life. Good friends are essential to both, and Capricorn will ensure her child is not a loner, but dashing out and about for the sake of it is low on both agendas. Neither mother nor child is highly emotional and communication on a deep level is most unlikely. Thus, these two talk a lot and think they know everything about each other. In fact they know very little. Perhaps the main bone of contention between them is the sometimes rather fussy and slightly neurotic Virgo manner (the Virgo child is often full of anxieties) that is incomprehensible to the down-to-earth Capricorn, and the mother's unbending and rather exacting attitude that grates against the child's more adaptable way of thinking. For these two the teenage years barely register as neither wants to threaten the cosiness of the relationship, and throughout their lives they usually enjoy a great friendship, with real understanding developing as the child gets into adulthood.

Virgo Child/Capricorn Father

A mutual admiration society often exists between the Capricorn father and his Virgo child. Each appreciates the other's diligence, patience and cautious approach to life and both are more than happy to deal with life on a practical level. Capricorn will thoroughly enjoy introducing his Virgo son or daughter to new interests and hobbies and, as both are usually good with their hands, they'll often happily shut themselves away in a workshop for ages. The rather stoic Capricorn can sometimes become a bit edgy in the face of Virgo's major dramas over small cuts and bruises, just as much as the child finds it difficult to deal with its father's rather rigid outlook. Capricorn can also despair of his child's lack of ambition and is not always understanding of its wider outlook on the possibilities in life. The child is often much more broad-minded than the father. Arguments around the meal table are not unknown because Virgo (especially a daughter) is often attracted to vegetarianism. To the meat and two veg Capricorn, this is just faddiness and an unnecessary expense! Generally, however, problems between father and child are no more than niggles: there is so much to unite them and difficulties are fleeting.

Virgo/Capricorn Siblings

Capricorn will always want to be the boss and won't take kindly to having its statements questioned. Virgo, with its more adaptable reasoning power can, in fact, run rings around its sibling but, as both tend to enjoy debate and neither goes into sulks or high emotional drama, arguments tend to be won or lost without a load of ill-feeling. Capricorn also takes advantage of Virgo's basically helpful nature, keeping its sibling running around at its beck and call. However, the painstaking Virgo approach to everything it undertakes often makes Capricorn wonder whether it wouldn't be quicker to do everything itself! In addition, Capricorn hates the Virgo hypochondria and constant criticism and Virgo seethes at its sibling's sometimes mean and snobby attitude. On the whole, however, these two are very compatible. Neither is particularly adventurous, both need stability and both understand about self-discipline and hard work. This is a relationship born to last.

Virgo and Aquarius

Virgo Child/Aquarius Mother

The Virgo baby arrives in the world with a very specific set of ideas about how it is to be looked after. The Aquarian mother, on the other hand, tends to take a much more laissez-faire approach and can be thoroughly disconcerted by her baby's slightly judgmental attitude. Right from birth, the Virgo baby expects everything to run like clockwork. Nappy changing, feeding, playtime – all should be done efficiently and in the right order! The Aquarian mother, whilst appreciating the need for some kind of structure to the day, will tend to wing it and juggle the timetable, thankful by bedtime that she has managed to fit everything in, including her social life and taking her baby out and about. The Virgo baby, therefore, can become fractious at what it perceives as a lack of order and its Aquarian mother stressed because she can't see what she is doing wrong. Virgo babies are also born with an innate need for cleanliness. The poor Aquarian, who feels there are more important things in life than worrying about a spot of purée on her baby's chin, is going to have a big wake up call with a little Virgo around! However, Virgo is a very adaptable sign and will happily fit in with the Aquarian routine once it has been established. With Aquarius a natural teacher and Virgo a willing pupil, these two will also enjoy time together exploring the baby's new environment, and although Virgo as an earth sign is quite tactile, it is not as needy in that area as, say, Taurus. This suits the Aquarian as she is not truly at home in the touchy-feely arena. Later on this relationship can founder on mutual criticism and misunderstandings between the conventional Virgo and the sometimes eccentric Aquarian. With a little bit of time and trouble, however, both can learn a lot from the other: Aquarius admires the Virgo hard work, painstaking approach and discrimination and her child appreciates its mother's honesty and objective thinking.

Virgo Child/Aquarius Father

The Aquarian father and Virgo child will invariably enjoy a meeting of minds. Aquarius will appreciate his child's analytical skills, mental application and hard-work ethos and the Virgoan will learn much from its father's original thinking and inborn humanity. However, Aquarius paints everything in life with a broad brush, in stark contrast to Virgo, who is often obsessed with the minutiae. This difference in outlook can sometimes become a problem, with Aquarius losing patience with the rather nit-picking and fussy Virgo approach and the child ignoring the father's sometimes contradictory and contrary statements. The Virgo need for order is also often at odds with the Aquarian's more freedom-loving attitude. Whilst these two may never enjoy a deep and unspoken closeness, they will respect the way the other thinks and, at best, will always seek the other's advice. The Aquarian father might even begin to question his certainties about life when he realises that his Virgo son or daughter is an equal in debate and that its views are well worth seeking. More to the point, his practical Virgo child is Mr or Miss Fix-it – and to the Aquarian that is wonderful indeed!

Virgo/Aquarius Siblings

These two children are radically different, and it's one of those sibling relationships that either works very well or there is no common ground at all. Aquarius takes an airy, independent and inventive attitude to life and needs lots of space and intellectual challenge. The Virgo sibling needs order and discipline, is conscientious, hard-working and discriminating. At best, Virgo can bring the Aquarian ideas down to earth, – and make them work – and Aquarius can broaden its Virgo sibling's thinking and attitude to life. At worst, this relationship can come to grief through the Virgo irritation with the Aquarian's unconventional and erratic approach to everything, and in particular to work, and the Aquarian's exasperation with its sibling's worries, criticisms and lack of vision. It's probably important for these two to develop totally separate interests and lifestyles and not to be forced into the same social scene. If handled carefully in childhood, these two can develop a real appreciation for each other's talents as they move into adulthood.

Virgo and Pisces

Virgo Child/Pisces Mother

For the Virgo baby, the Piscean mother can be a total enigma and vice versa. Virgo and Pisces are opposite signs in the zodiac, which brings an immediate attraction and yet the possibility of great incompatibility. The Pisces mother is gentle, kind and compassionate, qualities much appreciated by Virgo, but often vague, indecisive and escapist, traits that this particular baby finds unnerving and stressful. When Virgo doesn't feel grounded in the here and now it worries, becomes fractious and displays its fussiness, hypochondria and tendency to criticise in all colours of the rainbow! And the more Pisces seems to float off into her own world, the more likely it is that even the youngest Virgo will become even more died-in-the-wool and difficult to deal with. If the mother can get herself and her baby organised into a good routine for the early months, she will earn herself numerous Brownie points with her baby and find Virgo to be amenable and delightful – no trouble at all. Although Virgo will never really be at ease without good boundaries and firm foundations, it will love its mother's creative ideas, fun outings and the intuitive way she just seems to know exactly what it needs and how to relieve its worries. Pisces certainly knows how to comfort and, far more to the point, she'll never make a drama out of mealtimes and will happily fall in with Virgo's every fad. As a toddler and during the early years at school, Virgo will probably get in a state when Pisces forgets the games kit, misses the parent's evening and is the last to collect at the school gate. Pisces equally cannot understand how her youngster can be quite so pedantic and fret over such trivialities. Because these two are very adaptable, the relationship tends to improve with age when the initial problems are over. Virgo gets used to its mother's unworldly approach and learns to enjoy her flights of fancy, while Pisces respects her child's ability to organise and to cope. Above all, much love binds these two relatively modest signs closely together.

Virgo Child/Pisces Father

The Virgo child is painstaking in its efforts and hopes for a word of praise from its Piscean father. Whilst no Piscean would deliberately ignore his child's achievements, he can very often give that impression to his Virgo son or daughter. Virgo would like a lengthy discussion about the nuts and bolts of any project while Pisces just likes to swim in and out of situations. Virgo thus becomes disillusioned with its Piscean father who, in turn, becomes irritated at what he sees as a demanding and perfectionist child. The normal Virgoan tactic of using its intellect and verbal skills to make its point and clear up misunderstandings is also lost on Pisces, who just walks away from anything it doesn't want to hear! Despite the potential problems, this relationship usually stays the course. The Pisces father is highly sensitive and sympathetic to Virgo's innate fears and, because he isn't ambitious, isn't likely to push his child down roads it is reluctant to travel. He also revels in the fact that his child is so reliable and helpful and comes to depend more and more on its common sense and down-to-earth attitude as the years go by.

Virgo/Pisces Siblings

This can be a tough situation for Virgo who seems to do nothing but clear up after Pisces, whether it's literally putting the toys away and looking for lost pieces of the jigsaw or whether it's sorting out the general mess its sibling has made of a situation. Virgo's quick thinking and practical application usually bails Pisces out of problems brought about by its sheer lack of organisation! On the other hand, Pisces can think that living with Virgo is not easy as it copes with its rather fussy ways, its meticulous attitude to anything it undertakes (Pisces prefers the random, if not chaotic) and its singular lack of imagination. Virgo's ability to know what is good for its Piscean sibling is also singularly annoying: Pisces just sees it as rather harsh criticism, which it invariably is. All is not lost, however, as Virgo proves to be an absolutely wonderful rock around which Pisces can swim, a brilliant listener and enormous practical support. Pisces leads Virgo down some interesting and exciting paths, and understands its fears. This is a case where opposites attract far more than they repel.

LIBRA

The Libra Child 0-5 Years

Beguiling and enchanting, the Libra baby weaves a very special magic. Blessed with more than its fair share of good looks, it is usually all smiles and dimples and, from a very young age, is diplomatic, charming and thoroughly appreciative of the finer things in life. Ruled by Venus, the planet associated with love, harmony, social skills and the arts, the young Libran is determined to please and comes into the world with its peaceable and easy-going nature ready to be indulged and in the hope that its changeable and more frivolous moments will be ignored. John Lennon (9 October), who wrote and sang about a world at peace and was also a talented artist, epitomised two fundamental traits in the sign: ambition and a natural feeling for the arts. Contrary to popular belief, Libra is not one of the laziest signs in the zodiac but one of the most motivated and resolute: behind the great looks and charisma lies a very determined little soul and it's not known as the 'iron fist in the velvet glove' for nothing. Indolence, self-indulgence and sophistication hide strong aspirations and clear objectives.

From the start, the Libran baby knows exactly what it likes. It thrives in peace and quiet and hates hassle, tensions and tempers. Although not intuitive like the water signs (Cancer, Scorpio and Pisces), it has a wonderful ability to pick up on atmospheres around the home and quickly senses the onset of a 'domestic', the unhappiness of a parent, the irritations of a sibling or a general sense of unease. Once it realises that the overall goodwill has done a quick disappearing act, it tends to become fretful and thoroughly uncooperative, frequently going off its food (and this is the zodiac's sweet tooth and chocoholic!) and taking much time to regain its equilibrium. Its happy demeanour can also be shattered by the wrong surroundings and anything coarse. This is a child born to understand refinement and to live in a very pleasant environment. Garish colours, a messy highchair, a cluttered cot (even though full of favourite toys and teddies), or something else that grates against this child's aesthetic sense, can bring about a pout at best, or a real affront to its sensibilities and much wailing at worst. Give it, however, a glimpse of cashmere, softest leather or silk and Libra knows instinctively that this is what it is born to touch and to wear. This little magpie also instantly hits on anything that shines. Equal only with Leo, he or she is probably the king or queen of bling! The young Libran is usually extremely stylish, knows exactly what goes with what and often looks best in the pastel colours associated with Venus rather than the darker hues that suit, say, Capricorn or Aquarius.

Libra is the sign of the Scales which denotes a keen interest in fair play and a constant quest to get its life balanced. Whilst not in the assertive Aries league for championing a cause or a person, the young Libran can be just as quick to point out an injustice, to mediate in a quarrel and quietly to right wrongs. Its natural diplomacy and charm usually work wonders and all playgroups and playgrounds need a small Libran or two to act as referee and peacemaker! Where keeping its own world on an even keel is concerned, however, this can be quite another, and a much more difficult, story for Libra.

As soon as this baby understands about options, its love/hate relationship with making up its mind begins and parents of what they think is a thoroughly equable child are faced with its very changeable nature. This is a child who likes to weigh up the pros and cons of everything, from the best way to wield a spoon and, in fact, whether to use an implement or fingers at breakfast, to deciding which toy to play with first. Hurried into decision-making of any kind brings a display of frustration and temper at not being given enough time to think through every last alternative. The 'lazy' epithet for Libra often arises because it seems to take so long to do anything: it is anxious to try out things for itself (and therefore usually attempts to feed itself long before its contemporaries as well as put on its socks and shoes or do up buttons) and likes to do things slowly as it works out in its own mind all the different ways it could tackle the job in hand. Giving the impression that it is doing little, but in fact with its brain going at nineteen to the dozen to work out the optimum solution, patience is lost by those around and Libra dissolves into angry tears at having its contemplation interrupted – and just when it had worked out the answers!

The whole Libran concept of balance is, for the younger members of this sign, a constant yo-yoing between one extreme and another. When life is going well and it's on a high, the charm just oozes from every pore. When frustration sets in and the see-saw is on the ground, anger and generally very stroppy behaviour make life a misery for everyone. As Libra gets older it learns to modify the highs and lows but a two- or three-year-old battling to be independent and with so much to make up its mind about is often extremely difficult to live with. More annoyingly still, in company he or she will probably be sweetness and light and its poor frazzled parents or childminder will watch while it beams its beautiful smile to all and sundry, all angst completely forgotten.

The Libran baby usually has an inborn feel for the arts, not only finding music extremely soothing but also showing a natural sense of rhythm: he or she will soon be exhibiting its dancing skills. Although not in the Taurus league, it will not be shy, either, of having a good shot at singing and often manages to hold a tune at a very young age. Drawing and painting, perhaps more than making things, invariably come easily to this child and it usually shows its innate flair as soon as it can hold a crayon or paintbrush. Libra is instinctively drawn to beauty, whether it's clothes, lovely surroundings or an art gallery and this is a child who will be more than happy to accompany its mother on a spending spree at the shops, probably giving perceptive advice from the buggy! The Libran style should never be underestimated, nor should its love affair with cash. Getting this particular child to save its pocket money is often a lost cause. Far more likely is its insistence on issuing IOUs and a complete, but charming, loss of memory when it comes to settling its debts!

Both boys and girls are natural flirts and extremely romantic: in the nursery class they will profess undying love and make all sorts of unrealistic promises to their latest best friend, or probably the teacher, who is utterly enchanted by the little Libran's attractive personality. This child's magnetism is also maddening to those who look after it! Its ability to wind people around its little finger is legendary and there must be many who ask themselves why they are doing this little charmer's bidding and all the hard work while it looks on from the comfort of an armchair. Libra learns very young that it's possible to take the credit and get to the top of the tree when other people have done a lot of the work!

A good social life is very important to Libra: the youngest baby thrives in company and chit-chat and soon becomes a happy participant in any gathering. Flattery and diplomacy are Libran strengths that also show up very early. Many a three-or four-year-old member of this sign has come out with wonderful remarks that make a grandparent's day and comments that quickly defuse a tense situation. This child, too, responds to sweet talk: it can sometimes be gullible in the extreme and easily influenced, often falling prey to stronger characters in its efforts to be liked. This obsession with being liked by everyone is a singular Libran problem and often very worrying for its parents. In its easy-going way and in attempts to maintain harmony at all costs, the Libran child will give answers that it thinks will keep other people happy. A fear of being disliked and, therefore cut off from a group, is Libra's worst nightmare: this is a sign that has an inbuilt hatred of solitude. A foot-stamping, unhappy five-year-old has probably just made a decision in the interests of others rather than itself and is both regretting it and feeling unable to change its mind for fear of upsetting its friends. Thus, easily, do Librans get themselves into situations they'd prefer to be well out of! Instilling in the Libra child the importance of making a decision that is right for him or her, rather than worrying about what other people think, is a lesson that should be taught sooner rather than later.

Once at the school gates, Libra is invariably a thoroughly welcome member of the class. Socially adept, it will be a good mixer and its friendly, laid-back persona will make it very popular. Let no one, however, underestimate this youngster: if crossed, he or she will be fearless in attack while cloaking his or her every word or action in winning geniality!

Libra and Aries

Libra Child/Aries Mother

For the Libran baby, who'll happily settle for a peaceful existence and harmonious surroundings, its Aries mother can be quite a challenge. She, of course, just loves this wonderfully amenable baby but is blissfully ignorant of just how changeable and self-indulgent her little son or daughter is going to be. Libra faces a mother who is adventurous and impulsive and tends to rush rather noisily through life. Her baby stresses over dramas and tensions and dissolves into copious tears when its preferred congenial environment is so thoroughly jarred. The Libran indecision is also at odds with its mother's more direct approach and her tendency not to waste time over anything. The more Aries rushes her child and loses patience with its endless dithering over what to wear, which toy to play with or which friend to invite to tea, the more the Libran drama queen emerges. For this self-assured mother, the Libran's emotional highs and lows (charm one minute, anger and frustration the next), and its vacillation are very difficult to understand and to deal with. She will, of course, marvel at her child's natural tact and artistic flair, be extremely proud of its social confidence and revel in its generally rather easy-going nature. As both are inclined to spend liberally, a shopping spree often soothes both. If she's perceptive, Aries will also recognise that Libra is ambitious and do much to help it towards its goals. At best, Libra benefits greatly from its mother's enthusiasm and energy and learns a lot about having the courage of its convictions and the confidence to walk away from situations. Libra's tendency to be so gullible and easily led infuriates Aries! With a Libran child Aries often tones down her ego, learns to listen and becomes her youngster's greatest champion, while Libra gains much from the positive Aries approach to life. At worst, the mother despairs of her child's flippancy and vacillation while Libra can't cope with Aries' total inability to see anything from anyone else's point of view.

Libra Child/Aries Father

Aries is usually charmed by his little Libran, who instinctively knows how to flatter him, whilst his son or daughter is extremely proud of its dynamic and enterprising father. It doesn't take long, however, for the more diplomatic child to realise that its father is adept at treading all over people's finer feelings and for Aries to become exasperated with his child's changeable personality and its slightly self-indulgent approach to life. Aries gets on with things, usually with much energy, and he finds Libra's laid-back attitude thoroughly irritating. The Libran charm and smiles are one thing but its indecision and tendency to indulge in emotional drama is quite another, bringing on a dose of the quick Aries temper. With a little bit of patience, however, the father can do wonders for his child, instilling confidence and encouraging its ambitions. Time spent talking through the Libran decision-making process will never be wasted and he'll teach his child that it's sometimes important to put itself first rather than always trying to please everyone else. Aries often gives his Libran child a much tougher backbone, whilst at the same time learning a lot about other people's sensibilities.

Libra/Aries Siblings

The straightforward Aries, who likes decisions made and everything carried out immediately, finds the Libran fence-sitting and endless debate thoroughly irritating. Libra, in turn, cannot understand its sibling's leap before you look attitude to life and wishes it could be slightly more considerate. Aries, at home, usually gets angry at Libra's permanently laid-back attitude and at having to organise everything. Libra, in turn, cannot understand why Aries has to take such precipitate action when a little bit of thought would have brought about a better result. On the plus side, however, Aries does much to push Libra onwards and upwards in life, injecting a bit of oomph and courage, whilst Libra's social skills stop Aries from falling out with everyone it's upset with its thoughtless remarks. The Arian quick temper and Libra's tendency to shift from charm personified to silent sulking bring many difficult moments. At best these two are forever bailing each other out: at worst, they just can't tolerate each other's failings.

Libra and Taurus

Libra Child/Taurus Mother

With Libra and Taurus both ruled by Venus, mother and baby have a common interest in the good things in life. The Libran baby feels thoroughly comfortable with a mother who appreciates its need for beautiful surroundings, fine fabrics and a varied menu of delicacies and who wouldn't dream of indulging in raucous behaviour or impulsive action. Taurus, of course, knows she is thoroughly appreciated by her little Libran who is all smiles, charm and dimples and seems to be such an easy baby. Libra is also one of the most sociable children in the zodiac but the Taurean mother can be very possessive. When her child is starting to make friends, Taurus frequently resents its popularity, especially its easy affability with other adults. In order to be part of her child's social success she often insists on accompanying it everywhere, or tries to tighten her hold by ensuring that her own home becomes the centre for all entertaining. She is, after all, an excellent hostess and is usually extremely well organised. Libra thrives in the stability she provides, although gets distressed when her routines do not take into account the time Libra needs to make decisions. Libra's changeability and the swings from laughter to angry frustration are also a source of annoyance to the much more placid and practical mother who doesn't think too much about choices. She is a woman of great certainties and can appear extremely stubborn to a child who likes to debate everything. Spending money, however, is a joy to both mother and child and neither is known for financial moderation. Both are also artistically inclined and Taurus loves developing Libra's talents, whether it's music, painting, sandcastles or construction kits. Although Libra sometimes resents its mother's inflexibility and controlling behaviour, and Taurus thinks her child is far too easily influenced and idealistic, these two usually overcome any problems and enjoy a relationship where self-indulgence takes a wonderfully high priority.

Libra Child/Taurus Father

The easy-going Libran child and the practical, patient Taurean father usually have a very strong bond, which is firmly anchored in an enjoyment of the finer things in life. Taurus will be delighted that his child really appreciates the best restaurants and cafés where both can indulge their sweet tooth and liking for comfort. Even more, he'll love his toddler's affability and innate charm, which seem to endear Libra to absolutely everyone. Where these two can come unstuck is in the Taurean's dogmatism. Libra loves to weigh up the pros and cons of everything, wants to talk over every small issue and finds decision-making nigh impossible. The more realistic and pragmatic Taurus loses patience with his child's shilly-shallying and starts to lay down the law. Libra then feels bullied and Taurus gets further irritated as he watches Libra ignore his orders and take another, and to his mind, unsuitable path. Libra is always thankful for a reliable father who is such a rock at times of trouble, but with the Libran hatred of hassle, too many arguments with a stubborn Taurean can end up in a relationship that has cooled, although rarely do these two part company for good.

Libra/Taurus Siblings

Although these two are bound together in a love of luxury, sociability and much warm-hearted affection, this is not always an easy relationship for either of them. The Taurean is practical, likes to be well organised and is very persistent in everything it undertakes. Its Libra sibling is idealistic, easy-going and indecisive and, although ambitious, often gives up on situations at the first sign of trouble. Taurus frequently finds itself in the position of not only having to organise Libra but also having to second-guess its mood: is today about charm and affability or a load of angst? Libra, in turn, thinks its sibling is bossy and can't stand its resentment in the face of other people's success. The Taurean's obsession with routines and timetables also exasperates Libra. There is often much silent tension between these two but rarely does either want a complete break. Both prize harmony too much and, later on, Libra helps to dig Taurus out of his entrenched views while Taurus helps its sibling to make the right decisions and stick with them.

Libra and Gemini

Libra Child/Gemini Mother

Libra and Gemini both enjoy a busy lifestyle, full of chat, company and rushing hither and thither, so the Libran baby immediately feels at home with its thoroughly sociable mother. Life will never be dull for these two. Although Libra might get a tad worried about the absence of an organised timetable, and perhaps the slight irregularity of mealtimes, having lots of people around and endless opportunities to be admired will compensate the baby wonderfully. Gemini will definitely encourage her baby's intellectual development but find Libra is fascinated by the bedtime story one evening and bored to tears and restlessness the next. Both mother and child can be inconsistent: Gemini flits from plan to plan by the minute and Libra swings between great happiness and miserable frustration which bring days of total mutual incomprehension. The problems, however, are temporary: neither sits around sulking and both just tend to get on with things after any difficulties. These two talk a lot, but usually don't get involved in emotional depths, a situation that suits them both. Gemini will also take time and trouble to foster her child's skills, whatever they might be, and she'll certainly have no preconceived ideas as to her little Libran's interests. Like Aquarius, Gemini does not deal in stereotypes! Libra can sometimes feel pushed into things by its Gemini mother who likes to fill her child's every hour with some kind of activity. Because her youngster is not at all good at expressing views that might cause trouble or upset, it often puts up with situations it doesn't like and resents its mother for not being some kind of mind reader! Gemini taking time to talk through Libra's feelings and assuring her son or daughter that she'd like to hear the truth, can pay many dividends in helping her child to make decisions and not to be so easily influenced by stronger characters. On the whole this is a relationship that works brilliantly for mother and child who definitely appreciate, and benefit from, each other's qualities.

Libra Child/Gemini Father

The Gemini father will think his little Libran is excellent company and will be fascinated by his child's abundance of diplomacy and charm. What he'll find difficult to cope with, however, is his child's total inability to make a decision. Gemini is usually very certain of what he's doing and where he's going (before he equally certainly changes his mind again) and finds the Libran dithering over his every question utterly perplexing and annoying. He fails to understand his youngster's need to keep everyone happy. This is also a father who likes to be on the go from dawn to dusk and who sometimes thinks his young Libran is lazy beyond belief. His ambitious child just doesn't like to move into action until its plans are properly formulated! Libra's insistence on always having juice and biscuits at the best cafés doesn't go down well with Gemini either. He thinks his child is extravagant and that the people at the nearby greasy spoon are so much more interesting. Despite a few misunderstandings, this father/child relationship is invariably harmonious, each tolerating the other's quirks with much good humour.

Libra/Gemini Siblings

If silence reigns with these siblings, then Libra is fed up because it supported one of Gemini's failed schemes and Gemini is exasperated because Libra didn't stick to its guns. Whilst each invariably backs the other through thick and thin, and there is usually much chatter and lively goings-on with the two of them, both can be inconsistent and unreliable. Gemini's natural sales skills and Libra's innate diplomacy and ability to smooth troubled waters make them a formidable duo, but when things go wrong each is quick to blame the other. Neither, however, broods darkly or even mutters quietly for long. These two are air signs and know the importance of moving on. Both are naturally sociable and are usually very welcome arrivals at any playgroup or party and Libra is particularly good at calming Gemini down when it starts to get over-excited. Gemini is equally proficient at prodding Libra into doing its own thing and not just going along with the crowd. This is a relationship that rarely fails: as adults they are often best friends, respecting each other's opinions for better or worse.

Libra and Cancer

Libra Child/Cancer Mother

All Librans are blessed with immense charm and from birth the Libran baby is all smiles and dimples and on the fast track to learning how to entertain its parents. The Cancerian mother, given this utterly beguiling bundle of joy, is thrilled, little knowing just how many problems she might have to face from her enchanting son or daughter. For a start, her Libran baby needs an environment of complete harmony and will become fractious in the extreme when its equilibrium is jolted or the atmosphere becomes at all chilly. For a Cancer mother who is a mass of emotions and, even at the best of times, finds it difficult to take a thoroughly rational approach to life, this is a demand too far. The more worried and changeable she becomes, the more her baby will complain. Librans are super-sensitive to what's going on around them and can pick up distress signals of any kind within seconds. With the Cancer mother's self-confidence easily damaged, it doesn't take long for her to feel quite incapable of coping with this delightful baby, who in fact is very easy to please, but who she's seemingly unable to pacify. The little Libran just wants its Cancerian mother to relax and to enjoy having it around; it's as simple as that! As the Libran gets older, its total inability to make decisions as well as its tendency to weigh up the pros and cons of its every action and thought will grate on its Cancerian mother who just wants her child to 'speak from the heart'. Ultimately, however, these two signs are both very loving and very caring, and mother and child usually overcome any discord sooner rather than later. They also understand quite quickly that Cancer will always come from her feelings and Libra from its rational mind and, in the other, each has a great ally who can look at problems from a different perspective. In its Cancerian mother, the Libran child will know it has a true champion. In her sensitive way she will encourage her Libran child to achieve its true potential. She knows only too well that a Libran needs the gentle touch.

Libra Child/Cancer Father

To the Cancerian father, the arrival of this amenable baby will seem especially pleasing. Here is a child who will never make him feel stupid, never upset the social applecart and always be a credit to his parenting skills. However, the Libran who, from an early age, can work a room and understands all about networking, is often held back by a Cancerian father, who is reluctant to let go of the reins tying his child to home and family. The father's protective instincts can sometimes shelter behind quite autocratic behaviour and because the Libran child is so biddable and keen to please, it will give in rather than fight its corner. Although this may not be the easiest relationship it is, however, a very caring one. Libra hates any kind of upset and the Cancerian father loathes the idea of discord within the family. Each, therefore, will strive to understand the other and, as long as the Libran child is wise enough to acknowledge the Cancerian father's age, experience and good intentions, and Cancer his child's easy-going diplomacy and general popularity, these two can enjoy a very harmonious relationship.

Libra/Cancer Siblings

Libra and Cancer siblings can either be very helpful to one another or a mutual mystery. Each in its own way will prize family harmony and domestic security and neither will be looking to create unnecessary drama. The more outgoing Libran will be far keener to poke its nose out of the front door and to explore the wider world and could be a huge help to the more diffident Cancerian when it comes to socialising. However, Libra will find it very difficult to cope with the Crab's moods and irrational fears just as much as Cancer will be baffled by the Libran's seeming lack of deep emotions and its total reliance on logic, to say nothing of its time-keeping problems and vacillation. Because neither Cancer nor Libra will ever look for an out and out fight, both will tend to brood intensely on what they see as injustices, slights or misunderstandings, causing this relationship to degenerate into a total lack of communication if problems are not quickly identified and dealt with. Generally, however, these two usually maintain a happy and loving friendship and, ultimately, gain some idea of how the other ticks.

Libra and Leo

Libra Child/Leo Mother

Both mother and child have an inbuilt dislike of the coarse and vulgar and a sure and certain knowledge that they are destined for the finer things in life, thus making this a potentially excellent relationship. The Leo mother, to whom appearances matter and who has an innate sense of showmanship and drama, is thrilled to have a Libran baby who is blessed with a beautiful smile and such refined features. Libra, with its well-organised and warm-hearted mother feels totally comfortable and secure and knows, from the start, that its self-indulgence will be well and truly pandered to! With both mother and child also possessing artistic flair and loving a bit of glamour, they'll usually be first in the queue for the pantomime or a musical and will probably spend happy hours together indulging their creative talents. Spending sprees will also be high on both agendas as both mother and child have a blind spot about financial caution. Where these two possibly get into difficulties is the Leo insistence on the rightness of her opinions, and her slightly bossy interference, up against her child's seething resentment at being pushed around. Libra, to start with, will always seem amenable and ready to go along with its mother's plans. After the first two years, when Libra yo-yos between happy smiles and frustrated tears, it tends to give in to stronger personalities (of which Leo is definitely one!) rather than cause a fuss and a tense atmosphere. However, it quietly feels more and more put upon until the dam breaks, the iron fist appears from the velvet glove, and Libra makes its point very clearly. Leo also finds it difficult to deal with her child's indecision and its tendency to be rather gullible. Generally, however, this is usually a very affectionate relationship with Leo providing a wonderfully firm backbone for her more changeable youngster. In turn, she's highly flattered by Libra's charm and, later on, often very thankful for its diplomacy when, as with every fire sign, she really doesn't mean what she says!

Libra Child/Leo Father

The warm-hearted and enthusiastic Leo father is often slightly perplexed by his very laid-back Libran child, who goes about life in a much quieter way. He also wonders why his charming son or daughter always agrees with everyone rather than taking a stand on matters (as he did when he was five years old!). It often takes time for Libra to feel comfortable with its father's expansive personality and for Leo to understand his youngster's constant vacillation. These two, however, will thoroughly enjoy being out and about together and Libra will feel very confident with its Leo father when faced with new situations and making new contacts. In turn, Leo basks with pride as his son or daughter flatters all the right people. After all, both are ambitious and Libra learns a lot about 'who you know' from Leo. Both, too, expect the best in life and usually have much fun together buying things for themselves and for others. Leo is generous and Libra thoughtful. In the teenage years, Libra often feels controlled and over-organised by Leo who, in turn, frets about his child's seeming lack of concern about its future, but the long-term prospects for this relationship are excellent.

Libra/Leo Siblings

On the surface it's usually Leo who seems to be in charge of this relationship, tending to call all the shots and knowing that its Libran sibling will just go along with everything. In fact these two are equals. Although Leo will have the grand ideas it will be the Libran's cooler judgment and rational logic that will stop the plans from dramatically biting the dust, and Libra will always be the one who has to be the spokesperson for the two. Its knack of saying just the right thing, as opposed to Leo's dogmatic attitude, usually saves the day. Leo might well lose patience with Libra's endless attempts to please everyone and Libra resent its sibling's bossy and intolerant attitude, but their creativity and sociability make them great allies. They are also quite materialistic and there will be much competition between them over designer labels, the latest must-have toy or gizmo and the best place to go for pizza. Both are also blessed with a great sense of humour, which frequently saves the occasional difficult day.

Libra and Virgo

Libra Child/Virgo Mother

Any air (Libra) and earth (Virgo) relationship can stir up something of a dust storm and this one is no exception. At the beginning, the Virgo mother will see what she wants to see, a beautiful child who is calm, easy-going and a joy to bring up. Libra will feel extremely happy in Virgo's meticulously arranged domestic scene and feel that its every need is both anticipated and catered to. It doesn't take long, however, for the conflicts that occur with every astrological neighbour to show up. The Libran child is refined, very laid-back and desperately eager to please and to avoid hassle of any kind. Its Virgo mother is practical, values hard work and is certainly not afraid of saying exactly what she means if she thinks it's going to do some good. She, therefore, soon becomes impatient with what she sees as her young child's charming ability to get out of anything that seems like a chore, as well as the ages it takes to make a decision about anything: and the more she hurries and chivvies her Libran, the worse the situation gets. The three-year-old Libra starts to think Virgo is constantly criticising and worrying and, in its efforts to help out its mother, finds it even more difficult to decide what to say and what action to take. The rather extravagant Libran ideas certainly don't go down a bundle with its mother's more modest tastes and there are often many arguments over money and what Virgo sees as her child's rather frivolous obsessions. The innate Libran sociability is also often thwarted by Virgo, who can be shy and less confident in company. On the plus side, both can be very logical and once they start to communicate, Virgo encourages Libra to achieve balance in its life, and Libra soothes its mother's nerves and stress. At worst, these two can end up in a whirlwind of misunderstandings, but it's more likely that Virgo will use her analytical mind to work out how best to help her child and Libra will be thankful for its mother's common sense and utter reliability.

Libra Child/Virgo Father

The Virgo father is one of life's perfectionists and sets himself standards that are way beyond what anyone else would think is reasonable! His Libra son or daughter is quite the opposite and most charmingly goes through life hoping that someone else will do all the work. The father, who is often less socially aware than his child, finds its ability to work a room at five years old both unnecessary and mind-boggling but then likes to nit-pick about Libra's words and actions. Libra, in turn, gets thoroughly frustrated at its father's very conservative attitudes and further confuses things by see-sawing between huge smiles and contentment and resentful and simmering anger. However, on the educational scene these two have a meeting of minds and, with Virgo one of the best teachers in the zodiac, the Libran's rational intellect gets greatly stimulated. Libra finds it difficult to keep up with Virgo's busy lifestyle as this man is constantly on the go (or fidgeting) but is very good at calming him down and getting him to see worries in a realistic light. Libra knows it can depend on its Virgoan father who loves his child's ability to wind him round its little finger.

Libra/Virgo Siblings

Libra sits back and dishes out orders while Virgo rushes to get everything done. That is often how this relationship is seen by family and friends. However, a more honest picture is of the practical Virgo sorting out the endless Libran indecision, saving its sibling from going down unsuitable paths and being a thoroughly reliable shoulder to cry on. At the same time Libra is brilliant at listening to Virgo's endless worries and complaints and helping it along on the social scene as well as calming troubled waters after one of Virgo's more pertinent remarks. Virgo's rather conservative nature is seen by its sibling as stick-in-the-mud and sometimes Libra tires of encouraging Virgo to let its hair down. Virgo thinks Libra takes a very frivolous attitude to life and can't understand its penchant for very expensive material possessions, to say nothing of always having spent its pocket money at least twice! These two, however, thrive in debate and as long as they communicate, their relationship will survive.

Libra and Libra

Libra Child/Libra Mother

Same sign relationships can be a blessing, a curse or, more likely, a bit of both. From the start the two Librans will seem happily to drift through life, each very keen to please the other and both revelling in the other's company. Libra hates being on its own and thrives with other people around, whether it's family or a wider social scene. Thus mother and child will love a crowded, busy and happy environment where both can show off their charm, refinement and easy-going nature. Libra is the sign of the Scales which denotes a great sense of fair play and a strong need to keep life balanced. Both mother and child are acutely conscious of making life good for other people and just as aware that they come to resent putting their own needs in second place. This relationship can quickly develop into one where neither mother nor child ever really gets what it wants: they exist in a state of general dithering and often end up late at parties, school, the dentist or anywhere else, each blaming the other for the tardiness. Timing is not this pair's forté! Both can also be easily influenced by other people, often finding themselves in friendships that are made for all the wrong reasons. On the plus side, they both love beautiful things and the child quickly learns about its mother's love affair with the credit card (and takes note for the future!) and both are usually creatively gifted. They'll spend much time together in artistic pursuits of all kinds and from a young age the little Libran will probably be seen at art exhibitions or picking out luxurious materials in rather grand boutiques as much as in the playground. At worst these two can exist in a state of much confusion and, sometimes, complete frustration and inconsistency as no decisions are ever made and no one ever says what they mean. At best, of course, they have much in common and each understands the other perfectly, especially their mutual need for a quiet life. Most important of all, only this mother truly knows how deeply her ambitious little Libra wants to succeed.

Libra Child/Libra Father

This same sign relationship can either be one of endless muddle and disappointments or a wonderful friendship. Both father and child promise a lot, whether it's being there for a birthday party or parent's evening or remembering to put the books away or water a pot plant. Meeting those commitments is quite another story. The Libran father, in his efforts to please, will go along with the strongest demand made on his time, and his child will listen to the most recent requests. On a happier note, the father delights in his little Libran, who seems to be wonderfully sophisticated and charming at such an early age. Never mind that his son or daughter might be a bit gullible and impressed by the wrong things – he was too at that age! The Libra child is equally thrilled with such a laid-back father who knows all the best places to eat and where to buy stylish clothes and great toys. They often have a relationship of much bustle and fun but never spoil things by delving into the realms of emotions. Thwarted ambitions, however, bring them close to real communication: they truly understand the steel that runs beneath that easy-going persona.

Libra Siblings

The central ethos for all Librans is harmony. These siblings are not looking for trouble, arguments or any kind of domestic upset. As they are also consummate diplomats and rarely indulge in temper tantrums, two Librans can, and often do, enjoy a relatively quiet life within the family. However, their inability to make quick decisions (or any decision at all) and a general lack of enterprise and action can mean that these two often go through childhood in a state of quiet annoyance, as they miss out on opportunities, usually blaming each other for the problems. As they are also ambitious but very laid-back about their aims in life, each tries subtly to be boss of the relationship, hoping the other will do all the groundwork. Helping out with homework, coming to the rescue in the playground and making up excuses are all aspects of life in which one Libra expects help from the other, knowing it will be reciprocated at a later date. On the whole, this is usually a genuine companionship, with both being popular stars of the social scene and idealistic about each other and the world.

Libra and Scorpio

Libra Child/Scorpio Mother

Scorpio is deeply intense and prone to extremes whilst Libra is easy-going and rarely lets its emotions get to the surface, let alone take over. For this mother and baby, who are very different astrological next-door-neighbours, it can sometimes be an attraction of opposites but, more often than not, is a relationship of many misunderstandings. At the beginning, Scorpio provides a wonderfully strong and stable environment for the charming and affable little Libran and does much to advance her child in the world. She will be delighted to see how well her child does in company, although might get a little jealous if it shows any kind of favouritism to one of her friends. Like Taurus, Scorpio finds it difficult to share. She is also a woman of very firm opinions who doesn't have much truck with people who prevaricate and dither. Her Libran child, who finds decision-making almost impossible, often sees its balanced views rubbished and resents being pushed into situations far too quickly. Libra also finds it difficult to empathise with its mother's powerful and passionate feelings, while the determined and ambitious Scorpio gets thoroughly exasperated by her child who often seems frivolous, confused and far too laid-back. Libra is also a sign that doesn't need a great deal of discipline: it responds well to rational argument and wouldn't dream of upsetting its mother. Scorpio likes to control her environment (and her child) and often insists on rigid rules that brook no variation or discussion. The gentle Libran can sometimes feel totally overwhelmed by its mother's rather forceful personality just as much as Scorpio is flummoxed by her child's more changeable moments, its refinement and its inability to see through people. However, neither gives up easily on the other: Scorpio is famously loyal and Libra hates to cause unhappiness. At best, Scorpio learns a lot about tact and the middle road from Libra and her child benefits from its mother's energy, magnetism and sense of purpose.

Libra Child/Scorpio Father

The Scorpio father takes his role very seriously and is determined to see his child making the most of life. His Libran son or daughter, who takes a much more easy-going attitude to life, sometimes feels that it's being pushed down roads it would prefer not to take. Then, of course, it seethes with frustration and anger because it's never had the gumption to say 'no' to its father's plans! Scorpio feels strongly about everything: his Libran child rarely comes off the fence for long enough to have a firm opinion about anything. As a very young child, Libra benefits enormously from its father's enthusiasms: he'll be a good teacher and will do much to ensure his child is top of the class. In turn, Scorpio is enchanted by his good-looking youngster who charms everyone and makes him feel very special. However, his rather didactic approach is often at odds with his child's more even-handed attitude and he often wonders why Libra retreats well out of his way when he goes into lecturing mode. A Libran daughter usually feels very protected by her dynamic Scorpio father, but both son and daughter frequently tire of his manipulative and obsessive behaviour.

Libra/Scorpio Siblings

At first glance it would appear that Scorpio rules the sibling roost with its powerful and determined nature. Libra seems far too gentle and accommodating to stand up to its more dynamic brother or sister. It is frequently Libra, however, who comes out on top as it watches Scorpio's own machinations, secrecy and obstinacy bring about its downfall. Then Libra picks up the pieces, talks things through and puts Scorpio back on an even keel, to say nothing of smoothing its sibling's path with parents, friends, teachers and anyone else that the Scorpion has offended! In turn, Scorpio is a powerful ally to Libra, helping its unsure sibling to make important decisions and to realise that pleasing all of the people all of the time is an impossibility. Scorpio often frets because Libra just doesn't understand its deep feelings and need for privacy, while Libra gets fed up with Scorpio's derogatory comments about its love of luxury. Scorpio's loyalty and Libra's love of harmony and sociable nature are good starting points for a long-term relationship.

Libra and Sagittarius

Libra Child/Sagittarius Mother

The Libran baby is all smiles and will do its utmost to fit in with its Sagittarian mother's slightly disorganised lifestyle. Both naturally thrive in the company of friends and acquaintances and the Libran baby, from the first, is happy to make its mark on the social scene and to endear itself to all and sundry. Libra is ambitious but needs other people to help it reach the top of life's ladder, and, with a Sagittarian mother, the baby's natural instincts about 'it's who you know' are inadvertently and happily fostered with both zeal and panache. Libra has a need to be loved and to please and generally finds a very appreciative recipient of his or her basic good nature and happy demeanour in its equally optimistic and easy-going mother. Like all ambitious signs, however, the baby Libran also knows when it has had enough and will make no bones about it. Once its Sagittarian mother introduces an element of tension, disharmony or a complete sense of disarray into the proceedings, tears or temper and a picky approach to mealtimes can be expected. As the child gets older, the endless shilly-shallying and complete inability to make a quick, or any, decision can drive its Sagittarian mother to distraction, as can what she perceives as Libra's sometimes frivolous attitude to life. Libra often feels under a lot of pressure to do well at school, when it really prefers to take a more leisurely approach to achieving its objectives but is, in fact, much more attuned to getting on in life than its mother. Invariably Sagittarius will go along with whatever sensible decision her child makes but he or she can feel frustrated by a mother who is the eternal student and clearly doesn't understand Libra's aims in life. Both Libra and Sagittarius are spendthrifts and although a shopping spree could be a mutual pleasure it's never within budget! Generally, there's a wonderfully affectionate and contented relationship between these two: the child values the mother's advice and the mother her Libran's balanced viewpoint.

Libra Child/Sagittarius Father

The arrival of a Libra baby to a Sagittarian father must be bliss indeed for both. The baby beams and gurgles its approval of a father who is happy to chatter, take it out and about and generally appreciate its gregarious and accommodating nature. In turn the Sagittarian father feels loved and adored and wants to become very involved with the baby's development. Any Libran child, of course, knows exactly how to use his or her abundant charm to win over the father during good times and bad! As the child gets older, the active lifestyle and get-up-and-go attitude of the Sagittarian can often clash with the more laid-back and indecisive Libran approach and these two are often at loggerheads during the teenage years. Learning for its own sake, so important to the Sagittarian, can often bypass the Libran and that causes all sorts of hassle. The father can also be particularly hard on the Libran's attitude to money, usually because he sees his own spendthrift tendencies coming out in his offspring. The long-term outlook, however, for these two is excellent. Their differences are easily buried and they are quick to build on their similarities.

Libra/Sagittarius Siblings

One of the reasons these two tend to get on so well is the 'live and let live' attitude adopted by both. Neither is prone to temper tantrums or bearing grudges and both appreciate a good debate. Both are also very quick to recognise each other's skills. Sagittarius frequently needs its more diplomatic Libran sibling to get it out of a scrape and Libra is thankful for the Sagittarian's sense of humour and quick thinking when the going gets tough. Socially these two are usually an asset to any gathering and frequently work as a team as they get older. Any potential difficulties between them arise because of the Libran's fear of upsetting apple carts. The Sagittarian thus gets away with words and deeds that are uncalled for, causing the Libran silently to fret and fume. The Libran ability to charm also irritates the Sagittarian who can see right through that little ruse! Sagittarius, however, often saves Libra from dubious friendships. The issues that divide these two are relatively miniscule: the genuine affection that unites them is enormous.

Libra and Capricorn

Libra Child/Capricorn Mother

The Libran baby, so serene and laid-back even at the time of its birth, comes as an absolute joy to its mother who immediately sees her child's refinement, easy-going charm and eagerness to please. In Capricorn, the little Libran has a sure-footed and calm mother who will provide it with the pleasant surroundings in which it will thrive. Libran babies need harmonious conditions if they are to grow up happy and contented and, whilst Capricorn certainly provides a great sense of security and a congenial domestic situation, her busy lifestyle means the Libran equilibrium is frequently shattered! Tears and a loss of appetite quickly follow. A short period of calm restores the baby's spirits, but it can be difficult for the efficient and organised Capricorn mother, who is used to fitting a lot into her day, to slow down a little so as not to disrupt her baby's life more than necessary. She also comes to realise, while her child is still young, that they have very different ideas about what's important. Hard work is the core Capricorn belief and she hopes her Libran will feel the same. Whilst Libra is certainly ambitious, it relies on charm, contacts and natural talents to get on in life, and from a very early age this is more than obvious. Her child will love the social scene and be very popular, whilst Capricorn frets about books not being read and tasks left undone. Capricorn, who never finds it difficult to make a decision, will also become exasperated at the Libran inability to get off the fence. She'll see her child as either a time-waster, lazy, or frivolous, or often all three! In turn, Libra sees its mother as demanding, anti-social and probably rather stuffy. With the Libran penchant for the good things in life, there's also likely to be a major clash over spending. These two may never fully understand each other but, as neither would want to create a rift, they agree to differ and problems are always swept under the carpet.

Libra Child/Capricorn Father

For a Capricorn father and a Libra daughter, this relationship can work well. He fulfils his role as the provider for his family and she, all smiles and assuring Capricorn he's her absolute hero, happily spends his money, shines on the social scene and makes all the right contacts. However, Capricorn can still become exasperated at the Libran shilly-shallying and inability to make the best use of her talents and she rails against his stick-in-the-mud and demanding attitude. A Libran son, however, can be quite a different story for the Capricorn father. His son's airy, laissez-faire attitude grates with the more pragmatic Capricorn who thinks Libra should be taking life more seriously. Capricorn also resents the ease with which his son, from a very early age, socialises and captivates the people who matter. Libra, in turn, resents the narrow Capricorn viewpoints and its obsession with both proprieties and thrift. Earth (Capricorn) and air (Libra) can raise quite a sandstorm but when everything's settled down father and child will have found a way to co-exist, though mutual understanding may never be in their vocabulary.

Libra/Capricorn Siblings

Although these two are very different, they have a lot to offer each other. Capricorn can help its Libra sibling to become more focused and decisive, whilst Libra's abilities on the social scene and its appreciation of the good things in life can open up Capricorn's world quite dramatically for the better. Both are ambitious and will usually support each other's need to win a competition or get to the top of the class. The Capricorn bossiness and the changeable Libran moods, however, usually bring problems. Libra resents being organised and Capricorn is never totally sure of its sibling's commitment. Capricorn also tends to take advantage of Libra's good nature and eagerness to please, whilst Libra uses Capricorn to get it out of trouble, whether it's completing homework or sorting out one of its social dilemmas. Although Capricorn's patience and diligence are sorely tried by its more easy-going sibling, and Libra often thinks Capricorn is too proper and dull, they can often be very aware of each other's qualities and benefit from them.

Libra and Aquarius

Libra Child/Aquarius Mother

To the outside world, the Aquarian mother and Libran child look to be happiness and contentment personified! And that is exactly how it is. Both are air signs and from the moment of birth these two seem to have an unspoken and natural understanding. The Libran baby, all charm and eagerness to please, thoroughly enchants its Aquarian mother, who feels very much in tune with her easy-going, sociable and generally peaceful child. In short, she gets a terrific boost to her self-confidence and morale from a baby who clearly thinks she is just wonderful. Like it's mother, the little Libran loves company and therefore beams when taken out or is the centre of attention when she is entertaining. Very soon they are billing and cooing at each other and starting not only a life-long sharing of views but also a glorious mutual admiration society. So far, so good. The first slight hiccup in this perfect relationship usually comes when the Aquarian mother indulges in rather erratic behaviour or turns the daily timetable upside-down. Libra prizes harmony above all things and sudden upsets, changes and even boisterous behaviour can set this baby's nerves jangling. Suddenly the mother finds she has a very stressed baby on her hands who has probably gone off its food and is feeling right out of sorts. As the child grows up, the other potential stumbling block in this relationship is the Libran inability to make a decision. Aquarius, who is independent by nature and never afraid of taking a controversial stand, finds it taxing in the extreme to be faced with her Libran child, who thinks vacillation is the answer to everything. Libra wants to be liked by everyone and tries to please all of the people all of the time, something that is way beyond the thinking of its Aquarian mother! Generally, however, this relationship flourishes from beginning to end in much love and affection, general chitchat, spending sprees, a good social life and plenty of cultural stimulation.

Libra Child/Aquarius Father

In a Libran child, the Aquarian father has an almost perfect audience for his views on life and the world, particularly because, unlike Gemini offspring, his Libran will probably defer to his greater wisdom and knowledge and refrain from arguing every point! That is not to say there is no general communication between father and child: there is, but it is usually more about mutual interests and less about contentious issues. The Aquarian father will be keen to introduce his child to books, hobbies and culture and will love to arrange days out together where they can both learn something new. Where the relationship between father and child can come unstuck is during the teenage years, when the Aquarian contrariness and his total inability to see its effect on the child can cause major upsets. Equally, the Libran's need to please the father, rather than do what's right for itself, infuriates the Aquarian. This family dynamic works particularly well between an Aquarian father and a Libran daughter, but whether son or daughter, this is invariably an excellent and loving relationship.

Libra/Aquarius Siblings

With two air signs in the picture, there is bound to be plenty of chatter and busyness. Both like to be on the go, have an innate curiosity about life and enjoy the company of others, and neither suffers from either jealousy or possessiveness. In fact, both tend to be extremely helpful to one another and this can be a wonderfully laid-back relationship, characterised by much laughter, plenty of grand plans and constant demands on their parents' wallets! Both like the good things in life. Where problems can arise is in the Aquarian's need for independence and space against the Libran's dislike of its own company. Frequently the Libran feels rebuffed by the Aquarian and, equally, the Aquarian feels smothered by the attention of its Libran sibling. Whether older or younger, the Aquarian will tend to be the 'ideas' person and it will take all of the Libran diplomacy to talk its sibling out of some of its more bizarre plans! However, as the spokesperson for the duo, whatever the situation, the Aquarian will recognise that this is the Libran forté! These two are mutually supportive and usually enjoy a life-long friendship.

Libra and Pisces

Libra Child/Pisces Mother

This mother and child relationship is often made in a very indecisive heaven where both happily drift around in a bit of a muddle and are desperate to avoid any kind of confrontation. For Libra, its kind, sensitive and highly imaginative mother is bliss indeed: she'll never be rushing it into a busy schedule and forcing it to make up its mind about anything. Pisces is also delighted with what she sees as a wonderfully calm, easy-going baby who is unlikely to criticise or make her feel useless. Both, too, are usually artistically gifted and this is a mother who would far rather spend her time mucking about with paints and encouraging her child's creative talents than joining another mother and baby group. Libra is also very accommodating of its mother's haphazard timetable, her escapist nature and rather vague grip on the reality of any situation. At the start, the confusion that surrounds this relationship is not a problem for either of them, but once Libra gets a bit older, problems can emerge. The child is rational, the mother highly emotional and Libra will often wonder whether it can ever have a decent conversation with its mother without her dissolving into tears. She, in turn, wonders why her child can't just go along with things rather than constantly weighing up the pros and cons and hates the fact that it can be so changeable. Libra, with its naturally sociable nature, usually makes lots of friends, but its endeavours to be part of a group are often thwarted by a mother who forgets where she's meant to be or can't be bothered to join in. Her child is far more ambitious than she is and knows very early on that there are places to go and people to meet! The rather refined Libran is also sometimes slightly sniffy about the more cluttered Piscean look and it's often the case that the youngster tidies up after the parent, not the other way around. On the whole, this is a very loving relationship and if these two drift apart in later life it's almost by common consent rather than impatience with each other's foibles.

Libra Child/Pisces Father

In the early stages, with neither father nor child being particularly good at remembering diary dates, these two can exist in a constant state of being in the wrong place at the wrong time. For Libra, the frequently absent Piscean father can be very upsetting, although it will never say no to its father's apologies, which are usually in the form of very nice sweeteners, thank you! Where this father will also earn numerous brownie points is in his own artistic flair: from Pisces his child will love learning to draw, paint, play an instrument or just to see the world around. Both are enormously kind and often through misplaced compassion get themselves involved in rather dubious situations. It usually takes the more rational and diplomatic Libran child to tell its father not to bring home every lame duck! Sometimes Libra will wish its father was more pushy and less emotional about everything, and Pisces will despair of his child's obsession with the finer things in life. He'll never really understand, either, his child's ambition, let alone the quiet way it goes about getting what it wants, but generally this is an excellent and loving relationship and one which tends to improve with age.

Libra/Pisces Siblings

Libra and Pisces have much in common. Both can be indecisive, idealistic and easily led, as well as gentle and kind, and there's likely to be a certain measure of peace and quiet where these two are involved. Libra can be enormously helpful to its rather emotional sibling by pointing out the facts of a situation, and while Pisces is invariably a very good listener to Libra when its efforts to please everyone have made it resentful and angry. They are also likely to get into some hair-brained schemes, each egging the other on even while sensing that they are going down the wrong path: it is often the Piscean intuition that saves the day. On the creative front, however, their joint artistic ventures are usually very successful. Financially, Pisces fritters money away while Libra just overspends and there are often many IOUs passed between them. At worst, both can sulk and simmer over grievances but at best this is a loving and supportive friendship that survives both arguments and partings.

SCORPIO

The Scorpio Child 0-5 Years

Scorpio is considered to be the strongest member of the zodiac. It functions at the heights and in the depths, rarely contemplates anything that could be considered the middle road and has a determination and persistence that is second to none. This is never a sign to be taken lightly or trifled with. Its loyalty to those it loves is total until, of course, it's pushed across a line once too often and then it will walk away without a backward glance. Scorpio is certain of its loves and just as sure about its hates. Its most defining features are the mesmerising eyes that not only seem to see right through people but are also the windows to its own soul. Every Scorpio emotion is evident in its penetrating gaze, for better or worse, and every Scorpio has a passion, whether for someone or something.

The Scorpio child makes it clear right from the start that it considers life to be a serious business. It stares (and often glares) from the cot or car seat and takes in absolutely everything. Faced with new people and different situations it surveys each and every one with a rather lofty suspicion and never rushes into anything on a whim. In fact, the Scorpio child likes to be eased very slowly and gently into change of any kind. It is a fixed sign which likes the status quo and tends to be inflexible. Friendships are not made quickly: even the smallest baby likes to take its time in assessing someone's worth. However, having given the family a good once-over and tested the loyalty of friends, it beams happily and confidently at those who have passed the exam, and it'll stick with them through thick and thin.

From the start the Scorpio baby thrives on set routines, is very receptive to reasoned discipline and will always be happier knowing exactly what is going to happen during the day rather than following a rather vague timetable or haphazard arrangements. Although the Scorpio mind is strong on perception and analysis, it is also strongly intuitive, and this child's feelings about people and situations should never be disregarded, however odd they may seem. Its pertinent comments are often a case of 'out of the mouths of babes'! A quick appreciation of how things operate is also very evident in the young Scorpio, who is often way ahead of its contemporaries when it comes to toys and how they work. It may well be quietly amazed at some small feat of engineering but rarely for any length of time. Once it's figured out the mechanics, it wants to move on to something that is far more complicated! Like the other two water signs (Pisces and Cancer) Scorpio is usually very happy in that particular element. Baby swimming lessons and bath time are often very successful activities for the little Scorpio and splashing around in the bath before bed is usually a wonderful precursor to sleep (rather than a stimulant!). Equally, this is one sign that often greatly misses the evening water games if, for some reason, the routines have gone out of the window.

Even the youngest Scorpio will give its parents the occasional look that suggests it's being judge and jury of their every action which, particularly for the first-time mother and father, can be quite unnerving. That early strong, but silent, opinion is the forerunner of this youngster's obstinacy, which invariably makes its presence felt during the 'terrible twos'. This intransigency is the down side of the Scorpion's great sense of purpose and very difficult to deal with, as it's not easily talked out of anything. Appealing to its feelings rather than its rational intellect is often more productive as the Scorpio emotions run very deep and very strong. The thought that it could be upsetting people by its actions will possibly cut more ice than anything else, but it's often the case that the poor parent or childminder just has to wait patiently while this intractable bundle of pent-up fury decides to calm down! The other difficult emotions that are part and parcel of the Scorpio make-up are jealousy and possessiveness. This is a sign that finds it very difficult to share, whether it's a toy, a friend or an idea and often finds the arrival of a new member of the family very tough to cope with. It can also be resentful of other people's good fortune and even the youngest will be fully aware of its friends' belongings and wealth! (This, after all, is the member of the zodiac that understands big money: the world's financial markets are full of Scorpios.) However, rather than sit back and whinge, Scorpios, through fair means or foul, decide to get even! Ambition runs through their veins and, from the earliest days in the nursery, the young Scorpion wants to be top of the class.

Scorpio is often described as being secretive and certainly the youngest member of the sign delights in hiding away its toys, the mobile phone or anything else that is vital to family harmony. As the child gets older, it invariably has its secret camp or other hideaway, to say nothing of the two or three boxes which hold private treasures. It is, however, not so much secrecy that is the penchant for Scorpios, but privacy, and it is very important that this personal space is never invaded. Once it feels that everything is open to inspection, the situation often deteriorates into an obsessive need to keep things concealed and, when Scorpio shuts off, everyone knows about it. It's as though shutters come down and the child completely blanks everyone out. Once seen, this phenomenon is never forgotten and this is not the time either to continue a discussion or to force the little Scorpio into company. Usually, just left to its own devices for a short while, it comes back radiating sweetness and light.

These are powerful and passionate children who are never likely to go through life unnoticed, but they also have their vulnerabilities, which are usually well hidden. Forceful they may well be, but they are just as unsure as anyone else about certain aspects of life. It is, however, sometimes very difficult to help a little Scorpio who hides its feelings behind impenetrable barriers or a colossal temper tantrum. Like Taurus, anger builds slowly, but when the pressure cooker eventually explodes, it's a dramatic business. Where this child tends to be very amenable, however, is over food. As befits the idea of Scorpio being all or nothing, it invariably goes for either a very bland taste or the highly spiced and is often very adventurous about trying new textures and flavours.

All Scorpio children have a tendency to be a little aggressive. Before the discovery of Pluto, Scorpio was ruled by Mars and, like Aries (also ruled by Mars) little Scorpions see themselves as champions and knights in shining armour, ready to do battle for those they love and for causes they believe in. For most, an involvement in sport usually deals with a high energy level in the right way: boredom and too much time to brood about anything, as well as plotting to reclaim a favourite plaything, can mean that its strength is used in all the wrong ways. Learning to keep the formidable Scorpio emotional and physical energies under control can be a key part of its early education.

Scorpio loves to solve puzzles and from an early age its analytical and perceptive mind lends itself as much to jigsaws as anything that involves discovery. It's also fascinated by the bigger mysteries in life and this is usually the child who, early on, asks the questions parents hope will be delayed for a few years, whether it's about where babies come from or why stars twinkle! This child misses nothing and sooner rather than later its innate curiosity usually leads to a passion of some kind. Whether it's a hobby, a sport or a determination to win a competition, Scorpio never does anything by halves. On the other side of the coin, of course, is the possibility that the passion can become an obsession or compulsion but this child is usually open to reason.

Within its peer group, and often with adults too, the young Scorpio wants to organise. It'll rarely put itself into a position where it's at the beck and call of someone else and feels more comfortable when it thinks it's in control of situations. Early on, too, the Scorpio penchant for manipulation starts to show and its strong negative emotions, such as jealousy and a desire for revenge, make the youngster its own worst enemy. In its efforts to hurt others, it is usually very successful and easily inflicts tears and upset. The upshot, however, is different: Scorpio truly suffers when its machinations backfire and it is ultimately the unhappy loser, but this is the true survivor of the zodiac, daunted by nothing and ready to climb from the depths to the heights once again.

Loyal in the extreme to those it values and a powerfully magnetic and exciting friend and classmate, the little Scorpio is a force to be reckoned with. Its intuition, perception and persistence always keep it ahead of the game and in its eyes and smile it bestows its devotion on those it loves.

Scorpio and Aries

Scorpio Child/Aries Mother

To start with, Aries puts all her formidable energies into getting things right for her baby and Scorpio feels comforted with a steady routine and firm boundaries. Aries loves the way her baby's eyes tell the whole story and Scorpio delights in its mother's good humour and endless efforts to make its life interesting. Soon, however, the differences in the Aries/Scorpio personalities emerge. Aries has a short attention span, loves to be busy and usually needs plenty of company while Scorpio takes a long time to assimilate and approve of new situations. It doesn't have its mother's confidence or trust in human nature and is naturally suspicious. When faced with constant changes of scene and people the baby becomes fractious, which, of course, upsets its mother who thinks she is doing absolutely the right thing in involving her child in a wider world. Aries has its enthusiasms but Scorpio has its passions. Sometimes it's a favourite toy from which it won't be parted, sometimes it's an inability to share and sometimes it's slightly compulsive behaviour. Aries, who is constantly moving on in life, finds it difficult to comprehend her child's love of the status quo and its fear of letting go. Like all water signs, Scorpio is usually happy in baby swimming classes and, with its perceptive and analytical mind, enjoys construction toys and anything, in fact, that gives it a sense of achievement. Aries is certainly no slouch at getting involved with her child's activities. The Scorpio secrecy later on drives the more open Aries to distraction, as can her child's sometimes quite manipulative behaviour. Scorpio, in turn, resents its mother's forthright and 'me first' attitude. There is always the possibility of some major stand-offs between these two, especially when Aries comes up against her child's obstinacy and then tramples all over Scorpio's deep feelings. At best, Scorpio is loyal to its mother and Aries champions her child, but a good relationship between these two will always involve tolerance and much give and take.

Scorpio Child/Aries Father

Scorpio and Aries both have associations with Mars, the god of war, which is obvious when this father and child get themselves involved in team games or other adventures which test their mettle. Aries will be thrilled with his child's forceful and determined nature but Scorpio often feels chivvied into situations it would like to have a little bit more time to think about. The father's short, sharp temper is frequently ignited by Scorpio's fear of the unknown and reluctance to change. Aries is also baffled by his child's wilfulness and habit of either shutting itself off from confrontation or sulking after a disagreement. He just loves a short, sharp argument and certainly doesn't brood on situations. Whilst Aries will recognise and encourage his child's ambition, Scorpio would probably prefer a more subtle approach from its father and often resents his tendency to take control. Aries will hate the Scorpio secrecy and will never understand his child's deep feelings, vulnerabilities and intuition, although he will greatly respect its persistence and its intellect. In this relationship there are two strong characters and, without one or other giving in occasionally, it can end up as a long war of attrition.

Scorpio/Aries Siblings

This is a relationship where, to the casual observer, it looks as though the go-ahead, impulsive and forthright Aries gets everything its own way. In fact, it's usually Scorpio, after much plotting, planning and often fairly underhand behaviour, who leaves Aries trailing in the dust! Scorpio/Aries siblings tend to be all or nothing to each other. Both are ambitious and uncompromising, with the Aries ego and impatience matching up to Scorpio's obsessions and secrecy. However, Scorpio is also extremely loyal to Aries, who, in turn, will fight tooth and nail to defend its sibling and, once they work together, can be each other's greatest ally. Aries is brilliant at coaxing Scorpio out of its stubbornness and rather set ways while Scorpio teaches Aries a lot about staying power and respect for other people's feelings. The biggest barriers to their friendship are the Aries selfishness and the Scorpio jealousy: if those can be conquered there is nothing these two together can't accomplish.

Scorpio and Taurus

Scorpio Child/Taurus Mother

Opposite signs of the zodiac, as with Scorpio and Taurus, have many characteristics in common and yet enough differences to make the relationship both a comfort and a challenge. Both mother and child, at the beginning, instinctively feel at home with each other as Taurus provides her little Scorpio with a thoroughly stable environment, firm guidelines and a gentle, but very sociable, pace of life. She is also a fount of common sense, which is a wonderful foil for Scorpio's deeply emotional nature, and although she may not understand her child's intuition or its little obsessions, she certainly won't denigrate them. Her artistic interests and practical skills are also put to good use introducing Scorpio to anything from gardening, cooking and painting, to sculpting the best mud pies in the area! However, mother and child tend to be opinionated and stubborn and once locked in a battle of wills, there is no quick solution. After a total stalemate both will retreat, full of resentment. The child feels hurt and plans revenge (and a scheming five-year-old Scorpio is not to be dismissed lightly!) and Taurus becomes even more determined to get her own way the next time. Scorpio can also fail its mother in not honing its social skills quite as much as she would like. Scorpio does not put on an act for anyone and, if it doesn't want to entertain or to go out to tea, down come the shutters, on goes the mesmerising glare and Taurus despairs of her child ever developing anything in the way of her natural affection and charm. Both mother and child can be very possessive and often, when Scorpio is small, of each other, leading them into a very clinging relationship. Taurus will, however, always be patient and understanding of her child's worries about change and she'll be enchanted by her little Scorpio's fierce loyalty and analytical mind. At best, these two stick together through all life's ups and downs. Only when mutual obstinacy constantly blocks the path might Scorpio think of going its own way.

Scorpio Child/Taurus Father

Early on in this relationship the Taurus father cannot believe his luck at having a child who seems to hang on his every word. It's only when the equally intense Scorpio starts to get its own ideas that the father sees the start of many deadlocked situations. On the plus side, of course, he is delighted to see his child's staying power and sheer determination to get what it wants, and Scorpio is thrilled to have such a practical and reliable father whose patience it really values as it gets to grips with life. These two usually enjoy many interests in common, and Taurus is particularly good at encouraging his young Scorpio's ambitions. What Taurus finds difficult to fathom is his child's very secretive way of going about things just as much as Scorpio cringes at its father's self-indulgence and tendency to laziness. Although Taurus is far less emotional than Scorpio, he will make a good stab at trying to understand his child's feelings and, if possible, to do something practical to alleviate its worries. A Scorpio daughter is a real dilemma to Taurus as he's often in awe of her formidable personality and yet resents the fact that she consistently gets her own way.

Scorpio/Taurus Siblings

In one corner is Taurus who has all the practical plans and in the other is Scorpio who plays emotional games in order to get its own way. Although Scorpio thinks the Taurean's ideas are boring and Taurus is appalled at its sibling's manipulative behaviour, each secretly admires the other and together they can make quite a team. Both have great powers of endurance and determination and neither gives in easily: when it comes to facing a parental grilling, these siblings will stick by each other and cleverly get themselves out of trouble. Neither has a particularly adventurous spirit and each understands the other's obsession with the status quo. Jealousy and possessiveness are traits common to both. When they are young there can be a lot of tears and dramas over missing toys and the division of parental time and attention. Later on resentment causes arguments and brooding silences. These two can, and do, lose patience with each other and drift apart, but usually loyalty and affection ensure they help each other out for years.

Scorpio and Gemini

Scorpio Child/Gemini Mother

The inconsistent, adaptable Gemini and the intense, entrenched Scorpio make strange bedfellows and this is an astrological relationship that is likely to bring many difficulties before mother and child fully appreciate each other's qualities. Gemini takes on far too much and chases from one late appointment to the next, with routine never part of her lifestyle. Her Scorpio baby, however, needs a set of sensible directives and, most important of all in the early stages, an ordered day, without which it becomes fractious and uncertain. Scorpio is extremely uneasy about change, let alone sudden little adventures, all of which are the essence of life for its mother, and Gemini often has to struggle hard to bring some stability into her child's life. She is often amazed at the forceful Scorpio emotions and determination, which usually come out in strongly obstinate behaviour. To this thoroughly versatile woman, who is always interested in everything but rarely passionate about any single issue, the Scorpio intensity is truly baffling, and she often finds herself giving in to her child in situations where she knows she should be taking a firmer stand. Scorpio needs a great deal of attention and often becomes jealous of its mother's enormous fascination with other people and the time she spends on the phone or just chatting to her next-door neighbour. Gemini finds it difficult to give anyone, even her child, the depth of interest it craves. Thwarted, a three-year-old Scorpio will dream up some wonderful attention-grabbing situations which are the forerunners of the machinations that, later on, will take up much of its time and attention! Although Gemini will love her child's perceptive and analytical mind which chimes very nicely with her own rational intellect, and will also be charmed by Scorpio's fierce loyalty, she'll never comprehend its yearning for privacy and its very deep feelings. Scorpio, in turn, will love the fun it has with Gemini and the breadth of experience she offers, but will always feel that it's a complete mystery to its mother.

Scorpio Child/Gemini Father

The innately suspicious Scorpio is a stark contrast to its very open Gemini father. He is slightly unnerved by his son or daughter giving a new contact a quick (or even quite slow) once-over before making any opening remarks! In the same way, his son or daughter cannot cope with Gemini's broken promises, restlessness and inevitable changes of plan. The more chaos that develops, the more Scorpio retreats into moody silence and stubborn behaviour and the more Gemini tries to jolly things along. Where Gemini will score points is in his awesome knowledge of everything – or so it seems to his little Scorpio. Intellectually these two often develop a terrific bond and Scorpio loves its father's quick wit just as much as Gemini values his child's perception. The huge emotional depths of his child are completely lost on Gemini and the lack of real communication usually ensures that this relationship can only go so far, and no further. The sheer force of Scorpio's magnetic personality usually overpowers the father's lighter touch but his child will be loyal in the extreme and will eventually appreciate its father's ability to make life look a whole lot brighter.

Scorpio/Gemini Siblings

At best, Scorpio teaches Gemini a lot about staying power and persistence while Gemini helps its sibling to get out of entrenched positions and to modify its fixed opinions. Gemini is also happy to let Scorpio take the lion's share of parental attention, as it's usually far more sociable and less dependent on the domestic sphere than its brother or sister. Where these two usually come to loggerheads is over Scorpio's resentment at Gemini's success, especially if it appears to have been easily won, and Scorpio's very private nature. Gemini, who is open to everyone and everything, cannot cope with a sibling who finds it difficult to share and seems to plot and plan at every turn. Scorpio, in turn, finds the Gemini curiosity and nosiness unbearable and thinks its sibling is thoroughly two-faced, unable to hold an argument and far too cunning. Encouraged to develop different interests and to take diverse paths, these two usually get on very well. Distance can lend a lot of enchantment.

Scorpio and Cancer

Scorpio Child/Cancer Mother

This mother and child swim happily together in deep emotional waters. From the start there is a strong understanding and empathy between the two, and the Cancerian mother's intuitive nature will be totally attuned to her Scorpio baby's every need. In turn, her baby will turn its piercing gaze upon its mother with nothing short of the utter devotion, which, in time, will develop into one of Scorpio's greatest strengths – its complete loyalty. Scorpio's own sixth sense also gives it an immediate insight to its mother's worries and insecurities. The Scorpio baby thrives on set routines and likes to have changes introduced very slowly – something the Cancer mother understands perfectly. It would seem to be a very cosy arrangement but, on the other side of the coin, Scorpio can be quite judgmental, making it very clear if its mother is not coming up to scratch. Cancer, who is never that confident at the best of times, retreats into moody silence, hypersensitive to Scorpio's often very pertinent remarks. Resilience and an almost ruthless perseverance can also make this child quite a handful when it decides that things are not going its way! Cancer, equally, hangs on to its opinions and ways of doing things with a tenacity that defies belief. The possibility of a right royal battle of wills between the two, therefore, becomes evident and very often this mother and child relationship is dogged by stubbornness on both sides, to say nothing of a lot of tears and general upset. The worst-case scenario between these two is an over-abundance of emotional dependency with each reluctant to let go of the other. Cancer can also feel it's being pushed around by her child's more forceful personality. If Cancer can guide her Scorpio baby's formidable energies, these two will invariably develop a deep and loving relationship and an emotional bond that will not only sustain them both in good times and bad, but also allow them to respect each other's qualities and needs.

Scorpio Child/Cancer Father

A Scorpio daughter born to a Cancerian father can come as quite a shock! He hopes for a truly feminine addition to the family: she is likely to be not the slightest bit interested in everything he holds dear about the female of the species! He will often be far too protective of his rather forceful and determined daughter and, even when she is very young, she will startle him with her confidence and sense of purpose. A Scorpio son could be much easier for the Cancer father to deal with, as long as he takes a hands-on approach and gets involved in sports and other activities that keep his energetic and persistent son occupied and entertained. Whether dealing with a Scorpio son or daughter, the Cancerian father's greatest gift will be to understand his offspring's ambitions on the one hand and the insecurities and vulnerability beneath the Scorpio bravado on the other. Scorpio can sometimes get annoyed at its father's changeable moods, just as Cancer finds it difficult to forgive the Scorpio machinations. On the whole, however, this father and child usually develop a quiet understanding and, as both age, a sense of being totally comfortable with the other.

Scorpio/Cancer Siblings

Jealousy is often a major problem for Cancer/Scorpio siblings, particularly where the mother is concerned. Cancer, in particular, is usually very attached to the domestic apron strings and, although Scorpio is not too fussed at having its mother's attention, it just hates the fact that its sibling seems to have a stronger relationship with her. Scorpio's problems with sharing are brought quickly to the surface when there is a Cancer brother or sister on the scene. Both siblings are highly intuitive and pick up each other's moods, worries and insecurities very quickly. They therefore have an excellent communication system even though they frequently retreat into rather resentful silences when sharp, and very observant, comments have been made. Cancer is very kind and sympathetic, qualities that Scorpio fully appreciates as it recovers from disasters of its own making, whilst Cancer relies upon Scorpio's determination and persistence when tempted to give up on situations. Rarely does this relationship fall apart. It may go through some testing times but their empathy is total.

Scorpio and Leo

Scorpio Child/Leo Mother

Neither Leo nor Scorpio expects to go through life unnoticed: each is going to want its own way and has pretty firm ideas about how to achieve it! Early on, of course, as both are 'fixed' signs, mother and child thrive in a good routine, a steady pace and not too many sudden changes. Leo is extremely well organised and she'll combine a very secure domestic scene with an entertaining social life and plenty of interesting activities for her little Scorpio. She'll wonder, of course, why her child seems to be more tentative about things than she is, just as much as Scorpio will wish it was given extra time to assess people and situations but, on the whole, the first year or so usually goes quite smoothly. It's around the two-year stage that the Scorpio/Leo obstinacy starts to show, making immovable objects and irresistible forces look easy by comparison. Leo can be very fixed in her opinions, always knows she is right and can be quite intolerant of her child's different views and early attempts at making its own decisions. Scorpio can be just as determined and passionate about what it's trying to achieve and certainly won't back down quickly. Neither is open to negotiation and while Leo gets bossier, Scorpio retrenches and quietly prepares for round two. It's amazing to Leo, who is relatively transparent in her thoughts and actions, that her child can be so calculating and manipulative. She also finds her child's obsession with privacy very annoying. However, Leo is nothing if not both magnanimous and generous of spirit and, despite her frustrations, is often very admiring of her child's fortitude and ambition. Emotionally, however, it's not so easy as Leo wears her heart on her sleeve and Scorpio tucks its feelings well away and Leo hasn't the patience to find out what's really bothering her youngster. This is not going to be an easy relationship but Leo's warm-heartedness and Scorpio's loyalty often keep these two on a road that is blocked one minute and clear the next!

Scorpio Child/Leo Father

There is nothing complicated about the Leo father: he is the boss and knows best! At first his Scorpio child is in awe of what is often a larger than life character and loves being with him, although wishes he wouldn't show off as much as he does. Leo is also thrilled to have with him a son or daughter who takes such a quiet but intense interest in everything, and he secretly rather admires Scorpio's determination and persistence. As long as Scorpio goes down the path Leo has designated, life will be wonderful for both, but invariably Scorpio starts to resent being pushed around. Rather than indulge in a noisy argument (which is the Leo forté), Scorpio tends to retreat into silence, which produces a show of temper in Leo and causes yet further problems. But Leo is extremely generous, and if money can solve a problem, then he'll move heaven and earth to provide for his child, whether it's special lessons or an expensive hobby. Scorpio is inclined to bear grudges, but Leo certainly doesn't, and it's the father's ability to move on from the latest standoff that invariably saves this relationship.

Scorpio/Leo Siblings

Both Scorpio and Leo understand the importance of hard work and, as far as homework or other projects are concerned, neither is likely to interfere or upset the other and they'll tend to be mutually helpful and supportive. In every other aspect of life, they could well be at odds. Scorpio resents Leo's arrogance and its belief in the rightness of its every opinion while Leo gets upset at its sibling's rather underhand and obsessive behaviour. Neither is particularly accommodating or flexible and the more Leo seeks to gets problems out in the open, the more Scorpio distances itself from its sibling's temper. Breakdown of communication is frequent between them, particularly as Scorpio is highly intuitive and deeply emotional (which goes right over Leo's head) and Leo expects its sibling to pander to its very obvious feelings (which Scorpio chooses to ignore). If Leo can back off slightly and Scorpio open up a little, these two can benefit greatly from each other. Leo brings sunshine and glamour to Scorpio whose instinct for survival fascinates and encourages its sibling.

Scorpio and Virgo

Scorpio Child/Virgo Mother

Earth (Virgo) and water (Scorpio) signs have a natural affinity. Scorpio needs an ordered life and firm boundaries which its Virgo mother is well able to provide. She doesn't crave excitement and drama and isn't likely to subject her baby to sudden changes of plan or anything that could be considered over the top! The fact that she might fuss over her baby and perhaps worry over the minutiae of life isn't going to upset Scorpio in the slightest. After all, it's as discerning as she is and will be pleased that she is taking such a discriminating approach to its upbringing! These two will gently go through the milestones of Scorpio's development together, and Virgo will be particularly good at providing toys and entertainment that appeal to her child's perceptive and analytical mind. They'll also tidy out cupboards together, sort out the bookshelf and tackle anything that makes Virgo happier about her domestic scene. Whilst she probably won't be that enthusiastic about energetic sports, she'll encourage Scorpio to enjoy the garden, the swimming pool and probably the kitchen as well. Her rather finicky attitude to food (and her reluctance to be adventurous in her cooking) could frustrate the little Scorpio, whose tastes verge towards the spicy and the unusual. Both mother and child value privacy and neither would ever consider invading the other's space, especially when it's clear that doors are shut or serious thinking is going on. Although Virgo might never really understand Scorpio's very deep feelings, at least she'll be an ardent listener. She won't, however, have any time at all for the Scorpio jealousy and obstinacy, although will be good at talking her child through its intransigent moments, just as her child will resent its mother's hypercriticism and sometimes slightly stick-in-the-mud attitudes. Nevertheless, this relationship is usually one of much harmony and quiet contentment. The ambitious Scorpio will always be able to rely on its mother to support its aspirations just as Virgo can depend on lifelong devotion from her child.

Scorpio Child/Virgo Father

The straightforward Virgo is usually totally oblivious of his child's sometimes devious behaviour but admires its ambition, sense of purpose and very passionate take on life. Scorpio, in turn, loves its gentle father, frets over his worries and frequently gets irritated at his exacting demands. Both respect the other's need to be alone from time to time and hold each other's intellect in high esteem. The little Scorpio always knows it will get an honest answer from its father (combined, no doubt, with a lengthy commentary on the subject) while Virgo is quietly delighted at his child's perception. Scorpio's deep emotions and intuition are usually lost on Virgo whose rational mind is completely closed to any kind of sixth sense and, as with the other earth signs, he finds dealing with emotions very difficult. Where this father/child relationship can sometimes come to grief is through Virgo's tendency to criticise and to fuss. Scorpio takes exception, retires into silence and plans its revenge, which, in a five-year-old, usually manifests as a firm refusal to go along with any of its father's plans. A rebellious Scorpio is not to be trifled with!

Scorpio/Virgo Siblings

This is usually a very good sibling relationship. Scorpio will always be the stronger personality but comes to rely on Virgo to get it out of trouble, particularly when it's suffering problems of its own making. Virgo, in turn, knows that Scorpio will fight its corner through thick and thin and is invariably in thrall to its sibling's passionate views and sheer determination. Scorpio, however, can be its own worst enemy. Jealousy, possessiveness and intransigence lead it blindly down alleys that end in much unhappiness, and Virgo's practical realism, ability to talk things through and quick adaptability often manage to stop Scorpio in its tracks before disasters strike. Virgo worries and frets about everything, but Scorpio's perceptive mind and intuition can bring much comfort to its sibling. These two often spend hours talking together or in companionable silence and benefit from separate interests outside the home. Generally each values the other very highly and knows it has a totally reliable and discerning sibling.

Scorpio and Libra

Scorpio Child/Libra Mother

Like all astrological neighbours this mother and child are both fascinated and bewildered by each other! To the most easy-going and indecisive member of the zodiac is born the most forceful and passionate. The slightly laissez-faire Libran, who prizes a very comfortable life and never turns down an invitation, doesn't always understand that Scorpio needs a settled and organised environment and, although sociable, really values being on its own from time to time. A young Scorpio, more than most, will be very happy playing on its own, experimenting with its toys, making things and, later on quietly reading, while its mother seeks company almost for the sake of it. Consequently, Libra finds her child's need for privacy and its rather secretive approach to situations not only incomprehensible but almost an act of rejection. The more Scorpio retreats, the more Libra jollies it along into another outing or meeting, but a four-year-old Scorpio can be very perceptive and intuitively right about some of its mother's acquaintances! Scorpio's strong personality soon asserts itself and, rather than confront her child's stubbornness, she gives in – anything for a quiet life! She is also at a loss to understand the Scorpio inability to share and becomes almost embarrassed at her child's determination never to give up anything it's resolved to hang on to. Scorpio is intent on winning, no matter what the cost, and Libra's diplomatic skills are put to frequent use in sorting out the consequences of Scorpio's blunt remarks and resentful behaviour. Mother and child have a quiet sense of humour which can be a saving grace for both when tensions start to build and, although Scorpio has a better financial sense than its mother, it won't be averse to the occasional joint spending spree. Neither Libra nor Scorpio quickly gives up on anyone, let alone each other. Scorpio is endlessly grateful for its mother's charm and idealism whilst Libra is often in awe of her child's magnetism, emotional depth and sheer persistence.

Scorpio Child/Libra Father

To the debonair Libran father, its Scorpio child's penetrating and judgmental gaze is thoroughly unnerving. In turn, Scorpio cannot work out exactly what its father is thinking as he's constantly changing his mind and trying to please everyone. Scorpio knows what it wants and is determined to achieve its goals. Its Libran father, who shilly-shallies around, secretly admires his child's forceful approach but feels he has to make a stand about Scorpio's methods, including its obstinacy. Both father and child can be resentful of people who seem to have it all, and can mutter darkly together about the unfairness of life, but Libra doesn't understand the Scorpio jealousy any more than his child can fathom its father's faith in human nature and his frequent gullibility. Libra also finds his child's intensity about life very perplexing and is invariably immune to the depth of its feelings. Scorpio's need for privacy is also an enigma to the thoroughly sociable Libran. However, this relationship can and does survive despite the differences in personality. Scorpio loves its father's penchant for the good life and values his ability to look at all sides of a problem while Libra (with his vast social contacts) loves to foster his child's ambitions and passions.

Scorpio/Libra Siblings

Although these two are neighbours in the zodiac and therefore very different personalities, this relationship often survives many dramas and difficulties because Scorpio is steadfast and Libra hates disharmony. For a start, Scorpio needs its own space from time to time and gets exasperated when the Libran constantly interrupts. Libra, in turn, hates the way the Scorpion fumes obsessively about people and situations when things haven't gone right and can't understand why it gets such pleasure from planning someone's downfall. Libra knows only too well that, eventually, it'll have to smooth troubled waters and sort out its sibling's latest upset. On the plus side, Scorpio has a real talent for injecting a bit of staying power and determination into its laid-back sibling and values Libra's diplomacy, while Libra encourages Scorpio not to be quite so brooding and emotional and comes to respect its strong intuition. Fun and an enjoyment of life's finer moments also bind these two closely together.

Scorpio and Scorpio

Scorpio Child/Scorpio Mother

Same sign relationships tend to be all or nothing, and particularly so for two Scorpios who oscillate between bliss and heartache from the day the little Scorpion is born. Two very powerful personalities soon become locked in a battle for control and the mother usually knows she has met her match by the time her child is about six months old! Neither has any negotiating skill, as both will always insist on having their own way, and arguments, stubbornness, suspicion and retreating into brooding silences are likely to be a key feature of the relationship. As both mother and child suffer from major attacks of jealousy, there can be a lot of trauma for the little Scorpio when its mother gives her attention to someone else. Only this mother, however, truly understands the depths of her child's anger, hurt and envy when it's left out of a party, has to give up a favourite toy or resents someone else's good fortune. The mother wades into battle and the Scorpio loyalty has surfaced: this is one of the strengths that bind these two together. Mother and child also understand each other's need for privacy and their driven, powerful and intuitive emotions, and it's rarely through long discussions that these two solve problems. They look into each other's eyes and see the soul: no one understands a Scorpio like another Scorpio and the perceptive comments of her young child amaze and amuse its mother. Both are ambitious and the mother will do much to further her child's progress in the world, ensuring it joins all the right groups, gets involved in sports and makes plenty of good contacts. She'll run a fairly disciplined home, in which her child will find a great sense of security and stability but as both are fearful of change they can, and often do, get themselves bogged down in routines that have passed their sell-by date. When mother and child wallow in massive negativity they can be mutually destructive, but when they are both hitting the heights, this is a wonderfully loving relationship which survives many setbacks.

Scorpio Child/Scorpio Father

From the day his baby is born, the Scorpio father has usually mapped out its future, if not in absolute detail, then at least in broad outline. He's delighted to see, by the time his little Scorpio is about six months old, that it's got a formidably strong personality and is very determined to do things on its own. What he hasn't got to grips with, of course, is the fact that this strong-minded and powerful youngster's ideas might well not be in line with its father's. Early on, major stalemate situations develop between these two when the father orders and the child defies. His youngster's determination to tread its own path brings out the didactic in the father and they often end up either in brooding silences, with the shutters firmly down, or in highly emotional arguments when much is said that is hard to forgive. Despite these drawbacks to the relationship, there is generally a strong bond between them. The young Scorpio is fascinated by its powerful father, who is so passionate about doing the best for his child, while the father loves his offspring's perceptive and analytical mind and magnetic personality. The teenage years for this duo can often be difficult, the father desperate to retain control and the child eager for its freedom.

Scorpio Siblings

War and peace is often a theme of Scorpio siblings: they either seem to be worst enemies and at each other's throats, or best friends defending each other through thick and thin. As with any Scorpio relationship, there are likely to be some major disagreements along the way with jealousy, resentment, suspicion and possessiveness causing a lot of problems but their loyalty and ability to come to each other's rescue is second to none. At worst, of course, each can be so secretive and manipulative that no real relationship develops at all. With a lack of open communication neither really knows the other. On the other hand, their strong emotions and the fact that each sees behind the other's scheming behaviour often make them allies against the world and, with both determined to succeed, the siblings push each other onwards and upwards. It takes a great deal for these siblings to give up on each other. Pushed too far, however, they can turn their backs and never darken each other's door again.

Scorpio and Sagittarius

Scorpio Child/Sagittarius Mother

Zodiacal neighbours tend to have little in common and it takes hard work and patience for this relationship to work well. From the start, the Sagittarian mother is the recipient of Scorpio's strong sense of loyalty that is one of the hallmarks of the sign. She also tends to feel, however, that she is being judged by the piercing gaze of her adorable baby, who clearly thinks it is entitled to every minute of her time. It is the Scorpio possessiveness and jealousy, evident in even the youngest, that makes life so difficult for the freedom-orientated Sagittarius who simply cannot relate to such emotions. It takes the mother a long time to realise that her fretful and grizzling child resents her giving attention to anyone else. It is also difficult for her to realise that this demanding and sometimes self-centred baby is, like the other water signs, rather vulnerable and fearful. The Scorpion needs a great deal of reassurance to say nothing of a measure of routine, something that doesn't always come easily to the mother. As her offspring gets older, other character traits bring clashes between mother and child. Scorpio needs privacy and is quite secretive: Sagittarius is open and loves company. Scorpio can be obstinate and didactic: Sagittarius tends to be adaptable and 'wings it' when cornered! The Sagittarian mother is also adept at trampling over her Scorpio child's finer feelings, albeit unintentionally. This reduces the child to simmering silence, but the slight is never forgotten. At worst, these two go through many years in a love/hate situation which can, in later life, develop into total indifference. On the plus side, however, they often gain a lot from each other's attributes. Sagittarius lends a lighter touch to her child's rather obsessive nature, and equally learns a lot from Scorpio's determination and courage. She also has the ability to widen her child's view of the world and to revise its rather fixed opinions.

Scorpio Child/Sagittarius Father

It is not often that the Sagittarian father is made to feel that he's a child once again, but that serious, and sometimes rather judgmental, look from his Scorpio baby can make him think he's in a role reversal situation! These two get along really well if they are out and about keeping busy, and this relationship often thrives in a sporting environment or in competitive games of all kinds. The Scorpio is also a willing learner, particularly of anything practical, and a Sagittarian father is well able to cultivate those interests. Problems in the relationship develop through a genuine misreading of each other's character. Even more than the Sagittarian mother, the father usually fails to understand the Scorpio's sensitivities and insecurities and often pushes his child into situations that require his own abundant self-confidence and assurance. The secretive Scorpio child then resents what it sees as its father's intrusive and inconsiderate manner while the far more open Sagittarian is suspicious of his child's need for privacy. These two can develop a very close bond, but it takes time, and it can be a fraught journey to equilibrium and genuine affection.

Scorpio/Sagittarius Siblings

As these two are chalk and cheese, it's just as likely that they will get on famously as be involved in a life-long feud. Both are looking for totally different things from the family environment. Scorpio needs both constant reminders that it's loved and appreciated and someone who understands its depth of feeling. The much more emotionally self-sufficient Sagittarius needs someone to talk to and a busy social life. Both will probably enjoy sports and games such as chess, to say nothing of quizzes, general knowledge and reading. The bad news is the Scorpio possessiveness and seething silences coming up against the patronising and tactless ranting of the Sagittarian. Grievances fester as neither is going to climb down. Sagittarius also finds it difficult to deal with Scorpio's more manipulative side while the Scorpio sibling's jealousy is aroused by the Sagittarian's seeming endless ability to fall on its feet. Scorpio, however, will be supremely loyal to its sibling and in return will find its life enhanced by the Sagittarian optimism, joviality and philosophical outlook.

Scorpio and Capricorn

Scorpio Child/Capricorn Mother

A slightly calculating look emanates from the smallest Scorpio and, in its Capricorn mother, it immediately sees it has a bit of a challenge on its hands. This woman is clearly not going to give in to its every whim and allow it to act as a mini dictator. But Scorpio is not stupid: the baby works out pretty quickly that the Capricorn mother can really help it to make the most of its talents. Scorpio is a 'fixed' sign and is wedded to the status quo. It hates sudden change and flexible boundaries. A Capricorn mother instinctively understands those fears and provides very firm foundations and routines as well as a great deal of security. Both mother and child have a sense of purpose and hate wasting time, so they enjoy a busy, but often fairly mundane rather than glamorous, daily programme together. Scorpio, who can become quite jealous and possessive if it thinks its mother's attention is wandering to someone else, truly appreciates the Capricorn who always seems to be there for her child. Problems in this relationship arise through Scorpio's secrecy and Capricorn's need to control. Scorpio is a water sign and highly emotional, but these feelings are buried in hidden depths. Capricorn tries to avoid emotional territory at all costs and misunderstandings occur because neither feels able to confide in the other. Scorpio, therefore, has no way of unleashing its turbulent emotions in a controlled manner, and Capricorn has suddenly to deal with a major temper tantrum, or a sulk, or manipulative behaviour that she finds inexplicable. The Scorpio obstinacy also comes up against the Capricorn bossiness and the sheer determination of both signs to win the battle can cause major disagreements. The Capricorn pragmatism, accompanied by a gentle sense of humour, invariably triumphs. This relationship is usually one of great love, loyalty and respect and although it will have its more dramatic moments, it rarely fails to stay the course.

Scorpio Child/Capricorn Father

The Capricorn just loves his role as head of the family and expects to be obeyed and his status to be acknowledged. His Scorpio child, however, is prepared to question every tenet of its father's thinking which can, on the one hand, lead to very intelligent debate and a mutual admiration society or, on the other, a complete impasse, especially if Capricorn takes a 'do as I say' attitude. These two tend to tread quite carefully around each other, wary of getting into entrenched positions. On the plus side, they thrive in a busy environment, will probably enjoy shared hobbies and each will feel that it has a trusted companion. Capricorn will also encourage his child's ambitions – whether it's coming top of the class at the first swimming lesson or looking to a high-flying career. The father, who is usually very successful in life, will gain immeasurably by making great efforts to keep in steady contact with his Scorpio child. When Scorpio feels abandoned it can start to employ its talent for mischief! The teenage years, when the Scorpio's powerful emotions battle against the Capricorn rigidity, can be tense, but this relationship usually improves over the decades.

Scorpio/Capricorn Siblings

These two have many qualities in common. Both are determined, ambitious and persistent and neither wants to play second fiddle to anyone, even a sibling! So, from the start, there is the potential for a power struggle. Scorpio, in particular, gets particularly jealous about time given to its sibling. The Scorpio secrecy and its sometimes resentful and manipulative attitude are well matched by Capricorn's cool and calculating approach, though Capricorn usually fails to understand the depth of its sibling's emotions and, more importantly, the strength of its anger. Scorpio, who thinks that nothing in life is impossible, is often frustrated by Capricorn's more cautious and pessimistic views. Looking positively at these siblings, Capricorn can do much to guide the powerful Scorpio passions in a sensible direction while Scorpio can help Capricorn to conquer alien emotional territory. At best, these two make a formidable and fiercely loyal duo: at worst the relationship capsizes in a sea of resentments and intractable positions.

Scorpio and Aquarius

Scorpio Child/Aquarius Mother

Like its Leo cousin, the Scorpio baby arrives with the sole idea of ruling the roost. However, unlike the little Leo who reigns with charm and ego, the Scorpio tends to manipulate and control, and from its earliest days, when it fixes its beautiful eyes on its adoring Aquarian mother, it's already making its plans to take over! Aquarius is one of the most open and friendly signs of the zodiac, but in giving birth to a Scorpio, she is faced with the most secretive, jealous and determined member of the zodiacal family and one whose whole make-up is radically different from hers. They do, however, have in common a huge sense of loyalty and a great deal of perseverance, both of which can hold this potentially troublesome relationship together. The Scorpio baby is emotionally very needy and is often perplexed by its Aquarian mother's rather detached approach. By giving her little Scorpio as much attention as she possibly can during the early weeks and, all through childhood, giving her son or daughter special time during each day, she can alleviate some of her child's deepest worries. Scorpio babies also need strict boundaries and routines. The Aquarian mother is certainly good at setting some kind of structure to the day, but she's not usually a great disciplinarian. Without firm but kind handling, the Scorpio can often feel totally adrift and pushes its distracted mother further and further until the rules and regulations are set down. Despite their differences, there is usually a great sense of love and commitment between the two together with a willingness to make the best of what can sometimes be a complete mismatch. If the Aquarian mother can learn to fathom her Scorpio child's feelings and insecurities and the Scorpio can realise that its mother's coolly independent stance is nothing to fear, then these two can learn a lot from each other. For this relationship to succeed, it usually takes a lot of hard work but the effort will result in a depth of affection that others will greatly envy.

Scorpio Child/Aquarius Father

When Scorpio and Aquarius, two 'fixed' signs, are related there is always the potential for obstinacy and intransigence, but with an Aquarian father and a Scorpio son or daughter, this often manifests as an immovable object meeting an irresistible force! Whilst the Aquarian father is probably better than the Aquarian mother at setting ground rules and boundaries, thus giving his Scorpio child a greater sense of security, he is less likely to understand his son or daughter's vulnerabilities. He's particularly puzzled about his child's obsession with secrecy. At the same time, he'll probably be fascinated, on an intellectual level, at this amazing addition to his family. These two frequently talk a great deal and communicate not at all, and if there is to be any closeness between the two it usually comes through shared interests and education. When misunderstandings occur, the Scorpio child withdraws while the Aquarian father becomes ever more contrary in his efforts to bring the child to heel. The Scorpio loyalty to a parent and the Aquarian father's eventual pride in his Scorpio offspring frequently save this relationship from hitting the rocks.

Scorpio/Aquarius Siblings

As with any chalk and cheese relationship between siblings, this one can either work brilliantly or fail even to reach the starting gate. If the differences between the two are going to be the focus of the friendship, then Scorpio will be fascinated by its original and inventive Aquarian sibling, whilst the Scorpio depth, passions and magnetic personality will intrigue Aquarius. On the other hand, it's often the case that Aquarius becomes exasperated with the Scorpio secrecy and machinations, whilst Scorpio loathes its Aquarian sibling's perversity and emotional detachment. Arguments tend not to happen with this duo: if disagreements occur, Scorpio usually goes into a brooding silence and Aquarius finds itself talking into thin air – and getting more agitated by the minute! However, whatever the relationship between these two, both tend to be loyal and protective of the other in the face of adversity and although the relationship will probably never have great emotional depth, there is usually an underlying affection which may, or may not, be openly acknowledged.

Scorpio and Pisces

Scorpio Child/Pisces Mother

To the most gentle sign of the zodiac is born one of the most determined and forceful children and yet this is a relationship of two water signs who intuitively understand each other. The Pisces mother is not always the most confident in her abilities to cope with life's practical realities, including bringing up a baby, and her efforts frequently appear to be questioned by her little Scorpio who gazes at its mother with both love and a certain amount of critical shrewdness. Being a fixed sign and needing certainty and firm guidelines, Scorpio is often upset at its mother's sometimes rather vague grip on situations, to say nothing of her constant changes of plan and reluctance to enforce strict routines. She, in turn, can't understand why her child doesn't appreciate her selflessness at putting Scorpio first. On an emotional level, however, these two are at one. Pisces truly understands the Scorpio depths and vulnerabilities and these two often manage to say everything by saying nothing at all. The looks and the innate comprehension are all that matter. Scorpio, however, usually runs rings around its mother, who rather than cope with her child's seething obstinacy and sometimes obsessive behaviour, flees the scene, frequently in tears. As her child develops, a role reversal starts to occur and before too long it's Scorpio dishing out wise advice to Pisces and probably organising the domestic situation, while Pisces adopts the part of artistic teacher, outstanding listener and highly adaptable mistress of ceremonies! She will love her child's acute perception but find its secrecy and slightly manipulative behaviour very difficult to deal with. As Pisces is usually very content with her own life she is also puzzled at her little Scorpio's bouts of jealousy. Whatever faults Scorpio may find with Pisces, it'll be both protective and extremely loyal to its compassionate and sensitive mother, while Pisces will be eternally grateful for her child's constancy and understanding. These two muddle along happily with Scorpio in control!

Scorpio Child/Pisces Father

Scorpio thrives on consistency and firm boundaries. Pisces prefers to swim in unrestricted waters and is forever looking for change. Pisces sees his Scorpio youngster as too obsessed with routines and the status quo while his child thinks he is vague, unreliable and weak-willed to boot. Water sports, artistic pursuits and team games usually bind this twosome together, as does their innate understanding of each other's emotional depths. For a Scorpio son, it's often a revelation to have a father who has such an intuitive understanding of its worries. A Scorpio daughter happily winds her kind and gentle father around her little finger, tending to call more and more of the shots as she gets older! Pisces is often in awe of his forceful little Scorpio but has little truck with its obstinacy, preferring to swim away from conflict. However, he often gets caught in his child's machinations, of which he is totally oblivious until he finds he's agreed to situations right against his better judgment. Both father and child can be very secretive, and sometimes these two can drift apart in a sea of misunderstandings but, more often, they conquer their difficulties and strengthen their bonds.

Scorpio/Pisces Siblings

This is often a relationship of much deep emotional understanding but, where the practical realities of life are concerned, a total mystery! The intuitive bond between Scorpio and Pisces is very strong and each is the other's best friend and worst enemy when it comes to knowing what will work. Each can pour cold water on the other's plans or encourage it to greater heights, all because 'it feels right'. Where day-to-day living is concerned, Scorpio constantly has to run around after the disorganised little Fish, while Pisces frets at its sibling's attacks of jealousy and truculent behaviour. Both are capable of retreating into moody silences, and the Scorpio intensity and determination means Pisces usually has to seek a truce. To Pisces, Scorpio's powerful aura often makes it something of a hero, whilst Scorpio relishes its sibling's gentleness, kindness and unfailing ability to get it out of a rut. However many trying moments they experience, they'll spend a lifetime riding to each other's rescue.

SAGITTARIUS

The Sagittarian Child 0-5 Years

Bright-eyed enthusiasm emanates from every pore of the Sagittarian child, who not only sees life as a glorious adventure but also thrills to the challenge of every new hurdle that has to be conquered. From the moment of birth it is clearly evident that the baby is intelligently taking in everything that is going on, a wonderfully quizzical look indicating that it is already trying to grasp what this business of living is all about. Talking to a Sagittarian baby about anything, from a major news story to the minutiae of domestic routine, will invariably provoke an interested response: the sound of chatter generally, and of certain voices in particular, are extremely important to this member of the zodiac. Even at a very early age, Sagittarius thrives on communication, the acquisition of knowledge and a sociable lifestyle.

Sagittarius doesn't like to feel hemmed in and often gets quite tetchy in confined spaces. Fresh air and open places are often very conducive to its well-being and a fractious Sagittarian baby can easily be calmed by a trip in the pram or buggy or, later on, a short walk to the playground, the shops or just around the block. Even the youngest member of this sign takes a dim view of being cocooned too tightly. What is fine for the more security-conscious and emotionally needy signs is not so good for Sagittarius, who usually prefers to feel that its movements aren't totally restricted. The mother of a Sagittarian invariably finds that her baby has quickly acquired the knack of releasing its arms from a wrap and, later on, becomes adept at kicking off the bedclothes! Even as a toddler it will show the universal Sagittarian trait of hating formal, restrictive clothes and making some startling sartorial choices, usually in dark colours.

Whilst Sagittarius is not one of the most ambitious of the astrological signs (and it has a reputation for not making the most of its talents), it does appreciate having goals in life and thrives on challenge and a sense of achievement. A day without some kind of objective in mind is a day wasted as far as Sagittarius is concerned, and this attitude to life starts very early on. It is therefore very important for the little Sagittarian to end the day with a feeling of having learned something new or achieved something special. Because reading and language skills are often this child's forté, both should be encouraged and the reading of a bedtime story is extremely satisfying to this baby – not so much for the security and comfort of routine, but because of the excitement of the words, phrasing and vocal tones. Sagittarius is, after all, the zodiac's eternal student and from the start it's keen to learn.

Most Sagittarian children thrive in a fairly flexible routine and find it very difficult to obey rules just for the sake of it. Although their naturally rather noisy, excitable and happy-go-lucky approach to life can make it seem as though they need firm discipline, they are, on the whole, fairly amenable to anything sensible they are asked to do. This is certainly not the best member of the zodiacal family on whom to practise the 'do as I say because I say so' routine! It may take longer, but it's often a good move with a Sagittarian child to make the time to explain things: he or she will respond well to logic and reason. Whilst not in the Virgo or Capricorn league as far as common sense is concerned, the Sagittarian baby is blessed with an innate understanding of right and wrong and of fair play.

Perhaps the most charming trait of the Sagittarian child is its abundant joie de vivre and the sheer zeal with which it approaches life. For the parent this can bring a mixture of delight and exhaustion! This energy has to be fuelled and the interests sustained, as the worst thing any carer can do to this particular youngster is to crush this amazing exuberance and thirst for knowledge. At the same time, the formidable energy and gusto, which at times can become rather too boisterous and needs to be calmed, must also be channelled. It is very easy for Sagittarius either to start projects and never finish them or to fritter away its time and achieve nothing. Procrastination is a Sagittarian trait that is acquired young! Learning to see a task through to the end is vital to the Sagittarian child's development, just as much as it is to focus on a specific goal. Sagittarian energy is often best directed to sport, starting with anything from mother and baby swimming and the indoor climbing frame to dance classes and gymnastics for toddlers! In every way, for a Sagittarian child, achievement and success fuel its keenness to try something else or to take an interest to a new level.

Like the other fire signs, Aries and Leo, the Sagittarian is a very sociable child and needs the company of others. It is also one of the zodiac's best entertainers: it loves to show off and responds to an appreciative audience. However, the exaggeration that's involved in telling a good tale often spills over into daily life. Sagittarius doesn't deliberately lie; it just gets carried away, the story becomes more dramatic and pinches of salt should be taken with every telling. The Sagittarian child also has a lot to learn about thoughtfulness for others. Diplomacy and tact are never going to be its great strengths and even the youngest can be relied upon to demonstrate a massive case of foot-in-mouth disease. Where discretion comes naturally to some of the other signs, for the Sagittarian child it's something to be learned, just as much as sensitivity to other people's feelings. In addition, the wonderful Sagittarian smile very often hides its own hurt feelings, worries and anxieties and its natural joviality is frequently a mask for all sorts of unhappiness and insecurities. In the feelings arena there is much that will need to be said and taught, and parents of a Sagittarian need to be on the lookout for the 'tears behind the smile' and to help the child deal with his or her emotions. Thankfully, most Sagittarian children are not likely to be bullies or in any way physically rough. They prefer to reason than to get into combat and their weapons, if forced to use them, are usually verbal. After all, Sagittarius functions very much from the mind and the intellect. However, it shouldn't be assumed that this child will never resort to using force: in its quest for justice and as a champion of the underdog, all options will be open!

Although not naturally attuned to all matters domestic, most little Sagittarians will enjoy doing things around the home with a parent, childminder or grandparent as long as it becomes a learning experience. Once anything becomes routine or boring, the interest will wane and opportunities will be lost. As natural explorers and travellers, and relishing anything that challenges its thinking, a young Sagittarian will love to learn to fetch and carry, to run errands (even if it is only from one room to the next!) and will probably always want to set up some kind of camp, within which it will have its survival rations and everything necessary for its next expedition!

Generosity is one of the sign's greatest attributes and the young Sagittarian will probably be extremely open-handed with his or her pocket money and, even more so, with his or her parent's hospitality! From pre-school onwards, this child will be forever inviting friends home and volunteering his or her parents as chauffeurs, hoteliers and providers of good food! Financial management, however, is not a Sagittarian asset and planning to spend (or even save) pocket money sensibly can be a very valuable lesson to a child who, as it grows up, often thinks it can be bailed out of financial difficulty at every turn. However, most

Sagittarians tend to get by in life very well and, even as children, they know exactly when to take a chance on life and how to fall on their feet.

'Wise beyond his/her years' is often said about this child. Even at birth the little Sagittarian tends to give the impression that it is watching parents, relations and friends with sagacity and a deep inner knowledge. As a toddler the little Archer will probably come out with comments that give rise to an 'out of the mouths of babes' bout of laughter or perceptive remarks that make the listening adult cringe (usually because they're true and not particularly flattering!).

The straightforward Sagittarian child is often good humour and optimism personified. Energy and an avid interest in the world will never be lacking and nor will his or her open and generous attitude to life. With gentle instruction about other children's more delicate feelings and an understanding parental attitude to its problems in dealing with its own emotions, the Sagittarian will arrive at the school gates a more rounded individual. If it has also learnt the benefits of short periods of calm and the rewards that come from completing projects and attaining goals, then this child will be a most welcome arrival to his or her new environment.

Sagittarius and Aries

Sagittarius Child/Aries Mother

Both Sagittarius and Aries are fire signs: mother and child therefore share a wonderful enthusiasm for life, a love of action and a need to be at the centre of that activity. Immediately this is a relationship of much laughter, jollity and adventure, the prospect of which is obvious at birth. Aries is totally enchanted by the inner knowledge and wisdom of her baby, who, in turn, is thrilled to find itself with such an open and spirited mother. These two don't pussy foot around situations, tend to hate too much restriction and revel in a busy social life and an action-packed day. The little Sagittarian is never likely to complain if routine goes slightly to pot, as long as it is being entertained or putting its formidable intellect to good use, and Aries will never feel inadequate or guilty because she isn't running the totally perfect household. Her baby's first totally engaging smile will confirm that they are going to enjoy joyous and stimulating times together. Whether it's a walk in the country, visiting a local tourist attraction or museum, or perhaps a day at a theme park, Aries will love teaching her Sagittarian, who, in turn, will hungrily drink in the knowledge. Possible problems can arise when a four- or five-year-old Sagittarian finds its mother's fixation with doing things immediately (the NOW factor) and her short attention span somewhat annoying when it would love to linger over some exhibit or learn more about a subject. Equally Aries can become irritated at her child's endless questions and preoccupation with future goals. A spending spree usually makes both signs feel better and these two will always enjoy spending money, whether they have it or not! As neither sign is noted for tact, this relationship will always be full of very pertinent remarks, and yet both quickly forget a slight and neither sulks nor bears a grudge. The genuine warmth between this mother and child, to say nothing of a very deep understanding, sustains them through any difficult years. This is a relationship that is destined to last.

Sagittarius Child/Aries Father

The slightly gung-ho, adventurous Aries approach finds a very enthusiastic admirer in his Sagittarian child. This twosome will invariably be the noisy duo in the park, whether on the swings or kicking a football about. He'll also be delighted that his Sagittarian daughter is just as enterprising and energetic as a son and equally good-humoured when Aries wins at everything! Whilst he might get angry at the seeming lack of ambition in his Sagittarian offspring, at least there is no sense of competition between father and child and there is no clash of egos. Sagittarius, too, will certainly not cringe at its father's impatience and rather forthright manner as it knows only too well how easy it is to be tactless and, at five years old, to be unable to suffer fools gladly. Both father and child are naturally independent, but Aries can find it very hard to abandon control when Sagittarius wants to make its own decisions and to learn life's lessons. Despite a few glitches during the teenage years, this is usually a mutually beneficial relationship. Sagittarius learns much about courage and enterprise, whilst Aries respects his child's intellect and more philosophical mind set.

Sagittarius/Aries Siblings

On the surface, these two would appear to be ideal siblings as both enjoy an active lifestyle, are enterprising and straightforward and usually blessed with a good sense of humour. There are subtle differences between them, however, which can cause a few problems. Sagittarius is far more intellectual than Aries and values time spent reading, learning and acquiring knowledge generally. Aries, whose staying power is fairly limited, often gets impatient with what it sees as its sibling's self-indulgence and anti-social behaviour and frequently causes trouble by constant interruption and interference. Sagittarius then accuses Aries of being selfish and promptly demoralises its more egocentric sibling with a few well-chosen remarks. Aries is also competitive and ambitious and frequently rails against the Sagittarian luck and ability to land on its feet. More often than not, however, Aries relies on the Sagittarian wisdom, and Sagittarius is inspired by its sibling's courage and confidence.

Sagittarius and Taurus

Sagittarius Child/Taurus Mother

Astrologically these two are very different and this relationship doesn't slot neatly into place for either mother or child. The Sagittarian baby is born with an inbuilt love of freedom, a naturally optimistic and philosophical attitude to life and great adaptability. Its Taurean mother likes to be physically close to her baby, delights in routine and order, and is often stubbornly fixed in her opinions. From the start the baby will make itself feel comfortable by throwing off the blankets and looking dishevelled (its bid for freedom!). Taurus, who has a sense of style, takes pride in her appearance and wants her child to look good too, spends time tidying up her baby, cocooning it and giving it much demonstrative affection. The more Sagittarius is denied its space, the more it frets and, with her child manifesting such unhappiness, Taurus wraps it in an even tighter security blanket rather than just letting go and taking a more laid-back approach. At the toddler stage, Sagittarius starts to show its adventurous nature and need to explore the world. Taurus is much more concerned with establishing a cosy domestic scene, stability and security, all of which come very low on the Sagittarian list of priorities. While she'll certainly be keen to fulfil her child's educational needs, and is usually highly creative and well able to teach her baby, she tends to find the Sagittarian restlessness and its thirst for knowledge and debate thoroughly exhausting. Shopping trips for sports gear, books or anything that stimulates the Sagittarian intellect will be fun, as will days out together. At worst, these two drift apart later on, the mother often feeling rather rebuffed and rejected, and the child misunderstood. At best, each learns much from the other, Sagittarius about determination and staying power and Taurus about adaptability and trusting in life's goodness. Most important of all, Sagittarius will know that Taurus is constant: she'll always be there when her son or daughter returns from its latest (mis)adventure!

Sagittarius Child/Taurus Father

The very open, flexible and happy-go-lucky Sagittarian child is often a bit of a mystery to the practical, reliable and determined Taurean father. Sometimes he sees his son or daughter as irresponsible, superficial and tactless in the extreme, all so different from his innate charm, good taste and cautious approach to life. In turn the young Sagittarius thinks its Taurean father is a bit of a bore, self-indulgent and occasionally didactic, although equally well aware that he is wonderfully patient, affectionate and an absolute rock when it comes to defending and protecting his offspring. Problems mostly arise when the father's fears and worries hold back his adventurous child, thus frustrating Sagittarius who makes even more of an effort to do its own thing. The Sagittarian broad-minded and questing approach to life also tends to clash with the more fixed opinions of its father. At worst, Taurus can become resentful and jealous of his Sagittarian who appears to get such fun and achievement out of life with seemingly little effort. At best, he provides a solid and secure base from which his youngster can set off to conquer the world, sure in the knowledge that its father's practical skills and common sense will stand it in extremely good stead.

Sagittarius/Taurus Siblings

Sagittarius can be a great help to Taurus on the social scene as it is much more confident and adventurous about new situations and people. The charming Taurean will be just as vital to Sagittarius when it comes to getting its tactless sibling out of difficulties and smoothing troubled waters. However, the general line with these two is that Sagittarius sees Taurus as a wet blanket, forever frowning on its extravagant ideas and obstinate in the extreme, while Taurus thinks its sibling is both irresponsible and totally without depth. There can also be a lot of jealousy from Taurus, who thinks it works hard for everything while Sagittarius always seems to have it easy. Sagittarius equally thinks its sibling does nothing but look smug when another grand plan bites the dust. However, because these two are so very different and often provide a missing link for the other, it's quite possible that they can become good friends, especially if they pursue different agendas and interests when young.

Sagittarius and Gemini

Sagittarius Child/Gemini Mother

Sagittarius and Gemini tend to be very much on the same wavelength. Both are good communicators, have a tremendous thirst for knowledge and invariably put head before heart. For the Gemini mother it's usually a real joy for her to give birth to a Sagittarian. She instinctively feels that here is a baby who will understand her every move and thought and knows that they will have a great time together. Her baby, too, feels totally comfortable with this busy, adaptable, witty and sociable woman who will never impose stifling routines or an over-cautious approach to life. From the start the naturally inquisitive Sagittarius is intellectually fed by its mother: these two chat nineteen to the dozen even when the baby's response is merely a smile or a gurgle! As a toddler, the Sagittarian can be a lively companion for Gemini and they usually enjoy being out and about, revelling in lots of company. Both are sociable and confident. Later on, this mother and child will be at the forefront of the queues for libraries, museums, stately homes and anywhere they can gather new information. Where this duo can get into difficulties is on the emotional level: neither is good at dealing with feelings and very often there is much talk but little real communication, and even less understanding. Worries and stress are invariably covered up with even more activity. With the Peter Pan qualities of Gemini and the sometimes world weary wisdom of Sagittarius, this mother and child often seem to swap roles. Frequently the youngster comes up with the sensible solutions and encourages its mother to be more consistent. If the relationship fails, it's due to Gemini losing patience with her child's various quests and over-optimism and Sagittarius thinking its mother is superficial, with a limited attention span to boot. Mostly, however, these two prosper amidst much activity, debate and laughter and Gemini is brilliant at getting her child to look at the here and now, before concentrating on far-off dreams.

Sagittarius Child/Gemini Father

The Gemini father usually gets on famously with his Sagittarian son or daughter as he immediately finds a witty companion, an intelligent pupil and someone who is more than happy to listen to his endless chat and repartee! Sagittarius loves the rational, logical Gemini mind, the fount of knowledge its father seems to have about everything and the excitement of spending time with him. However, Gemini is always busy and sometimes fails to understand how much his Sagittarian child is relying on a promise that was probably made in too much Gemini haste. To his youngster, who has a tremendous sense of fair play, cancelling plans for no good reason is devastating. This can also be a relationship of sharp or thoughtless comments and although neither bears a grudge, each soon learns that words are an effective weapon! Gemini is also inclined to become impatient with his child's big plans and sometimes blindly optimistic views, just as much as Sagittarius despairs of its father's lack of staying power. Generally, however, this develops into a life-long and very happy friendship and laughter is always their best medicine.

Sagittarius/Gemini Siblings

Sagittarius and Gemini thrive on action, chatter and a good social life. Sagittarius might complain about its sibling promising more than he or she can deliver, while Gemini sometimes thinks Sagittarius is both irresponsible and prone to foot-in-mouth disease, but these are blips in what is basically a very good relationship. Sagittarius is particularly good at calming the Gemini nervous tension, whilst Gemini's logic helps to put the Sagittarian's grand plans on a firmer footing. The innate Sagittarian wisdom and honesty is, of course, up against the more cunning Gemini nature, but Sagittarius usually takes a philosophical attitude to its sibling's duplicity whilst Gemini learns a lot from its sibling's very forthright remarks. Both tend to love the sound of their own voice and are witty and brilliant in debate, so this is never going to be a quiet and peaceful twosome. Basically, these two have a lot of fun together and it takes something totally beyond the pale for these two to drift apart.

Sagittarius and Cancer

Sagittarius Child/Cancer Mother

Sagittarian babies tend to greet the world with a wisdom beyond their years, which is either rather daunting for the Cancerian mother or tremendously comforting. If she is facing the idea of motherhood with a certain amount of trepidation, then it's as though her Sagittarian baby is almost trying to help her along and has no intention of making her feel stupid or inadequate! Sagittarians are happy-go-lucky and optimistic, qualities that are evident even in the youngest member of the sign, who immediately sees life as an exciting challenge and is more than keen to find out what the world has to offer. But it is this natural curiosity and sense of adventure that can be baffling for the Cancerian mother. She just wants to shelter her child within the comforts and confines of her nest and can't understand why it's so attracted to the outside world. Bestowing huge smiles upon all and sundry, the Sagittarian baby wants to befriend everyone and fails to understand that it should be singling out its Cancerian mother for special attention! Cancer is a water sign (all emotions, moods and hidden depths) and Sagittarius a fire sign (all action, enterprise and upfront attitudes). The Cancer mother wants to cuddle her baby and keep it close to her in every way: the baby wants to explore, whether it's on all fours or being deep in conversation with the childminder. Faced with this extrovert child, the Cancerian mother can sometimes feel she's not needed or, worse, unwanted, but just like the Aries baby, Sagittarius needs somewhere to rest after a day of excitement and conquering new heights and the Cancer mother provides exactly the right environment. Equally, her Sagittarian child can motivate her to greater success and achievement in the outside world and encourage a more positive attitude to life. In the long run, these two often benefit greatly from each other, especially when the Cancerian mother has the courage to let her child go out into the world and to learn from its own mistakes.

Sagittarius Child/Cancer Father

The ambitious but cautious Cancerian father finds himself parent to an energetic Sagittarian adventurer who throws itself into life without a coherent strategy or a care in the world. In order that the Sagittarian does not drive its poor Cancerian father to the verge of a nervous breakdown, it's important for Cancer to understand that his child will never take his responsible attitude to either life or a career but will successfully reach different peaks. Despite being a natural wanderer, Sagittarius will always rate its family, and family life, very highly but will never want to feel tied. Cancer is reluctant to encourage his Sagittarian child's need for freedom, often provoking rebellion and, at worst, complete loss of contact later on. The sensible Cancerian provides a secure base from which his child can set forth into the world and to which it can return to re-charge its batteries. In return, the Sagittarian will be thoroughly appreciative of such a stable and comforting base and will bring much joie de vivre into the home. A Cancer father can either crush its Sagittarian child's spirit or bring out the very best in his son or daughter. This is a relationship that needs very careful handling.

Sagittarius/Cancer Siblings

Differences repel or attract and Sagittarius/Cancer siblings tend to find each other absolutely enchanting and invigorating, or thoroughly unapproachable and incomprehensible, and usually a bit of both. Faced with the confident and bubbly Sagittarian personality and seeing a competitor for its mother's affections Cancer frequently withdraws into its shell and carps about its sibling. As far as the Sagittarian is concerned, its aspirations lie in the wider world and in no way does it want to be king or queen of the domestic scene. The Cancerian moods and tendency to sulk can drive the more open Sagittarian to distraction, just as Cancer despairs of the Sagittarian's restlessness, tactless remarks and rather boisterous behaviour. On the plus side, Sagittarius finds Cancer a willing and sympathetic listener who helps to put emotional issues into perspective, while Sagittarius is able to jolly Cancer out of its negativity and worries. With patience and good humour, they can be very supportive to each other.

Sagittarius and Leo

Sagittarius Child/Leo Mother

Sagittarius and Leo are warm-hearted, generous and confident and this mother/child relationship is usually as much about great style and drama as it is about affection, enthusiasm and sociability. Leo is immediately appreciative of her Sagittarian baby's naturally inquisitive approach to life whilst her child revels in its mother's big-hearted personality and her pride in showing-off her newborn. After all, this is a child who wants to explore the world and it starts in the cradle: all those interesting people to meet! The Sagittarian also appreciates its mother's busy lifestyle and, to start with, her well-organised day. Later on it can fret at Leo's slightly inflexible attitude, to say nothing of her insistence that she is right and, at worst, her bossiness! Leo will make it her business to introduce her youngster to the arts, sports, shopping and anything else that she thinks will take its fancy and, as she is a naturally good teacher, she'll find her Sagittarian to be an extremely willing pupil. Sagittarius is born with grand plans and a thirst for adventure, and its Leo mother understands the larger than life scenario better than most and, more particularly, goes along with the Sagittarian exaggeration and over-optimism about everything. Therefore she gives her child all the confidence it needs to go out into the world, sure it can conquer any given situation. Problems can arise when the Leo obstinacy kicks in and she, in her child's opinion, interferes, lays down rules just for the sake of it and refuses to listen to anyone else's point of view. Sagittarius can also exasperate its mother with its rather capricious and irresponsible behaviour and Leo becomes adept at glossing over her child's tactless remarks. Nevertheless, these two invariably club together to laugh at life's more difficult moments and are each other's most fervent champion.

Sagittarius Child/Leo Father

The Leo father is often secretly proud and in awe of his Sagittarian child who seems to have so much innate confidence at such a young age. In turn, Sagittarius revels in its father's King of the Jungle attitude, his broad-mindedness and loyalty. For these two, life is often a big adventure: they are the ones queuing at the biggest rides, hogging the best seats and making sure they are on the winning team. However, the Leo father's big ideas on life are usually at variance with his child's. He sees success as being number one in an organisation or situation whereas Sagittarius looks at more personal goals and is not that interested in reaching the top of the ladder. When Leo has dictated a route for his child that it is reluctant to travel, Sagittarius sees its father as interfering, inflexible and controlling. The Leo ego, however, can be firmly dented by his child's devastatingly accurate and uncharitable comments. Despite these glitches, this father/child duo works extremely well. Leo loves his child's enthusiasm, good judgment and optimism and Sagittarius can always count on its father's support and encouragement.

Sagittarius/Leo Siblings

This is usually an extremely good sibling relationship. Both are naturally outgoing, broad-minded and positive and love a busy schedule and doing things in style, especially when it comes to financial matters. Neither is particularly good at saving and they are usually early converts to the principle of robbing Peter to pay Paul, to say nothing of doing deals with each other. Sometimes Sagittarius becomes irritated with Leo's rather fixed views and inability to indulge in a proper debate, while Leo frets about its sibling's restlessness and lack of organisational skills. As both are fire signs, each likes to get its own way and there can be times when neither will give in. Short, sharp tempers are the hallmark of both, although Leo might brood about a situation far more than Sagittarius who is always keen to move on. The sunny Leo nature and the Sagittarian jollity are usually far more in evidence, however, and these two will often be each other's mainstay throughout life. Leo relies on the Sagittarian wisdom and Sagittarius benefits from its sibling's generosity of spirit.

Sagittarius and Virgo

Sagittarius Child/Virgo Mother

To the Virgo mother her little Sagittarian is something of an enigma. She's providing a wonderfully cosy and ordered environment, is spending hours preparing the best, often organic or vegetarian, food and is ensuring that there is a certain amount of peace and quiet during the day. Unfortunately, her rather frustrated Sagittarian likes space and freedom to move, loads of rather chatty and noisy company and is generally not too concerned about what it eats. Faced with this singular lack of appreciation, Virgo becomes stressed and agitated and introduces even fussier routines. Worse, her sense of duty starts to override her ability for fun, just when her Sagittarian has decided that good times are at the top of its agenda. Sagittarius also has a big vision of what life is all about, whereas Virgo tends to concentrate on the detail. The toddler often gets irritated at its mother's insistence on focusing only on one toy, tidying the cupboard or completing the jigsaw when it wants to embrace so much more. For Virgo, who prefers a stable existence and little in the way of risk, to see her Sagittarian relishing challenge and prepared to gamble on situations, is something akin to a nightmare. And, rather than gently steer and encourage her child's adventures, she tends to put blocks in its way, guiding it into what she sees as safer waters and her youngster views as a stagnant pool. Both mother and child can be verbally sharp – the Virgo criticism and the Sagittarian tactlessness – and this relationship can be marked by intense arguments, though rarely a show of temper: Sagittarius, however, does a good line in door slamming! At best, Sagittarius is thankful to Virgo for putting the brakes on some of its wildcat schemes and for providing a sound foundation to life, while Virgo gains from her child's sense of humour and positive outlook. At worst, both resent the other's way of going about things and Virgo finds, to her cost, that her Sagittarian has no fears about leaving home.

Sagittarius Child/Virgo Father

The Virgo father is often shocked to find that his Sagittarian daughter is very determined to go her own way and doesn't rate decorous behaviour that highly! A Sagittarian son, who has such confidence and good judgment, is also rather alarming to the Virgo father who can immediately see that his word is probably not going to be law at all. Father and child, however, are both keen students and often vie with each other as to who can learn the most about a subject. As his little Sagittarian gets older they often spend happy hours together debating anything from the state of the world to the Premiership. The difficulties in this relationship occur because father and child have very different attitudes to life. Virgo paints miniatures and Sagittarius vast landscapes. The child finds its father's nit-picking and criticism very difficult to handle and Virgo is horrified at his child's lack of diligence and discernment to say nothing of its cavalier attitudes. At worst, Virgo totally gives up on his free-spirited and seemingly thoughtless child while Sagittarius sees him as over-conventional and prissy. At best, Virgo appreciates his child's positive attitude to life and the Sagittarian comes to depend on its father's practicality and common sense.

Sagittarius/Virgo Siblings

Sagittarius and Virgo are both adaptable and it is this quality that usually enables these siblings to get along despite the fact that Sagittarius revels in the challenge of the largest climbing frame while Virgo worries over health and safety. Sagittarius loves open spaces, freedom and lots of noisy company. Virgo values its privacy, prefers a cosy environment and is far more discerning in its friendships. It takes time for the Sagittarian to realise it's sometimes best to leave Virgo to its own devices, and for Virgo to stop fretting over its sibling's latest adventure, and for both to realise that they have much in common. Both are naturally keen to learn, debate and teach, and have an innate sense of fun and often end up being very good friends. Virgo frequently bails out Sagittarius from another financial crisis (at six years old!) and lends very practical support. In turn, Sagittarius encourages its sibling to get more out of life and injects a good dose of optimism.

Sagittarius and Libra

Sagittarius Child/Libra Mother

The easy-going, sociable Libran mother and the adaptable, versatile, philosophical Sagittarian child are made for each other. Libra is fascinated by her inquiring and outgoing baby who equally adores its refined mother. Not only will she do anything to make her child's life comfortable but she is also thrilled to find that her baby thrives on the social scene and, more importantly, on a fairly relaxed schedule (though nothing akin to chaos!). The natural Sagittarian curiosity about life and its ability to be a great companion at a very early age is meat and drink to its mother, who rates spending time on her own as one of life's great miseries. She is also delighted that Sagittarius responds to reason and usually doesn't have to be reminded more than once about rules and boundaries. Libra hates to say 'no' and relishes having a child who seems, intellectually, to understand so much at such a young age. In turn, her Sagittarian child responds well to the calm environment she has created, her gentle charm and the strength of personality that is hidden beneath her idealistic nature. However, as with any relationship, there are a few glitches. The Sagittarian penchant for speaking its mind, which is obvious from the time it starts to talk, can drive the more diplomatically minded Libran to distraction: she feels she is permanently having to apologise for her perceptive but tactless offspring. Equally, the Libran indecision is frustrating for the little Sagittarian, who finds plans for the day continually subject to chop and change. Neither, however, is likely to put the other under extreme amounts of stress and both will enjoy, sooner rather than later, extravagant spending sprees. Most important of all, Libra will be a wonderful listener to her often over-excited and over-optimistic child, never pouring cold water on its plans but encouraging it to think of all the options and all the angles. This is a relationship that starts well and usually just gets better.

Sagittarius Child/Libra Father

The urbane and gracious Libran father is invariably delighted to have a Sagittarian son or daughter at his side. This child radiates sincerity and optimism, is prepared to take on a challenge and is often a real star on the social scene. Sometimes, of course, Sagittarius is a little too boisterous for his liking but it doesn't take much for his youngster to understand what is acceptable and what isn't. If problems arise in this relationship, it's invariably to do with the father's ambivalence about discipline and his sudden changes from total affability to rather dictatorial behaviour. Libra is known for being an 'iron fist in a velvet glove' and just as Sagittarius has decided it has splendidly wound its father around its little finger it is unexpectedly faced with a bout of autocratic behaviour that wipes that wonderful smile well and truly off its face! The easy-going Libran is soon back on show, but to his Sagittarian child, it's all very confusing. Libra can also get annoyed at his child's lack of ambition and tendency to jump from one enthusiasm to another. Nevertheless this is a relationship that is founded in genuine understanding, and often a lot of idealism, and the bonds usually strengthen with the years.

Sagittarius/Libra Siblings

Rarely do these siblings come to blows, although there are definitely moments when resentments seethe away beneath the surface. Sagittarius, who likes to get on with projects and life generally, finds it very difficult to fathom its Libran sibling's vacillation, more particularly when it reneges on agreements (especially when trouble looms) in the hope of a quiet life. In turn Libra despairs of the Sagittarian's blindly optimistic attitude to life, its sometimes capricious nature and insistence on saying exactly what it means. On the whole, however, these two usually get along very well. Sagittarius often has cause to be thankful for the Libran tact and diplomacy getting it out of another embarrassing situation, while Libra relies on its sibling's good judgment and thorough dependability when about to make a totally wrong decision. Both siblings are open-minded and have a great sense of fair play, ensuring that there are no mind games, just gentle teasing. These two are usually mutually supportive all through life.

Sagittarius and Scorpio

Sagittarius Child/Scorpio Mother

As with all zodiacal neighbours, Sagittarius and Scorpio are totally different and this relationship is never going to be easy for either mother or child. At birth, Scorpio will be fascinated by her baby's innate sense of fun and inquisitive gaze whilst her little Sagittarian will probably be mesmerised by its mother's beautiful eyes and magnetic, exciting personality. The Scorpio mother will make it her business to get her baby into a good and disciplined routine, will spend time organising her child's social life and ensure that it is at the forefront of whatever is going on, whether at nursery, in a playgroup or in the neighbourhood. If Scorpio is not ambitious for herself, she is for her child. Unfortunately, however, her Sagittarian usually fails to show any gratitude for her efforts to push her child forward as it has no game plan for life and certainly doesn't share its mother's determination to get ahead. The youngest Sagittarian thrives on being able to use its initiative, on having its own space and on being trusted. Scorpio is happiest going down well-defined paths, is innately suspicious about people and their intentions and, although secretive herself, is not inclined to respect her child's privacy. It's not long before Scorpio finds Sagittarius difficult in the extreme. Her child doesn't conform, doesn't understand her feelings and blithely seems to go about life on a wing and a prayer. In turn her child feels hemmed in, controlled and equally misunderstood although realises that its innate jollity and optimism does wonders when tensions develop between mother and child. At best, Sagittarius gains enormously from its mother's passion and determination, while Scorpio learns to respect her child's good judgment and sincerity. Despite the likelihood that each will end up puzzled, annoyed and ultimately disenchanted with the other, Scorpio will always show unstinting loyalty to her Sagittarian child, just as much as she will be able to depend on her son or daughter in times of trouble.

Sagittarius Child/Scorpio Father

The open and versatile Sagittarian child and the forceful, secretive Scorpio father can make a powerful and positive duo or a twosome heading for disaster. At first, Scorpio will certainly be proud to have his Sagittarian son or daughter by his side: its beaming smile, joyous nature and adventurous spirit will delight everyone. Sagittarius will be equally admiring of its strong, determined father who seems to radiate power and great depth of feeling. Scorpio, however, would like to direct and control his child's every waking moment, an approach that goes firmly against the freedom-loving, Sagittarian grain. Even the youngest Sagittarian likes to feel it is trusted to take the initiative, to make the right decisions and to deal intelligently with any consequences. It's not long before Sagittarius can feel it's being manipulated into situations against its wishes whilst Scorpio fights a seemingly losing battle in getting his child's cooperation. At worst, Sagittarius flees the Scorpio father's regime as soon as possible, but if Scorpio can trust his child's judgment and let go of the reins, Sagittarius can surprise and delight him with the scope of its thinking and successful outcome of its adventures.

Sagittarius/Scorpio Siblings

Unlike the parent/child dynamic, two very different siblings can often work quite well in a family. These two will certainly have their misunderstandings and, from time to time, feel utterly frustrated by each other. Scorpio resents the constant Sagittarian invasions into its privacy, to say nothing of its tactless remarks and irresponsible behaviour, while Sagittarius can't stand the obsessive and obstinate Scorpio nature, its jealousy and its resentfulness in the face of other people's success. On the plus side, Sagittarius is wonderful at jollying Scorpio out of its dark moods and injecting optimism, while Scorpio has a marvellous sixth sense about its sibling and seems to come up with the right encouragement at the right time, as well as being loyal in the extreme. The versatile and adaptable Sagittarian sibling is also good at encouraging Scorpio to be slightly less rigid about everything. At best, these two make a formidable team.

Sagittarius and Sagittarius

Sagittarius Child/Sagittarius Mother

From the first glance these two gaze at each other in a happy bubble of intimate recognition, knowledge and secret wisdom that is utterly private to the two of them. The Sagittarian mother and her Sagittarian baby have an immediate intellectual rapport and do their utmost to make life easy for each other. They revel in each other's company and the mother will treat her baby immediately as a little adult, something that comes to her naturally, and exactly the role her baby wants to assume as well. Living in a slightly disorganised environment and yet proving to her baby that she can be depended on, the Sagittarian mother fills both her life and her baby's with plenty of mental stimulation, lots of laughter and a wide variety of activities. Both can be quite restless and have a fairly low boredom threshold (but nothing like as low as Aries or Gemini!) so life is invariably busy and very sociable. This relationship usually gets off to a brilliant start and gets even better as the child gets older. They can happily spend hours in anything from encyclopaedias to philosophical discussions and also spend plenty of time making tactless and, sometimes, quite inadvertently hurtful remarks. Neither, however, bears grudges and although both can get very heated and throw a grand display of temper when pushed too far, nothing lasts very long and grievances are never allowed to fester. Both mother and child are, on the whole, honest and sincere which is another reason why they tend sometimes to talk from the hip. Both will respect each other's need for freedom and space and that rite of passage when the Sagittarian child leaves home is seen as a thrilling challenge for both, rather than a time of anxiety or depression. And the mother knows, anyway, that her child will definitely be back from time to time for a great chat and to put the world to rights!

Sagittarius Child/Sagittarius Father

The responsibilities of fatherhood don't always come easily to the Sagittarian, who by nature can be a tad irresponsible and a bit capricious, but in his Sagittarian son or daughter he truly finds a kindred spirit. Here is a child who values its independence, and therefore respects his, and enjoys lots of outdoor activities with which he can join in. With luck, his child will also be an avid learner, which will enable him to use his teaching skills. Best of all, of course, for him is the knowledge that his Sagittarian offspring shares the notion of life being a great adventure and a constant challenge. There is an easy understanding between them which, with a Sagittarian son, tends to develop into a 'boys' club', father and son enjoying many of the same activities. With a Sagittarian daughter, he will not only encourage any sporting interests, but also her academic ones: this father/child duo set great store by the development of the mind. Sometimes their mutual need for freedom or a surfeit of insensitive and even arrogant remarks can mean an eventual parting of the ways, but generally this is a father/child relationship that is hard to break.

Sagittarius Siblings

Sagittarian siblings tend to be either great friends or indifferent to one another. There can be quite a strong competitive edge between these two and it's often best if they have totally different interests and activities in which they can each shine. Neither wants to feel that it's being pushed into the other's territory or timetable and both will thrive in their own individual space. They have a great sense of humour, will be devotees of the social scene and, at the same time, won't need much forcing to complete homework or any other tasks they are set. More to the point, both learn a lot from their own mistakes and, in each other, invariably have a great source of common sense, wisdom and a sound and well-judged outlook on life. Thoughtless behaviour and a total lack of diplomacy can drive a wedge between these two, as can having to pick up the pieces of each other's blind optimism about people and situations. No Sagittarian sticks around when his trust and basic good nature have been imposed upon once too often, even when it is a sibling.

Sagittarius and Capricorn

Sagittarius Child/Capricorn Mother

Although the Capricorn mother will look with much wonder at her Sagittarian baby, who, even at birth, appears wise beyond its years, these two signs are very different and therein lies the problem. Capricorn thrives in a safe, secure environment and in an orderly existence. Her Sagittarian baby loves space, freedom and a lifestyle that is full of challenge and adventure. In no time at all the Sagittarian baby feels constricted, frustrated and often bored, and the poor Capricorn cannot understand what she's doing wrong. After all, she's provided a very safe nest and is taking such small, sensible steps with her baby. Sagittarius comes into the world with a 'can do' attitude and it's all too easy for its Capricorn mother unwittingly to hold it back and crush that wonderfully inventive and optimistic spirit. On the social scene these two also have very different agendas. Capricorn is very choosy about friendships while Sagittarius is thoroughly enthusiastic about meeting everyone and wants to get involved with everything. As her child grows up, it becomes increasingly irritated with its mother's caution, innate pessimism and prudence, whilst Capricorn in turn is exasperated at her child's extravagance and sees its happy-go-lucky, restless behaviour as nothing short of irresponsible. Capricorn is also rather appalled by her offspring's lack of overt ambition and yet secretly resents the fact that her child always seems to land on its feet. However, the Sagittarian sense of humour does wonders for Capricorn and the mother can teach her child a lot about circumspection and determination. Capricorn also quickly learns that her child is dependable and has excellent judgment, whilst Sagittarius comes to respect its mother's patience and perseverance (both much needed when dealing with this particular child!). These two either benefit greatly from each other or go through life thoroughly mystified by each other.

Sagittarius Child/Capricorn Father

In many ways the Capricorn father often sees his Sagittarian child as an excited and inquisitive puppy, all action and straining at the leash but not that easy to bring to heel. Capricorn would really love to train the Sagittarian to do things the right way and to steer its life in a sensible and secure direction. This falls on the completely deaf ears of his child who takes a happily optimistic attitude to life and has no plans whatsoever to do with career ladders or being first past any particular winning post. In fact, everything the father holds dear is almost dismissed by his child! His Sagittarian offspring is a seeker of information and usually chatters endlessly. Capricorn can often be quite taciturn, especially in the face of trivialities, thus eventually bringing about a lack of communication. The Capricorn thrift and the Sagittarian extravagance also bring these two into conflict. If each can respect the other's qualities, rather than despair at their differences, these two can jog along very happily together. The father should admire his child's honesty, sincerity and open-mindedness, while Sagittarius should be grateful for its father's reliability and tremendous efforts to do the best for his child.

Sagittarius/Capricorn Siblings

The Capricorn child takes a very serious attitude to life, works hard and is very conscious of its responsibilities. It also tends to think that around every corner is someone or something that is going to knock him or her off track. The Sagittarian, in contrast, believes that life is always going to be good, puts as much effort as is needed into anything, and no more, and doesn't respond well to any situation that spells commitment. This innate Capricorn seriousness and pessimism, versus the Sagittarian jollity and optimism, can make them very incompatible siblings, except that a great sense of humour usually sustains the relationship when all else fails. Capricorn is also very good at bringing the Sagittarian dreams gently down to earth, whilst Sagittarius eggs on the Capricorn ambitions and brings some sunshine into its sibling's dark moods. They rarely tread on each other's territory, particularly when it comes to parental time and attention. This relationship is frequently an attraction of opposites, but sometimes they exist in a state of mutual incomprehension.

Sagittarius and Aquarius

Sagittarius Child/Aquarius Mother

The arrival of a Sagittarian baby to an Aquarian mother is an utter joy: these two will instantly feel totally comfortable with each other and enjoy an innate understanding. Both are extremely sociable and neither tends to be clinging or possessive. In fact, the more people around mother and baby, the better, and the little Sagittarian just loves the sound of laughter and the buzz of conversation that is usually part and parcel of the Aquarian mother's lifestyle. Mother and baby also need space and independence, and the little Sagittarian feels this from the start. It is much happier sitting and watching what's going on than being swaddled and cuddled. However, ignore a Sagittarian baby and its mother will know she's made a mistake. This baby likes to feel it is part of the family, and indeed of any occasion, and loves to indulge in conversation. The sound of its mother's voice is music to its ears, especially when she is in her teaching role. The Sagittarian child is a thoroughly willing pupil and these two often have much fun together exploring the world of museums, historic houses, books and the internet. Where this relationship can sometimes get into trouble is when the Aquarian mother, who secretly likes the status quo despite her modern outlook and seeming need for change, fails to understand the truly adventurous spirit of her Sagittarian. This is a child who sees life as a challenge and is, in fact, far more versatile and adaptable than its mother. Sometimes the Sagittarian feels frustrated by its mother's inflexibility and the Aquarian alarmed at her offspring's devil-may-care attitude to life. Generally, however, these two usually enjoy a marvellous friendship and truly understand each other's independent nature. They tend to take life as it comes and rarely get tangled up in emotionally muddy waters but, if feelings do intrude, both talk a lot, hope the problem has been sorted and usually fail to get to the heart of the matter.

Sagittarius Child/Aquarius Father

This father/child duo usually enjoys an excellent relationship. The sunny-natured Sagittarian with its great sense of humour, honest and straightforward personality and keen intellect delights its Aquarian father. Like him, his child does not want to delve deep into the emotional depths and is much happier with rational debate and philosophical discussion. And can these two talk! Equally, the Sagittarian child delights in its freedom-loving, forward-thinking father who understands its need for a challenge and adventure (though may not encourage it!) The Sagittarian is also adept at skirting around its father's more dogmatic moments and can deal very effectively with the Aquarian stubbornness. In turn the Aquarian father is well able to teach his Sagittarian child about loyalty, perseverance and humanitarianism. Father and child will probably share many interests and enjoy being out and about together. Where this relationship can become stressful is during the teenage years when Aquarius can set boundaries that are too rigid and his views are not open either to discussion or compromise.

Sagittarius/Aquarius Siblings

Sagittarius and Aquarius are the two most independent and freedom-loving signs of the zodiac and this sibling relationship will work brilliantly if each is allowed to develop well away from the other's shadow. Left alone to pursue their own path, they will probably happily gravitate towards one another, drawn by a quick intellect, sense of humour and a genuine love of knowledge. On the social scene these siblings are usually extremely popular and both thrive amidst a large circle of friends. Whilst not averse to the occasional heated argument, neither child sulks or bears grudges and a witty remark or a pertinent and pithy comment usually breaks down any barriers. Both, however, can be very opinionated and the Aquarian perversity and sometimes eccentric behaviour can rile the Sagittarian. In turn, Aquarius dislikes the patronising, even arrogant, air of its Sagittarius sibling and is frequently appalled (but mesmerised) by its risk-taking adventures. These two will always be supportive of one another and be there in times of trouble.

Sagittarius and Pisces

Sagittarius Child/Pisces Mother

To the Sagittarian child, who dreams of far away places and big adventures, its imaginative and unworldly Piscean mother must seem like a gift from the gods. For Pisces, who can immediately sense her child's intellectual curiosity and freedom-loving outlook, this is clearly going to be a wonderful relationship. Unfortunately the situation is often very different. Pisces lives in the realms of emotion, is probably not the most practical in the zodiac and rather drifts her way through life. Her child is not too comfortable with the whole feelings business, is dependable and has very grand plans for its life. Early on, the baby can stress over its mother's rather vague way of going about things and, whilst not in the Virgo or Capricorn league for needing routine and order, at least would like some semblance of organisation. The more her baby frets, the more Pisces wants to swim away, and a whole vicious circle begins. As a toddler, Sagittarius thrives in a rather noisy and sociable environment with plenty of activity and intellectual stimulation. Pisces prefers to get herself into a good book or the latest celebrity magazine and to ponder the greener grass everywhere else in the world. Thus Sagittarius finds it more and more difficult to gain its mother's attention, never knows whether plans for the day will ever materialise and starts to play up. As a result Pisces starts to think her child is irresponsible, capricious and inclined to exaggerate every small blip in the day. Sagittarius, of course, will always benefit from its mother's compassion and kindness and the fun that comes from her artistic endeavours and general creativity. Pisces, in turn, will love the bright-eyed enthusiasm, humour and optimism that are the hallmarks of her child. At worst, Pisces never manages to rein in the Sagittarian energy or fully develop its talents and then wonders why her child is so dissatisfied. At best, Pisces understands her child's need to take life as it comes and Sagittarius appreciates her selflessness and her ability to listen.

Sagittarius Child/Pisces Father

A Sagittarian child is invariably highly active, noisy, full of good humour and thoroughly over-optimistic about everything it takes on. The Pisces father, who is one of the most imaginative and sensitive in the zodiac, is often exhausted just watching his energetic child, let alone getting involved in its sports and interests. To Sagittarius, Pisces never seems to be quite grounded enough and there is often a lot of disappointment in this relationship. Sagittarius is honest and direct but Pisces can be vague and secretive, which thoroughly frustrates the child who finds it impossible to have a constructive conversation with its father. Although all Sagittarians are known for their good judgment, the younger ones need a lot of sensible direction if their talents are to be beneficially developed and the Pisces father finds it so much easier to leave his child to its own devices. At best, Pisces will introduce his child to water sports and take his son or daughter around the art galleries and other exhibitions which are meat and drink to his Sagittarian youngster. He might not be the best at taking the initiative or adopting an enterprising approach to life, but he'll astound his child by his deep understanding of any problems.

Sagittarius/Pisces Siblings

Sagittarius and Pisces are adaptable and versatile and neither likes to take too rigid an approach to anything, leaving plenty of room to manoeuvre in any situation. It is this flexibility and, equally, their ability to walk away from stressful situations that help to make this a relatively constructive relationship. Sagittarius, of course, becomes exasperated at the Piscean emotionalism, negativity and general escapism whilst the Fish has to put up with its sibling's tactless and hurtful remarks, its superior attitude and constant restlessness. However, Pisces is invariably grateful for its sibling's wise advice, buoyant optimism and sincerity when times get tough, just as much as Sagittarius knows that the Piscean will lend a sympathetic ear and intuitively come up with the right answers when another of its plans bites the dust. These two will always have an understanding and will often choose to consult each other at critical moments.

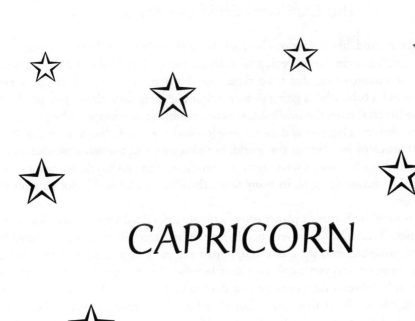

CAPRICORN

The Capricorn Child 0-5 Years

For the Capricorn child, life is a serious business from the moment of birth. It comes into the world absolutely certain that it's going to reach the top of life's ladder and the studious, slightly superior, countenance, that is so typical of the sign, is developed within weeks. After all, this is not a baby who is going to worry about keeping up with the Joneses: he or she will BE the Joneses! Even the smallest Capricorn tends to beam happily when it's taken to large houses, driven in big cars and meets people who have clearly 'made it' in life. With this total confidence of its place in the world, but also aware of the work needed to get there, Capricorn doesn't want to waste time on frivolities, fun and anything that will not be important to its future lifestyle. In many ways, therefore, childhood is not particularly easy for this sign.

Capricorn is ruled by Saturn, a planet often wrongly associated with doom, gloom and many difficulties. In fact, Saturn is very much like the best teachers who are respected by everyone, instil discipline into the classroom, impart the most knowledge, set the hardest homework and from whom every pupil ultimately benefits. The Saturnian creed is that hard work brings wonderful rewards, a concept that does not sit easily on the shoulders of very young children, whose life, at that stage, should be full of sunshine and joy and certainly free from responsibilities and duty. Capricorn children, however, seem to understand all about their Saturn legacy. They happily and naturally accept that they have an important role to fulfil, which will probably include taking charge of situations, being a reliable and conscientious member of the family and learning to manage their life with efficiency and order. And all this before they go anywhere near the school gates!

Far from going on a sit-down strike when asked to tidy up toys, lend a hand or keep an eye on a situation, the little Capricorn proves delightfully willing to accede to parental requests: it just loves being thought of as grown up and capable of helping. He or she will also develop its own routines and organise its life with a thoroughness that makes its poor parents feel less than adequate at best, and downright stupid at worst! Even the youngest member of this sign knows what it wants and, despite being faced with a few setbacks en route, will eventually attain it – whether the goal is the biscuit tin or a decision to wield its own spoon (and even a fork) long before it is really able to do so. The Capricorn determination is never to be underestimated. On the whole, this child of the zodiac does not throw temper tantrums and does not indulge in a lot of tearful scenes. Instead it frequently wears down the parent or childminder with its patient, dogged perseverance and failure to give up on anything it's set its heart on. Its smile, at the point of success, tells its own story and it doesn't take a lot, either, for the Capricorn sense of humour to emerge. Whilst not innately attuned to fun and laughter, the Capricorn child has a wonderfully dry wit. A few well-chosen words from an under-five can defuse many tense situations.

Even as adults Capricorns are not garrulous: if they have something to say, they speak, otherwise they often prefer to remain silent. The child is no different and, whilst keen to get on the move (after all this is the mountain Goat, who is desperate to climb to the summit), is frequently less obviously willing to indulge in endless chatter. Capricorn will learn the right words and use them correctly when it has something important to impart. For this reason, the sometimes worried parents of what they assume to be a rather taciturn child are frequently astonished when it comes out with a thoroughly lucid sentence and makes its opinions very clear. Where Capricorn is more than likely to be well ahead of the pack, however, is in stacking bricks, making models, and building sandcastles. Like the other earth signs, this child has a real feel for construction. It's often also quite musical, though not always artistic as such.

Whilst it could never be said that Capricorn is possessive and unable to share, it usually finds it difficult to be a team player (unless it's chosen as captain and can boss everyone around!). Generally, it's quite diffident on the social scene and needs a lot of encouragement to make friends and to get involved in any kind of get-together. Frequently, the little Capricorn will stand on the edge, usually feeling light years older than its contemporaries and, at the same time, a cut above! It is not, by nature, a loner, but chooses its friends very carefully and often functions better in one-to-one situations than in a large crowd. Although Capricorn does lend its time and its toys, it is not one of life's real givers – either of itself (emotionally effusive is definitely not its style!) or of its money, and this is where the little Goat needs much help in its early years. Most signs of the zodiac need to learn about discipline and patience: Capricorn needs education in the pleasure that can be derived from seeing someone's happiness at receiving affection, a present, or both. Pocket money for this sign will be saved rather than spent and Capricorn needs to be encouraged to enjoy what it has. It's a sign that can become a little mean, and at worst miserly, and an understanding in early childhood of a sensible mix between saving, spending and the sheer joy of giving is a valuable lesson. It's never going to be spendthrift and its first venture into a shop will be an indication of its future buying habits. Something that will last and is good value is likely to be clutched very firmly in the small Capricorn fist.

The most difficult aspect of the Capricorn personality to deal with is its pessimism. Despite its determination and ambition, the mountain Goat is easily discouraged and behind its strong and silent façade there often lurks a much more uncertain character. The bossy child who seems to be in control of all it surveys is often putting on a great act and, in fact, needs careful nurturing and plenty of support. It also needs a strong dose of positive thinking: whilst not wanting to be as over-optimistic as its neighbouring sign (Sagittarius) it certainly needs something to balance that tendency always to look on the gloomy side of situations. An early understanding of life's shades of grey, rather than black and white, stops the Capricorn child from developing a fear of failure and a lack of self-confidence that can hamper its progress in life. At worst, it can feel tethered to a stake in the ground, which is often the fate of the domestic Goat. Without the challenge of the mountain peaks Capricorn becomes frustrated and unhappy and much talent goes to waste. 'No emotion in public' is often the mantra of the older Capricorn but this rather stoic attitude to feelings is implanted at birth. It is sometimes extremely difficult to fathom exactly what is going on in this child's mind, and it is all too easy to trample over feelings that are rarely evident. A quivering upper lip is often the only sign that something is badly wrong and all young Capricorns could benefit from having someone around who encourages them to talk about their emotions.

It is all too easy to think that the little Capricorn is the personification of someone who is all work and no play. Nothing could be further from the truth. The Capricorn child is rarely dull: it frequently has great charm, a keen intellect, a thoroughly willing attitude to life and a certain knowledge that if something is worth having it's worth both working for and waiting for. Its delightful sense of humour and that wry smile are also enchanting.

Unlike perhaps its Gemini or Sagittarius cousins, who are usually too busy dashing about to be truly interested in anyone or anything for any length of time, Capricorn makes an excellent companion from a very early age, taking a huge interest in what's going on and listening intently to what it is being told. It is also highly conventional: this child instinctively knows what is right and proper and what is likely to make it look ridiculous, and will make no bones about it to a parent it sees as being slightly too loud, too outlandish or too laid-back. Out of the mouth of a babe ...!

Capricorn is born old: often the new baby has the wrinkles and rather tired skin more usually found in someone very much older. In personality it already has the reliability, perseverance, sense of duty and even a touch of the world-weariness that are going to be the mainstays of its character. However, all good things come to those who wait and Capricorn knows this better than anyone. Life definitely improves for Capricorn as it gets older and it eventually becomes one of the youngest senior citizens around, both physically and mentally. When Capricorn eventually starts to kick up its heels, it does so in grand style. At that stage it's those early lessons in balancing the serious with the more flighty, in the giving and receiving of affection and presents, together with the encouragement of both optimism and that perceptive dry wit, that it will remember and, for all of which, be truly grateful.

Capricorn and Aries

Capricorn Child/Aries Mother

For the Capricorn child, who comes into the world determined to make its slow and steady way to the top without too much in the way of show and drama, it can be quite unnerving to have an Aries mother with her fiery temperament, high energy level and me-first approach. This particular baby thrives in a relatively disciplined and ordered environment, appreciates a low-key, but choice, social life and a steady pace to everything. Its vibrant, disorganised and extremely busy mother, to say nothing of her impatience, comes as a bit of a culture shock, but at least her positive attitude does wonders for her baby's pessimism. Capricorn often becomes deeply unhappy when plunged into chaotic scenes and with no road map whatsoever as to future plans, whether it's who's coming to play today or the possible visit to grandparents next week. In her delightfully egocentric way, Aries often fails to notice her child becoming quieter by the minute and the stiff upper lip just starting to quiver. A short time spent reassuring and comforting her less confident child can do wonders. Aries, in turn, can find her little Goat very difficult to deal with. She constantly has to bolster her child and quickly tires of its ultra cautious attitude. After all, she leaps into the unknown with spectacular verve and cannot understand Capricorn's innate prudence and carefulness. She also finds it irritating when her son or daughter is clearly appalled at her latest adventure, loud behaviour or new risqué outfit. Capricorn is just so conventional and it starts at birth! On the plus side, of course, Aries benefits from her child's practical skills, quiet, dry sense of humour and seeing its ambitious nature come to the fore. Capricorn will always have a champion in Aries and knows its mother will never fail to penetrate the dark moods and jolly it along. Generally these two go through life not always in harmony but with the same ultimate goals – and success is music to their ears.

Capricorn Child/Aries Father

The Aries father, with his adventurous attitude to life can initially find it difficult to understand his rather conventional and often endlessly complaining Capricorn. Worse, his five-year-old sometimes seems openly to despair of its father! Capricorn also baulks at being pushed forward and seems to have to weigh up all sorts of issues before joining in anything. With patience not being this father's strongest suit he can easily give up on his child before realising that they have many similar qualities, ambition being the most important. From the start, Capricorn knows who and what is important and the clued-up Aries father will just love taking his child to all the right places and introducing him or her to the best things in life. Both, after all, thrive at the top of the ladder! The Arian quick wit is also a good match for the dry Capricorn humour and these two often indulge in happy repartee and all sorts of in-jokes. If Aries can give his young Capricorn plenty of encouragement and Capricorn learn from its father about the direct approach and the sheer joy of living, these two can be of great mutual support – but it takes time and patience on both sides.

Capricorn/Aries Siblings

Capricorn and Aries are both inclined to be bossy, and, in any sibling relationship, they will jostle for position and insist on getting their own way. Compromise is rarely an option, so there can be some spectacular confrontations. Aries will tend to do a lot of shouting and probably chuck a few toys around, while Capricorn will be more measured and verbally deadlier. Although Aries will quickly forget an argument, Capricorn is likely to brood darkly about everything, and it usually falls to Aries to drag its sibling out of its pessimism and to haul the wonderfully dry Capricorn wit to the surface! Capricorn frequently finds the Aries gung-ho approach utterly tedious, while Aries becomes impatient with Capricorn's cautious and prudent attitude, to say nothing of its lack of enthusiasm. Money matters can also divide these two. Aries is always on the scrounge and Capricorn resents its piggy bank being raided! At best, Aries benefits from Capricorn's practicality and common sense while dishing out encouragement and inspiration to its sibling.

Capricorn and Taurus

Capricorn Child/Taurus Mother

Capricorn and Taurus are earth signs and both value stability and security. Common sense and feet firmly on the ground are ingrained and neither looks to anything in the way of seismic shocks to liven things up. For the Capricorn child, a Taurean mother is an absolute joy. She totally understands her child's needs, will never subject it to erratic schedules or an over-crowded day and, being extremely tactile, will show her little Goat plenty of demonstrative affection. Equally, Taurus will delight in her youngster who seems to be so responsible and sweetly conventional at such an early age and is showing signs of a shy smile and a slightly dour sense of humour. Although Capricorn is ambitious by nature, sometimes its self-confidence is more fragile than would appear and Taurus has the patience and persistence to ensure her child is gently encouraged towards success and to realise that disappointments are seen as lessons in life rather than total catastrophes. Both mother and child are very practical by nature and will relish doing things together around the home, whether it's growing seeds in the garden, coping with a construction kit or making decorations: Taurus is highly creative and in her little Capricorn she will have a willing student. Into every good relationship, however, a little shower occasionally has to fall. Taurus, who is highly sensual and loves to have a good time, can get irritated by her child's seeming inability to put pleasure before business and sometimes really upsets Capricorn when she dismisses homework or something else to which it is devoting time and attention as 'unimportant'. She can also find her child's dark moods very difficult to cope with. Capricorn frets about its mother's self-indulgence, inflexibility and inability to enter debate. Her opinions are fixed! Nevertheless, these two really understand each other and, despite the occasional Taurean bout of temper or wet blanket attitude from Capricorn, are usually happy to be firmly anchored to each other.

Capricorn Child/Taurus Father

The Taurean father will move heaven and earth to provide for his child and in Capricorn he at least has a son or daughter who will truly appreciate his efforts. His reward, of course, is seeing his offspring doing very well in the world. As both take an innately cautious approach to life and neither wants to rush into change or new ventures, Capricorn feels immensely comfortable with a father who doesn't take risks and would rather be seen as plodding or boring than adventurous and impulsive. These two will take a quiet pleasure in each other's company and, as both usually have a very practical streak, will enjoy making things together. From construction kits to assembling a wardrobe, they'll work as a team! The one potential difficulty in this relationship is the father's tendency to think he knows best versus his child's disciplined determination to get its own way. There can be some splendid impasses between them as Capricorn gets older. On the plus side, of course, Taurus loves the finer things in life and Capricorn is very aware of status and labels: these two will never quarrel over where to be seen and what to buy!

Capricorn/Taurus Siblings

Practical, patient, persistent and disciplined are adjectives that describe both Capricorn and Taurus, which suggests a mutual need for stability and security that, for them, comes with material possessions. There is usually much financial planning over how best to spend pocket money and savings, Taurus more likely to go for the luxury end of the market and Capricorn for the sensible and necessary! Taurus will always be the more self-indulgent and Capricorn the more industrious, and Capricorn often feels it's pulling its rather lazy brother or sister along in its wake. It is Taurus, however, who will be marvellous at digging its sibling out of its pessimistic thinking and whose natural warm-heartedness will delight Capricorn and restore its wonderful dry wit. Taurus also has a natural business sense that Capricorn admires. At worst, these two can just find each other rather boring, but usually they jog along happily together, trusting each other's judgment and thankful that neither is going to rock the sibling boat.

Capricorn and Gemini

Capricorn Child/Gemini Mother

At the arrival of her Capricorn child, the Gemini mother will immediately notice her baby's serious countenance and a rather worried look in its eyes. To the Peter Pan of the zodiac is born the 'old before its time' baby, and the totally different attitudes to life of this mother and child can make it one of the more trying astrological combinations. Gemini lives life at quite a pace and with a certain amount of panache: Capricorn favours routine and a steady, calm existence. With Gemini organising a great social life and probably an overcrowded timetable, the little Capricorn becomes thoroughly unnerved and fractious. Thinking that she's not doing enough for her child, Gemini crams even more into her day and in the face of her endlessly cheerful and chatty approach to life, her baby seems to become even more depressed! For Capricorn, life is a serious business and it's invariably thoroughly confused and discomfited with a mother who takes such a positive and energetic attitude and tends to flit through life with no real sustained interest in anything. Gemini is also quite unconventional, whereas Capricorn has an innate sense of dignity and of what is right and proper. The mother then gets annoyed and probably puzzled when her child won't join in anything which makes it look silly or which it thinks is beneath its station. (Like Leo, the Capricorn child can be snobbish!) On the other hand, she cannot believe how much her child loves anything competitive: she is not ambitious but her child is determined to get to the top. The natural Gemini curiosity is also not necessarily exciting to Capricorn who sometimes feels its privacy is invaded. At best, Gemini encourages her child's wonderfully dry wit, injects optimism and digs Capricorn out of its rigid approach while she learns a lot about patience and sticking with situations from her little Capricorn. At worst, these two exist in a state of total incomprehension, but the child will eventually take on the role of responsible parent to its delightful but inconsistent mother.

Capricorn Child/Gemini Father

To the Capricorn child who likes to live by timetables and has a great sense of honour about promises being kept, the Gemini father is often a total enigma. Exciting he may be but, to a Capricorn, reliable he ain't! From an early age Capricorn learns not to put too much trust in its father, who in turn tends to think of his son or daughter as demanding and endlessly grumbling about his failure to keep dates or his tendency to change his plans on a whim. At the same time Capricorn clearly benefits from the light Gemini touch. Without his spontaneity and versatility, his little Capricorn would tend to wallow in a famously 'can't do' and negative attitude, and fail to have a shot at sports, hobbies or anything else which might look a bit daunting to start with. He or she also gains enormously from its father's social confidence: he can ease his child beautifully into the larger world. For his part, Gemini learns to respect his child's patience and fortitude and secretly envies its ambition. A sense of humour often keeps this relationship on the rails, especially when mutual exasperation is the order of the day.

Capricorn/Gemini Siblings

This is a chalk and cheese sibling relationship and one that can occasionally work better than expected because each sign has a totally different agenda within the family. Gemini thrives on a busy social scene and on being out and about, while Capricorn prefers the domestic environment and taking life at a much slower pace. In theory, each could learn a lot from the other but, in reality, Capricorn will carp endlessly about having to bail out its Gemini sibling from another scrape, while Gemini will be thoroughly irritated by Capricorn's tendency to rubbish its ideas for fun and games. Capricorn has staying power and self-discipline and is often resentful at being made responsible for (and normally blamed for) its sibling's misdemeanours, whilst the adaptable and rather intellectual Gemini gets utterly frustrated by Capricorn's conventional views and constant moaning. However, Capricorn is usually very protective of Gemini and gives plenty of practical advice when its brother or sister's nervous system goes into overdrive, while Gemini widens Capricorn's horizons.

Capricorn and Cancer

Capricorn Child/Cancer Mother

For a Capricorn child to be born to a Cancerian mother must be a dream come true. Life is a serious business for a baby Capricorn and from the start it's keen to learn the rules. It takes in everything slowly but surely and thrives in a domestic environment that embodies security and stability. For the Cancer mother this is wonderful: she is able to provide everything her Capricorn needs and will be rewarded with a contented baby who feels it's found the right parent to guide it on its upward path through life. So far so good! Capricorn is an earth sign and as such is concerned with practical issues and the tangible. Order and discipline are also bred into Capricorn's every bone and if timetables go wrong and routines go out of the window, the Cancerian mother can find she's got a very fractious baby on her hands. She, in turn, then feels she's failed her baby, goes on one of her famous 'guilt trips', and makes Capricorn feel insecure. This baby will not find it easy to understand her more emotional nature and will certainly not appreciate it if her feelings get in the way of his or her mealtimes or in any other way disrupts the daily schedule. With a Capricorn baby, it's essential that the domestic scene runs like clockwork! Generally, however, these two usually enjoy a very congenial and affectionate relationship. Both need and value stability and both hold the home and family in high esteem. The Cancerian mother will understand her Capricorn child's need to succeed and also its steady approach to everything it undertakes. Capricorn will blossom with a mother who doesn't rush him or her into new ventures, but at the same time gently encourages. Later on, when the Capricorn ambition is fuelled, there can sometimes be problems between mother and child, especially if the Cancerian has devoted all her energies to the home and family. Capricorn, who is prone to snobbery, can make her feel inadequate. More likely, though, is the Capricorn child who puts its Cancerian mother on a well-deserved pedestal!

Capricorn Child/Cancer Father

This father and child tend to be extremely good for each other. Both are ambitious and equally determined to make it to the top. Capricorn is also extremely well equipped to cope with a Cancerian father who hides his sensitivity beneath much bluster and bravado. Like the other earth signs, Capricorn is not always comfortable in the realm of feelings and is certainly able to understand a parent who has the same difficulty dealing with his emotions. From an early age, the Capricorn motto is 'no emotion in public' and preferably no emoting at all! On a more mundane level, they will both enjoy being out and about together, and will find they have mutual interests, of which music, history and collecting things are but three. At worst, Cancer sees Capricorn as too concerned with appearances and the child worries about its father's moods and negativity. As Capricorn gets older it starts fully to appreciate the sympathetic and sensitive side of its Cancerian father and is often able to offer a great deal of practical support, mostly in the form of a lot of common sense. The Cancer father, in turn, can unlock Capricorn's feelings without making his child feel vulnerable.

Capricorn/Cancer Siblings

This is a case where opposites are more likely to attract than repel. For a start, competition for the attention of a parent is avoided because Cancer veers towards the mother and Capricorn to the father. Secondly, these siblings usually have much in common: neither tends to want to excel in the sporting arena, both will like reading and spending time in quiet pursuits and both will be very content in the domestic world. Problems arise when Cancer starts to brood on hurt feelings and grievances and Capricorn decides to go into strong, silent mode, thus ensuring a breakdown of communication. Neither gives ground easily and without the benefit of mediation, these two can drift apart through sheer stubbornness and pride. On the plus side, the Capricorn sibling does much to allay Cancer's fears just as the Crab can give tremendous emotional support to Capricorn. Both have a tendency to let problems build up and to hug cares to themselves, but in each other find someone who can stop the molehills from becoming mountains.

Capricorn and Leo

Capricorn Child/Leo Mother

To the Leo mother, her Capricorn child is a bit of a puzzle from the start. It certainly doesn't seem to share her joie de vivre and displays far too much caution, common sense and reserve for her liking. Capricorn, while usually vastly impressed at a young age by its stylish mother is often unappreciative of her extravagant gestures, grand plans and self-importance once it gets to school. Luckily, in its Leo mother, Capricorn has one of the better-organised members of the zodiac, and it certainly appreciates the routines that she puts in place from the very beginning. She's also brilliant at getting her child involved on the social scene and encouraging it to make friends. Trouble looms for this duo when each realises that the other is as opinionated, and possibly as snobbish, as the other. Neither gives in quickly or easily over anything and, from the 'terrible twos' onwards, Capricorn and Leo can have massive arguments and grand displays of intransigence. Worse, Leo can feel the faint whiff of disapproval from her four-year-old when she goes on a spending spree and is reminded of how it would be more sensible to save money, or at least to buy something that will accumulate in value or has a better label! On the plus side, Capricorn's dry wit invariably keeps Leo entertained and her child is always appreciative of its mother's enthusiasm and broad-minded attitude. At worst, Leo constantly feels she is dragging Capricorn out of its personal Slough of Despond and trying to convince it of the sheer enjoyment of life, while her child finds itself up against its mother's ego and her reluctance ever to step down from her throne. This relationship often needs much give and take on both sides but, once Capricorn understands its mother's more sensitive nature and Leo starts to value her child's practicality and keenness to do the right thing, a better rapport can be reached. Eventually, of course, Leo takes all the praise for her child's success when Capricorn reaches the top of the tree!

Capricorn Child/Leo Father

The little Capricorn just loves going around the town with its Leo father, who has such style and confidence. Equally, Leo is enormously proud of his child, who instinctively knows exactly how to behave and takes such a serious interest in everything he undertakes on behalf of his family. However, Leo is extremely self-centred and the little Goat can dig in its heels at its father's insistence on doing everything his way. Leo gets just as cross at Capricorn's inability to take a risk or indulge in a little lightheartedness! In their worst moments, Leo thinks his Capricorn child is sometimes boring in the extreme, while Capricorn sees its father is a patronising show-off. Their ambitious natures and sense of humour, however, tend to keep the relationship on an even keel and Leo frequently comes to admire his child's persistence, diligence and sheer determination to get to the top of the class. During the teenage years there can be a lot of jockeying around for position in the family, especially with a Capricorn son. Patience and perseverance are needed to get the best from this relationship and the ultimate reward of a great deal of mutual admiration.

Capricorn/Leo Siblings

In this sibling relationship there is often the question of who is king/queen of the castle? Both like to be boss and neither gives in gracefully when playing second fiddle. At worst, these two exist in a state of resentment and rivalry. Leo complains about Capricorn's boring work ethic and miserly attitude to money, and Capricorn detests Leo's pushy, dogmatic and somewhat pompous behaviour. As with any stressful astrological relationship it often takes time for these two to appreciate each other. Leo has the knack of making Capricorn see a bigger picture, while Capricorn can fine-tune Leo's grand plans or, if necessary, put a stop to them. They both understand the need to get to the top of life's ladder and are often mutually supportive in their efforts to succeed. Capricorn will always be the more responsible of the two, and Leo the more joyous and enthusiastic, and as long as neither is pushed into some kind of role reversal, these two will learn to respect and possibly even to truly admire each other.

Capricorn and Virgo

Capricorn Child/Virgo Mother

For a mother and child who both value stability, security and a prudent lifestyle, this relationship seems like a gift from the gods. Capricorn relishes the routines, sensible rules and huge efforts put in by its mother, and Virgo can't believe her luck in having such an appreciative baby who clearly thrills to her every word and action. They happily dance through life together in a stately waltz rather than a spirited quickstep. Virgo soon gets her little Capricorn involved in doing things around the home, putting her child's practical aptitude to good use and thus, at the same time, instilling a great deal of confidence into her son or daughter. She certainly won't fuss and fret about Capricorn's rather studied and slow way of doing things: after all, she's a perfectionist and likes things just so. Capricorn, who is fully aware from birth as to what matters in life, especially status, is charmed by its mother's discernment and discrimination: she will never lead it down showy or raucous paths. Where these two can come unstuck is in getting too attached to a very limited comfort zone. Neither is particularly adventurous and it's often easier for Virgo to keep her Capricorn entertained at home or on outings of her choosing (and her child's delight) rather than get involved in the bigger rough and tumble. The Virgo tendency to worry and the Capricorn penchant for looking on the dark side can also be a problem for these two if the 'down' moments coincide. Mother and child can sit quietly huddled in misery, often relieved by a witty comment from Capricorn to which Virgo responds with quick repartee. Virgo rarely has much to criticise about Capricorn but her perfectionist nature sometimes makes her demanding. On the whole her son or daughter usually responds well to constructive comments but pushed too far and Virgo is faced with a despondent and extremely pessimistic child and hours of coaxing her offspring into a more positive mood. On balance, this is invariably a relationship that starts well and improves over the years.

Capricorn Child/Virgo Father

A Capricorn child feels immensely safe with its Virgo father, who, in turn, is utterly charmed by his son or daughter who seems to be diligent, disciplined and practical, all traits that, to him, are totally admirable. Virgo is one of the best teachers in the zodiac and finds in Capricorn a thoroughly willing pupil. Not for Capricorn a quick rush through the museum or a new book at bedtime. He or she will be making notes, asking questions and causing Virgo to think on his feet more often than not! Neither father nor child is totally comfortable in the realm of emotions and although they will talk about anything and share a sense of humour, real understanding between them is often missing. Sometimes this relationship gets into difficulties over Virgo's nit-picking or Capricorn's rather rigid attitude to life (as opposed to its more adaptable father), and Virgo often forgets that Capricorn, despite being ambitious and status-conscious, is not as confident as it might appear. On the whole, however, this father/child relationship, despite a few blips over Virgo's fussy behaviour and Capricorn's pessimism, is invariably steadfast and loyal.

Capricorn/Virgo Siblings

Capricorn and Virgo siblings thrive in a disciplined environment, a good routine and plenty of practical challenges and neither ever wants to get involved in high drama or emotional fireworks. Both tend to be conventional and very grounded, although Virgo sometimes thinks its sibling's mindset is far too rigid while Capricorn cannot understand how Virgo can be so hypercritical and finicky. Virgo, who is also much more gregarious than Capricorn, often despairs of its sibling's rather snobbish attitude and, even more so, of always having to make excuses for its sometimes socially inept behaviour. There is always the possibility with these two that Capricorn takes on the role of boss and Virgo of servant but it is equally likely that Virgo takes great pride in being the power behind its sibling's throne – running the ship but letting Capricorn think it's the skipper! Both will be prudent with money but Virgo often sees Capricorn as miserly. These, however, are small problems in what is usually a constructive and happy relationship.

Capricorn and Libra

Capricorn Child/Libra Mother

To the easy-going Libran mother, her rather serious-minded Capricorn baby will be both an enigma and a pleasure. She'll love the fact that it seems to be taking in everything she says and is clearly keen to get itself into an organised routine. As a toddler, Capricorn will start to show its ambitious nature and leadership potential, qualities that are inherent in its mother: she'll also be relieved that her son or daughter doesn't want to upset any apple carts through fiery tantrums or irresponsible behaviour. Capricorn likes a modicum of order and discipline and is comfortable in the knowledge that there are certainties in life – whether it's the routine of a nursery or childminder, tea with friends or going to the library on a Wednesday afternoon. Libra, by contrast, hates to say no to anyone, often takes on too much and chops and changes her plans from minute to minute in the hope that she'll please everyone. She might well gain applause from some, but her little Capricorn won't be at all impressed and quickly goes into one of its silent moods. Apologies in the form of Libra's little treats and presents also tend to cut no ice with a four-year-old Capricorn, who is much more prudent and cautious about money than its free-spending mother! On the plus side, of course, Libra will always be the most charmingly pushy parent Capricorn could wish for, probably ensuring that teachers who fall under her spell give her child a great deal of extra attention. Although getting her son or daughter to enjoy the social scene will seem an uphill struggle, Libra won't give up easily on introducing her child to those who matter and developing its people skills. Although Libra may never really understand her child's rather serious approach to life, its strong work ethic and rather reserved behaviour, she'll move heaven and earth to do the right thing by Capricorn, just as much as her child will come to rely on its mother's ability to inject sunshine, refinement and style into its much cooler personality.

Capricorn Child/Libra Father

The charming and invariably rather urbane Libra father is often totally perplexed by his rather serious-minded and reserved Capricorn child. He constantly wants to cheer up his son or daughter who cannot fathom his total inability to make up his mind about his plans for the day. Capricorn isn't likely to appreciate being told it's off to the playground only to find its father suddenly changing tack and ending up at a café where Libra holds court with friends while Capricorn glares darkly! Whilst thoroughly encouraged that his child seems ambitious and has a good notion of what is important in its father's life (money, status and knowing the right people) he despairs of his child's lack of flair and its over-conventional attitude. Capricorn's delightfully dry sense of humour certainly saves Libra from losing patience entirely, especially when the more disciplined and organised child starts to run rings around its father. However, Libra has a wonderful ability to smooth his little Capricorn's path in life, something of which his son or daughter is very appreciative. Equally, later on, Libra loves to bathe in the glow of his child's success.

Capricorn/Libra Siblings

The practical Capricorn and the idealistic Libran can either love or exasperate each other. Capricorn is always thankful for its sibling's diplomacy and easy-going nature when it gets in a state over social occasions or having to suffer fools gladly. Libra is often dependent on Capricorn's application and self-discipline when it has put pleasure before business and there's still work to be done. Capricorn can also be immensely patient with its more easy-going and sometimes unreliable sibling, while Libra is skilled at defusing Capricorn's negative thinking. Libra, however, becomes irritated with Capricorn's total inability to go with the flow: even at a very early age the little Goat must be in control of situations. Capricorn in turn finds the Libran indecision absolutely maddening and cannot understand how its sometimes gullible sibling manages to be lead down all sorts of garden paths. At best, these two quickly work out how they can benefit from each other's talents and Libra will always do its utmost to keep the relationship on an even keel.

Capricorn and Scorpio

Capricorn Child/Scorpio Mother

In this mother/child relationship two of the strongest signs of the zodiac are meeting head-on and far from being a disaster, this is usually a huge success. Capricorn absolutely relishes its mother's disciplined and ordered approach to looking after her baby and, as with everything she undertakes, she's going to make a success of this particular role. Her baby feels thoroughly secure with its persistent, determined and purposeful mother and, far from resorting to Capricorn shyness and reserve, shows early signs of a self-confidence that normally takes much longer to foster. Both mother and baby also have a fortitude that enables them to conquer any mountain they choose to climb and each senses that from the very beginning. In her determination to push her child to the front, Scorpio will arrange days out, a social life (to include the local great and good!) and the best childcare she can manage. Her Capricorn baby will measure up to all her hopes and, although some might think she's perhaps over-demanding, to Capricorn she's expecting the best and her son or daughter is just thrilled to make her proud of its achievements. Both understand the nature of hard work, and her natural feel for discipline falls on Capricorn's very receptive shoulders. Scorpio's opinions tend to be quite fixed and Capricorn is naturally conventional, so neither is likely to upset the other with outrageous ideas and bohemian behaviour. Scorpio's passion for life can sometimes be lost on her more prudent and serious-minded child, just as Capricorn's pessimism can grate with Scorpio. Long silences can be a feature of this relationship, especially during the teenage years. Scorpio resorts to sulks and usually empty threats in the face of any Capricorn challenge, and her child, faced with its mother's resentment and obstinacy, retreats into a black mood. Generally, however, Capricorn delights in its mother's zest for life and Scorpio thinks her child's dry humour and application to getting on in the world is just marvellous.

Capricorn Child/Scorpio Father

This astrological duo invariably faces the world as an unbeatable team. Scorpio might worry a little about his slightly taciturn child, who certainly can't fathom its deeply emotional and secretive father, but generally these two share a determination to succeed. Scorpio is absolutely delighted to find that his child intends to get to the top of life's ladder and seems to have the same application as he does, whilst the young Capricorn instinctively knows that its father will steer it in the right direction. Neither tends to look on the frivolous side of life and time spent together will be productive. Problems can arise when Capricorn starts to develop its own ideas and to tread its own path in life. Scorpio, thinking he's losing control of his child, can become didactic and fixed whilst Capricorn, mountain Goat that it is, leaps onwards and upwards, away from its stubborn father. At worst, Scorpio schemes and manipulates in order to stay top dog, but at best is wonderfully supportive of his Capricorn offspring and becomes a powerful ally. A Scorpio father and Capricorn daughter usually develop a very close relationship but, with a son, a lot depends on how Scorpio handles his success.

Capricorn/Scorpio Siblings

As with any Capricorn/Scorpio relationship the general outlook is good, although in a sibling situation there is a possibility of the Scorpio jealousy rearing its ugly head, particularly if it feels that Capricorn is getting more attention. Capricorn can also become grudging and damning if Scorpio seems to be doing better at school or is successful in sport. On the whole, however, each recognises the other's ambition and will be thoroughly supportive. Capricorn also has a wonderful knack of grounding its more emotional sibling, providing a shoulder to cry on and a few practical solutions at times of trouble, while Scorpio understands exactly how to dig Capricorn out of its negativity. Capricorn will never fathom Scorpio's secretive and sometimes suspicious nature and frequently tramples over its sibling's vulnerable emotions. In turn, Scorpio frequently thinks Capricorn is unfeeling and a bit of a stick-in-the-mud. Despite this potential problem, these siblings appreciate that together they thrive – and usually win.

Capricorn and Sagittarius

Capricorn Child/Sagittarius Mother

The Capricorn baby expects, on arrival, to find a structured, disciplined and ordered environment. The Sagittarian mother takes an easy-going approach to life, certainly doesn't plan for months ahead and uses her powers of persuasion to instil order if and when it arises. The baby needs stability and security and its mother's sometimes haphazard approach and lack of a set routine can leave the little Capricorn feeling totally at sea. Thus, the child can feel thoroughly unsettled with Sagittarius, who, in turn, can't understand why her baby doesn't seem to respond to her lively ways and relaxed notions of running the home. It takes many years for the Capricorn child to appreciate that its mother (perhaps despite all signs to the contrary!) is dependable and blessed with perception, honesty and a wonderfully straightforward attitude to life. Optimism and sociability are the Sagittarian mother's strong points, while pessimism and reticence often define the Capricorn child. It can therefore be difficult for the gregarious mother to get her child to join in with social activities and even partake in family discussions. Her limited patience can be tried to breaking point when it comes to jollying along her rather uncertain little Capricorn. She is also slow to realise that her child favours the conventional just as much as she espouses informality and from an early age the child can get quite twitchy about how its mother is going to behave, what she'll wear and what she might say. On the plus side, the Sagittarian mother can inject warmth and liveliness into the Capricorn lifestyle and encourage her child's naturally dry wit. She will also be absolutely brilliant at defusing the Capricorn fatalism. Where these two can come unstuck is over Capricorn's constant negativity and, later on, over its snobbishness and frequent miserliness. After all, its mother is one of the friendliest and most generous in the zodiac.

Capricorn Child/Sagittarius Father

At a relatively early stage the Capricorn child often seems to treat its Sagittarian father with a certain amount of disdain. This open, outgoing and somewhat boisterous man isn't quite what it was expecting as a father figure! Equally, the Sagittarian father probably wasn't ready for such a serious-minded child. Sagittarius is a father of many words, Capricorn a child of few, and communication can quickly grind to a halt when the father starts to lecture and the child takes refuge in silence. In the same way the child's sometimes 'wet blanket' approach to life leaves the Sagittarian fuming. After all, he trusts in life's bounty and it's never let him down! The sensible Capricorn quickly realises that his or her father is a mine of useful information and wise words, just as the Sagittarian respects his ambitious child's perseverance, patience and prudence. Unfortunately, not all Sagittarian fathers and Capricorn children are that perceptive. Frequently these two exist in a state of complete misunderstanding, the father seeing the child as a boring stick-in-the-mud and Capricorn viewing Sagittarius as shallow and irresponsible.

Capricorn/Sagittarius Siblings

These two either have a great relationship based on mutual respect and an understanding of their differences, or go through childhood (and adulthood) thoroughly confused and irritated by one another. This sibling relationship often works best when Capricorn is the older child. In this way the innate Capricorn sense of responsibility, and five going on fifty attitudes, are given full rein and the Sagittarian happily trots along in his or her wake. Because these two will generally have very different interests both can develop very nicely along their own lines. However, Capricorn will often resent the fact that its Sagittarian sibling always seems to fall on his or her feet, whilst Sagittarius will see Capricorn as mean, rigid in outlook and lacking in dash and verve. On the plus side, Sagittarius will be brilliant at encouraging Capricorn's ambitions while the Capricorn sibling steadies the rather restless Sagittarian nature. These two, if nothing else, usually share a good sense of humour and quick wit, something that can sustain them during their more difficult times.

Capricorn and Capricorn

Capricorn Child/Capricorn Mother

The Capricorn baby, from the very first, sees life as a serious business and in its mother knows it has found someone who thinks exactly the same. The Capricorn mother also instinctively knows that her baby is going to flourish in the disciplined and orderly environment she creates. Thus mother and baby start out together in the way they mean to go on – cautiously, prudently and patiently. Both thrive in routine and certainties and neither wants to get involved in emotional dramas, take risks or rush hither and thither just for the sake of it. Life's frivolities are something they are happy to ignore, but both enjoy a busy and purposeful schedule. Whilst not in the Aquarius league for socialising, these two make friends in all the right places (the baby Capricorn enchants its mother by noticing the bigger house or smarter car!) and both are quick to join in with charity ventures. The child's ambitions are readily fuelled by its mother who moves heaven and earth to get her child into the best school and involved in exciting holiday ventures. She's also adept at entertaining her child and is an excellent teacher to a diligent pupil. It isn't long, either, before her child picks up the dry Capricorn wit that quickly unites them in a very droll outlook on life. Despite their understanding of the outside world, the Capricorn mother and child are totally unable to talk about their own feelings. In fact, they rarely communicate at a deep level at all. Neither likes to let its guard down nor be seen to be out of control, but misunderstandings and grievances that have been simmering under the surface for ages can suddenly explode. Mother and child do not indulge in raised voices and heated argument but are usually astonished at what has been said. Then, they dust themselves down and carry on, just as unable to resolve the real problems as they ever were. Rarely, however, does this relationship reach a dead end, as each values the other's qualities and understands its failings.

Capricorn Child/Capricorn Father

The Capricorn father can scarcely believe his luck at the arrival of his Capricorn son or daughter. Here is someone who takes life as seriously as he does, is going to be just as ambitious and is certainly going to hang on his every word. That is invariably how it starts with the Capricorn father and his Capricorn child and they stride along happily together working out how to conquer the world. As the child grows up, of course, it starts to develop the same traits as its father. Suddenly both father and child know best and what had been intelligent discussion becomes heated argument. They then take refuge in silence and brood in a pessimistic fashion about the other's narrow viewpoint or didactic attitude. At worst, the Capricorn father pushes his child up ladders that are totally inappropriate, but at best he'll be extremely supportive of his child's efforts and do much to smooth his offspring's path through life. The Capricorn child usually holds a Capricorn father in great esteem. Only if a mean-spirited attitude emerges or, worse, a resentment over his child's success, will his son or daughter decide that the father's input is no longer needed.

Capricorn Siblings

When these two live under the same roof there is usually a strong element of competition and a great sense of mutual support. At best they can function very well together: they both understand about hard work, self-discipline and making plans for the future and will take time and trouble to help each other with school work and anything else that's important. They will also aid and abet each other on the social scene, making sure they get invited to the best parties and meet the right people. Each knows it can depend on the other and both understand each other's reluctance to explore the emotional arena. On the other side of the coin, they can drown in a sea of negativity, exacerbating each other's deepest fears and refusing to look at life through anything but the narrowest lens. Because they value their home comforts and domestic security, they usually make an effort to get along while young. As they get older, the competitive drive can force a wedge between them but their sense of humour and pride in each other's achievements often save the day.

Capricorn and Aquarius

Capricorn Child/Aquarius Mother

Neighbouring astrological signs tend to show radically different characteristics and Aquarius and Capricorn are no exception. To the most unconventional sign is born the one most concerned with proprieties and doing the right thing; a baby, moreover, who seems to be well aware that this is all going to be hard work and wonders whether Mum can manage! Capricorn thrives on discipline and order and is being lovingly cared for by a mother who is more inclined to take life as it comes and who is most unlikely to live by a strict routine. Without a sense of certainty, the little Capricorn can get quite fractious, which, in turn, upsets its Aquarian mother who can't understand why her constant chatter and exciting plans for the day are failing miserably to keep her baby entertained. Like the other earth signs, Capricorn likes to take life a little more cautiously than Aquarius and on the social scene can tend to be quite diffident. The mother, far from just handing her baby over to granny, friend or nursery helper, has to take things much more slowly if she is going to have a contented child on her hands. Time spent in reassuring her Capricorn child will help to develop the baby's self-confidence, which is always much more fragile than it appears. The Aquarian's optimistic and sometimes zany approach to life is radically at odds with the innate Capricorn reservation and pessimism and this can cause many misunderstandings between mother and child. Capricorn frequently thinks its mother is foolhardy, irresponsible and eccentric, and Aquarius despairs of her sometimes rather gloomy, rigid and unadventurous child. On the plus side, these two can help each other along splendidly. Capricorn can be a very stable influence on its slightly contrary mother whilst the Aquarian can stimulate her Capricorn child and develop its ambitious nature. Neither sign delves into the realms of deep emotions and a shared sense of humour can also break down any barriers in this relationship.

Capricorn Child/Aquarius Father

Frequently in this father/child relationship a role reversal occurs with the Capricorn child being more responsible and prudent than its more unpredictable and unconventional father! The child frequently smiles indulgently, or despairingly, at the antics of its opinionated parent! Early on, however, Capricorn is delighted with its intellectual, friendly and inventive father, who does much to encourage his more serious-minded child. The Aquarian, in turn, sees in his child a willing pupil and admires its patient and careful approach. It is ultimately, however, the Capricorn's more disciplined nature, to say nothing of its love affair with convention, that becomes a total mystery to the more individualistic father. Capricorn can also become almost embarrassed by its parent – a particular problem in the teenage years – and the Aquarian finds the Capricorn snobbery and social climbing (from a very early age!) quite insufferable! Loyalty and respect often keep these two in a workable relationship but, whilst some Aquarian fathers and Capricorn children understand and tolerate their differences, others retreat into entrenched positions from which they find it very difficult to emerge.

Capricorn/Aquarius Siblings

The Capricorn child is very conventional and likes to take life slowly and cautiously, but at the same time is determined to get to the top. The Aquarian is a true individual, with probably a slightly bohemian nature struggling to get out. Frequently, the Aquarian sees its Capricorn sibling as stodgy and boring and Capricorn despairs of the Aquarian's erratic way of life and contrary attitude. However, Capricorn can also be charmed by the Aquarian friendliness, loyalty and ingenuity, just as Aquarius values the Capricorn diligence and practical attitude to life. These two also share a good sense of humour, although the Capricorn wit tends to be much drier than the Aquarian's. Aquarius can also be a tremendous help to Capricorn on the social scene, as it is generally much more at ease in company. In turn, Capricorn can teach its Aquarian brother or sister about patience, prudence and getting on in life. A certain amount of distance will lend a better understanding to this sibling relationship.

Capricorn and Pisces

Capricorn Child/Pisces Mother

Pisces is the most unworldly sign of the zodiac and Capricorn the most materialistic and practical and therein lies a big problem in this relationship when Capricorn is young. The little Goat can't cope with the chaos, lack of routine and general indecision of its mother. It likes to know what's what in life and that includes a timetable for the day. Its loving, kind and sensitive Pisces mother, who tells her baby stories, looks at it with her beautiful, dreamy eyes, makes bath-time particularly special and fills the home with music and all manner of creative masterpieces, is at a loss to know why her baby is so fractious. In an effort to please, she usually adds in more to the day and further confuses her little Capricorn with even less in the way of order and structure. Capricorn also thrives in a fairly disciplined environment and likes to know the rules and where its boundaries are: the Piscean mother swims happiest in uncharted and infinite waters and really doesn't want to know anything about shorelines. In the early years of this relationship, mother and child often do no more than muddle through as Pisces is baffled by Capricorn's ambitious streak and rather reserved personality just as much as her child becomes unnerved by its mother's vagueness and inability to cope with practical matters. By the age of five, however, Capricorn has probably mastered many of the routine chores in the home and is probably far more aware than Pisces of what has to be taken to school, when it's playing football/netball and whose party it is on Saturday! As Capricorn gets older, this relationship tends to improve. Pisces is brilliant at digging Capricorn's feelings out of rather sterile earth, developing its dry humour and fostering a warmer personality. Capricorn, in turn, often takes on the parental role and has wonderfully broad shoulders on which its mother can unburden her feelings. Only in exceptional circumstances do these two give up on each other.

Capricorn Child/Pisces Father

For Capricorn, who tends to like his life to run like clockwork and who is conventional in the extreme, its Pisces father is often a bit of a mystery. For a start, nothing is ever organised: Capricorn, desperate for a father of strength and purpose, finds its compassionate and adaptable Pisces exists in a glorious state of confusion and muddle. Eventually, of course, the father provides a day or excursion of wonder, imagination and probably enormous creative excitement. Pisces is also prone to breaking its promises, something Capricorn finds very hard to cope with: this is a sign that has a strong sense of duty and commitment. Home life and the role of the father are also very important to Capricorn and the Piscean tendency to take a much more casual attitude to both can be quite upsetting. At worst, Capricorn has little time for what it sees as a loving but irresponsible parent and Pisces gets tired of the Capricorn pessimism and snobbery. At best, and this is far more usual, Pisces takes great pride in his Capricorn child who learns to appreciate its father's gentle personality and his intuitive guidance.

Capricorn/Pisces Siblings

Whilst this is usually a sibling relationship of great mutual affection it isn't without its more difficult moments. Capricorn feels it is forever sorting out Pisces' muddled existence and clearing up after its sibling, whether it's toys or a misunderstanding. Pisces finds Capricorn's rather straight laced behaviour and inability to do anything on the spur of the moment thoroughly irritating and boring. Different attitudes to money can also cause a few problems: Capricorn gets used to bailing out Pisces when it's overspent, while Pisces often sees Capricorn as rather mean and miserly. The better side of this twosome is shown in Capricorn's endless practical advice and help when another Piscean dream crashes to earth. In turn, Pisces has a sixth sense about what is bothering Capricorn and is enormously helpful at keeping its sibling's worries and negativity at bay. It also knows just how to bring the Capricorn sense of humour to the surface. This relationship works best if Capricorn is the older sibling but, if it's the younger one, it soon establishes itself as boss!

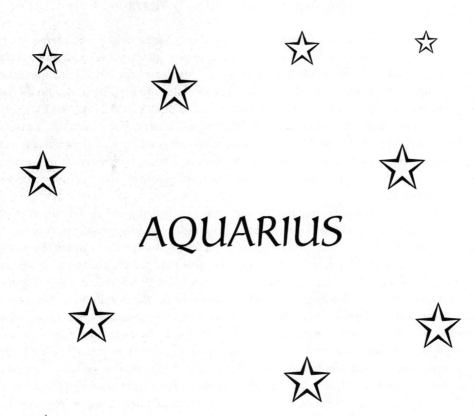

AQUARIUS

The Aquarian Child 0-5 Years

From the moment of birth the Aquarian child will show that he or she is in a league of its own: this is the true individual of the zodiac. Independent, determined and curious about everything around it, the little Aquarian amazes, delights, frustrates and alarms as it makes its often unpredictable way through life. This is not a child who is going to fit into one, or any, particular mould: throw out the received wisdom of the baby books and take the achievement guidelines with a pinch of salt. With most Aquarian youngsters, it's a case of 'expect the unexpected'. He or she will do all the right things and tick all the correct boxes, but in his or her own way and own time. Perhaps more than any other sign, the Aquarian baby makes great leaps of progress on the one hand and rigidly refuses to change patterns of behaviour on the other.

Charm, smiles and laughter one minute and a cold, challenging and slightly unforgiving stare the next: 'contrary' should be every Aquarian's middle name and from a very early age the innate rebelliousness and obstinacy swiftly interchanges with the wonderfully sunny nature. Nothing, where Aquarius is concerned, is a foregone conclusion and from minute to minute, let alone day to day, it's a matter of guesswork as to whether the baby is going to be accommodating or downright difficult! Much of the Aquarian wilfulness comes from either frustration or worries. This baby wants to be into everything and finds it impossible to believe that there are rules, regulations and boundaries. Its quick mind is also way ahead of its physical abilities – a sure recipe for disappointment and annoyance. Despite its progressive outlook and freedom-loving attitude, the Aquarian also suffers from great uncertainties. It is a 'fixed' sign and therefore tends to favour the status quo and has an inbuilt dislike of change. Rushing any Aquarian baby or toddler into new routines just brings out the worst in them. Change has to be tackled slowly and surely if there is not to be a major case of tantrums and digging in of heels. The removal of what the child has come to see as safe and secure structures can be very unnerving.

All Aquarians thrive in company and even the youngest is often at its best when there are plenty of people around. This can mean anything from a gathering of its peers, or family, to smiling cheerfully at everyone in the supermarket. On a shopping spree, especially if in the buggy, or in a highchair in a café, it needs to see what is going on. Turn its back on the action and suddenly there'll be wails which indicate temper rather than unhappiness. This is one of the zodiac's most companionable and trusting children and it'll be looking for new friends everywhere. It is also one of the easiest children to take out and about. It is rarely fazed by new surroundings and usually has a very healthy appetite and an interest in all sorts of food combinations. Only when feeling slightly under the weather will an Aquarian child become fussy at meal times. With a fairly low boredom threshold, the little Aquarian also needs plenty of distractions, probably in the form of a large toy cupboard. In the rather perverse Aquarian manner, however, it will probably become attached to a favourite item that has no place in the nursery whatsoever, and it could well be the TV remote control. From a very early age the Aquarian begins its love affair with gadgets and gizmos.

Aquarius is not only a keen learner but is also very interested in how things work. A first Lego kit will probably lead to a beginner's chemistry set much further along the line. However, its attention span is often limited and it will tend to acquire knowledge in a fairly erratic fashion. Most Aquarian babies and young children (unlike perhaps their Virgo, Gemini or Sagittarian cousins) do not appreciate being taught anything when they are just not in the mood. It's often a matter of the parent twigging that the child is in learning mode and taking advantage of it, rather than organising set play times and hoping to make progress with the shape sorter, the building bricks or the delights of a new book. Pick the wrong day and the Aquarian intransigence will become very obvious! Science and modern technology are particularly associated with Aquarius (expect it to fathom the rudiments of the computer fairly early on!) but that does not mean that the arts are a no-go area. Lewis Carroll (with his wonderfully vivid imagination) and the original rebel without a cause, James Dean, were both Aquarians, as was Charles Darwin (a scientist of radical thinking). This sign will not be pigeonholed!

On a good day, the Aquarian child will take an interest in everything and, perhaps before full-time education, it could be important to encourage it to finish something it's started and to tackle anything from a painting to a jigsaw at a steady pace, rather than in fits and starts. By the time the five-year-old Aquarian arrives at the school gates, it will be a mine of information, some appropriate to its age and the rest gleaned from all sorts of sources and probably unusual in the extreme. It will also think of itself as an expert in the clothing stakes. Left to its own devices, the Aquarian can make the latest and zaniest fashion statements look staid! Even in the smallest school uniform Aquarius will find a way of making itself unique. These children never blend in with the crowd if they can possibly help it!

From an early age the Aquarian shows its innate kindness: it is in no way possessive and tends not to cling, unless feeling out of sorts. Whilst not in the Pisces or Cancer league for picking up atmosphere, it's usually well aware of any sadness and its concern usually shows in the baby's eyes and in the toddler's or older child's efforts at giving comfort. Aquarius is not particularly tactile: it doesn't look for kisses and cuddles and can be sparing in its own overt affection: it isn't unknown for a two-year-old to remove itself from a cosy embrace, making it clear that such a loving gesture is quite unnecessary! However, when it comes to its own feelings it's on shakier ground. A natural understanding of its own emotional nature is not part of the Aquarian make-up and the child will need much help in dealing with both its own vulnerabilities and the deeper sensibilities of others. Otherwise, tactless and opinionated remarks tend to burst forth from the little Aquarian when a more sensitive approach is called for.

Personal space is of paramount importance to two signs of the zodiac, Sagittarius and Aquarius, but it is the formidable Aquarian independence that really makes it imperative for this particular child to have lots of room to manoeuvre. From babyhood, Aquarius is determined to do everything on its own and often gets furious when offered a helping hand. Although loving company and sharing time with friends and family, the Aquarian often wanders off, seemingly detached from the rest of the party. It will return in its own good time, its natural friendliness and love of the social scene ensuring that it won't spend too much time in solitude. Forcing the Aquarian free spirit into a tethered situation often produces nothing more than a show of temper or a cold, distant and defensive attitude.

Whilst the Aquarian emotions are often rooted in somewhat sterile territory, its intellect is definitely planted in very fertile ground and it has no difficulty dealing with logic. Therefore, from the earliest age, it's very easy to have a rational discussion and to get a point across through intelligent argument. Of course, there are likely to be more than a few perverse comments along the way (including saying 'no' to every suggestion) because that's the Aquarian way of doing things, but this child respects sensible debate and good reasoning and will eventually respond in a positive manner.

Trust, honesty, friendliness and originality shine out of the Aquarian child, and the world would be very dull place without its naturally reforming spirit, progressive outlook, inventive approach to life, and even its slight penchant for rebellion. Parental reassurance and understanding can greatly help the rather bossy confidence that often masks the Aquarian child's insecurities, thus giving it much more genuine self-assurance when it joins the classroom. Most Aquarians become very popular members of the school community although, perhaps more than some of the other signs, they can take a little longer to settle down into a new timetable.

It takes much patience and probably a good sense of humour to bring out the best in an Aquarian child, who, in turn, will forever be a joy and a total enigma. Its loyalty to those it loves, however, is never in doubt.

Aquarius and Aries

Aquarius Child/Aries Mother

Aquarius (air) and Aries (fire) are astrologically compatible: fire warms the cool Aquarian air, which, in turn, fans the Aries flames. The little Aquarian will be enchanted with its go-ahead, lively and enterprising mother who makes each day so interesting and exciting. She certainly won't bundle up her child in a load of restrictions and seemingly inexplicable rules and regulations and is instinctively aware of her baby's need for space and freedom of action. The Aquarian curiosity about life and its extremely friendly demeanour is obvious from day one, and Aries is more than happy to pass her child around friends and family. She's not usually the most maternal of the zodiac's mothers and it often comes as a relief that her child is never likely to be clinging or over-dependent on her for any reason. The Aries 'me-first' approach to life and its mother's impatience, however, can start to grate with the more charitable and loyal Aquarian, just as much as Aries becomes frustrated at her child's penchant for bringing everyone it meets home for tea. Aquarius' unpredictable and often contrary behaviour is also in stark contrast to her thoroughly straightforward, and often blunt, attitude. Despite its determination to do things differently, the Aquarian, in fact, likes the status quo and hates to get involved in showdowns of any kind. Aries, with her quick temper and love of clearing the air, frequently finds her admonishments a waste of time and energy as her child decides to disappear from view rather than get involved in an argument. The rather cold and unforgiving Aquarian stare can also thwart Aries who suddenly starts to see the funny side of a situation. She can also be puzzled by her child's difficulty in accommodating change when she loves to live at a fast pace and with a constantly varying agenda. On the whole there is much more to unite this mother and child than divide them. Both value their independence, and the Aries enthusiasm and the Aquarian rationality make them a very positive duo.

Aquarius Child/Aries Father

The Aries father is always on the go and full of plans for today, next month and two years hence. His Aquarian son or daughter, who is totally open to new experiences and to meeting lots of interesting people, is often a wonderful companion for him, although the child can sometimes become unnerved by his more impulsive decisions. The father's abundant enthusiasms, however, aren't always appreciated – frequently he'll think his young Aquarian is rather cool towards his latest adventure, and it's this sometimes rather aloof attitude that Aries finds immensely irritating. Aries can also find his child's keenness to befriend the world and his wife very odd: he's extremely self-centred and his child the zodiac's humanitarian. Problems often arise in this relationship when Aries can no longer control his child's every action. He becomes frustrated at Aquarius' lack of ambition and despairs of his child's unconventional behaviour. Aquarius, in turn, is embarrassed by a father who seems to upset its friends with his forthright remarks. The Aries father and Aquarian son can go through some difficult moments before a real friendship develops, but an Aquarian daughter often adores her warm-hearted father.

Aquarius/Aries Siblings

This is usually a very good relationship, although not without a few inharmonious moments. The straightforward Aries becomes irritated with the Aquarian's eccentricities and what it sees as perverse behaviour. Aquarius, in turn, hates the Aries fiery temper and impatience and resents the fact that it invariably has to pick up the pieces, after one of Aries more volatile moments. The cool and rational Aquarian temperament is also an enigma to Aries, who is so much more up-front and emotional about everything. On the plus side, of course, Aquarius is able to be thoroughly honest with Aries who may not like what is said but invariably comes to see its sibling is right, while the Aquarian learns much from Aries' enterprising attitude. Neither sibling wants to be mollycoddled and both relish independence and although short, sharp quarrels are likely when both think they are right, neither will ever resort to manipulative or underhand behaviour. Theirs is a friendship that lasts and is beneficial to both.

Aquarius and Taurus

Aquarius Child/Taurus Mother

Aquarius and Taurus like the status quo and can be stubborn in the extreme, and from the start of this relationship mother and baby can make it subtly clear that each wants its own way. The young Aquarian will certainly have no quarrel with its mother's ordered lifestyle and the daily routine she has put into place for her baby. The stimulating social life will also go down well since Aquarius just loves meeting people. However, Taurus can be very possessive about her baby and finds it difficult to cope with a child who seems to want to go to anybody in the room but her. The more threatened she feels, the more she clasps her baby, and the more the little Aquarian feels bound to one particular person, the more it protests. Taurus is also one of the most tactile and sensual people in the zodiac and Aquarius is emotionally rather cool and doesn't rate cuddles and touch all that highly. It prefers to talk its way through life and gives up little about its inner self. The Aquarian toddler soon becomes very independent, not only in the way it takes itself away from its mother and gets on happily with some activity or other, but also in its attitude. This is a child who says what it means and means what it says! In turn, Taurus takes to being more controlling and opinionated and thus a potentially stressful situation opens up between mother and child. The usual Taurean solution to emotional problems is to go on a bit of a spending spree and enjoy some self-indulgence. Again, this is lost on her Aquarian who is probably one of the least materialistic people in the zodiac! However, all is not lost for these two, as the little Aquarian is kindness personified and will hate to see its mother upset: she'll be charmed by her child's loyalty and fascinated (but often appalled!) by its original thinking. Despite moments when each finds the other quite impossible, once Taurus realises that her child functions in a totally different way from her, her natural affection and patience will ensure this relationship never hits the buffers.

Aquarius Child/Taurus Father

To the practical, reliable and very solid Taurean father, his Aquarian son or daughter usually comes as a mixture of shock and delight. He is enchanted by what he sees as a rather quirky personality and an inquisitive nature but is a little concerned by its rather independent stance. The Aquarian feels very secure with its affectionate father, who is so grounded and so absolutely certain about everything but worries about his slightly obsessive nature. It's not long before both realise that they are as inflexible as each other. Aquarius resents being ordered about and Taurus fails to understand his contrary son or daughter, who is never prepared to take the safe route. Taurus also hates the fact that Aquarius tends to walk away rather than indulge in argument and its emotional detachment is a total mystery to him. In the Aquarian's mind, there is no point discussing anything with someone whose views are so fixed. Aquarius also finds it difficult to cope with its father's unadventurous attitude to life, although later on is grateful to have a parent who is steadfast. Loyalty and friendship usually bind these two firmly together – eventually.

Aquarius/Taurus Siblings

Taurus and Aquarius are united in their opinionated thinking and general inflexibility but they are radically different personalities. Aquarius definitely livens up its more placid sibling, just as Taurus lends common sense to the Aquarian's every new plan. However, Aquarius frequently complains that its sibling has no sense of adventure, while Taurus fails to understand the Aquarian's insistence on being original and its love of the unpredictable. Although the more intellectual of the two, Aquarius often comes to rely on Taurus to finish its school work or come up with good ideas. Taurus, who is far more self-indulgent, depends on Aquarius to invent excuses and talk the talk to get its sibling out of trouble. Within the family, Taurus needs the demonstrative affection and Aquarius the meeting of minds, so neither treads on the other's domestic territory. With obstinacy being a mutual trait, these two can retreat into corners and stay there but with careful guidance they relish each other's qualities and gloss over the more annoying traits.

Aquarius and Gemini

Aquarius Child/Gemini Mother

This air sign duo are instinctively in tune with each other, understanding that communication is the key to any relationship and that delving into emotional depths is probably best left to other people. The Aquarian baby will love the fact that its Gemini mother has so many friends and contacts and is clearly not going to spend her time cocooning her baby or indulging in a lot of tactile bonding. It'll also be delighted that it has such a chatty mother: this baby loves the sound of the human voice and wants to get involved in an exchange of views as soon as possible. What Gemini sometimes forgets is that an Aquarian is not as naturally adaptable as she is and needs to be slowly introduced to change of any kind. If her baby is fretting or, as a toddler, behaving in a totally contrary manner, it's usually because it's fighting against too many new situations coming all at once. Both mother and child are intellectual by nature and will enjoy reading together – this duo is probably well known at the local library – and will flourish in any situation where education is the key. Museums, stately homes and galleries are but a few of the places where this mother and child will feel thoroughly at ease and have a great deal of fun. Sometimes Aquarius gets annoyed at its mother's broken promises because she either overfills the diary or decides to change her mind at the last minute, whilst Gemini finds it difficult to deal with her child when it adopts an aloof, detached manner and doesn't seem to be on her wavelength at all. Arguments tend to arise between them when Aquarius becomes stubborn and Gemini knows she is right: it is normally Gemini who backs down in the face of her child's intransigence! Although these two frequently go through life never fully understanding each other, they usually have the most marvellous friendship and in later years spend much time out and about together and hours on the phone indulging in gossip.

Aquarius Child/Gemini Father

Where a meeting of minds is concerned, this father/child relationship is often highly productive. Gemini will be thrilled to find his little Aquarian hanging onto his every word whilst Aquarius will marvel at its father's endless knowledge about absolutely everything. More to the point, Gemini will be genuinely interested in what his three-year-old has to say, but then make it his business to interrupt and correct (though rarely indulging in outright criticism!). Trouble can come from Gemini's thoroughly restless and changeable attitude to life which results in him promising more than he can deliver, much to the chagrin of his Aquarian who sets great store by honesty and loyalty. The Gemini father is, himself, also bemused by the sudden Aquarian contrariness and obstinacy, failing to understand that his child is neither as versatile nor as quick to change tack as he is. Both, however, are extremely assured and happy on the social scene and Gemini is usually very confident in his Aquarian's ability to hold his or her own in conversation. This may never be a really deep relationship, but it is one of mutual respect and genuine affection. Father and child will be seeking each other's opinions for years.

Aquarius/Gemini Siblings

Chat, communication and busyness generally are the hallmark of this relationship but it's the frenetic Gemini lifestyle that frequently irritates Aquarius who cannot understand its sibling's often rather superficial attitude to friends and situations. Aquarius rates loyalty very highly and would never dream of letting friends down in Gemini's cavalier manner. Gemini equally despairs of the Aquarian's often unpredictable behaviour, unable to believe that anyone can be so inflexible or so perverse! These, however, are but small issues in what is usually a genuinely happy sibling relationship defined by wit, friendliness and good times. Aquarius and Gemini are both inventive thinkers: grand ideas and an adventurous spirit unite these two in the occasional scrape from which they extricate themselves most eloquently. Gemini is especially good at bluffing its way out of tight corners. When they eventually go their own way, they usually remain in constant contact.

Aquarius and Cancer

Aquarius Child/Cancer Mother

Astrologically Cancer and Aquarius are chalk and cheese. Cancer prizes security and the family unit and takes a cautious approach to life. Aquarius is the true individual of the zodiac and, from the moment of birth will refuse to be pigeonholed and will befriend all and sundry. For the Cancer mother, who wants to keep her baby close to her and needs not only to feel loved by her baby, but also to have gained its approval, an Aquarian can come as something of a shock. Of course it loves its mother, but that's something it feels the Cancerian should take as read! This is one of the most sociable babies in the astrological family and, once aware of someone new in the room, will push away from its devoted mother and seek to make another friend. The vulnerable and worried Cancerian immediately sees this as personal rejection and feels hurt and useless. Far from feeling wounded, she should appreciate that she has provided her Aquarian child with a wonderfully safe and solid base from which it can venture forth, all the time knowing that its protective mother is there to return to. On the plus side, of course, her Aquarian baby is never likely to cling, be fearful of life or lack friends: in fact it'll love bringing all and sundry home and will be a star among its peers because of its mother's generous hospitality. A Cancerian mother will also provide one of the essentials for the Aquarian baby – a reliable routine. Despite its independence and seeming disregard for all things safe and secure, Aquarius in fact needs a firm base and boundaries within which it can experiment and safely rebel! For a Cancerian mother, having an Aquarian baby is akin to taking a crash course in a totally alien subject but, when conquered, takes her into a new realm of understanding. It also brings her a great relationship with a child who will amaze and delight her. If she is open to its very different personality and handles it with care, her Aquarian child will not only like her, but probably also worship her.

Aquarius Child/Cancer Father

This is a classic relationship where one party comes from the heart (Cancer) and the other predominately from the head (Aquarius), and it takes time for the middle ground to be reached. Few Cancerian fathers want their children to grow up and leave the nest but for the Aquarian child it's the world outside the home that is of paramount importance. Very often Cancer has a real problem with his Aquarian son or daughter's frantic social life and its avid interest in other people's lifestyles and thinking. Because of what the Aquarian sees as an over-protective stance from its father and all sorts of unnecessary restrictions, its perverse and unpredictable side comes to the fore. This twosome functions best on the intellectual level and, as the Aquarian gets older, there is often much earnest discussion between the two, even if little agreement. With its rational thinking Aquarius can often soothe its father's troubled brow and, best of all, is usually impervious to Cancer's rather snappy temper. Despite their differences, the possibility of a lasting bond between father and child is excellent. Both are innately kind and any trust the Cancerian father places in his child is usually richly rewarded.

Aquarius/Cancer Siblings

At best these two can get on brilliantly, Cancer enchanted by the witty and talkative Aquarian, who, in turn, finds Cancer to be a mine of kindness and sympathy. That is the theory! In practice, Aquarius finds Cancer to be moody, subject to long silences and thoroughly self-pitying, and Cancer thinks its Aquarian sibling insensitive, perverse and emotionally detached. On the plus side, of course, the Aquarian will never threaten Cancer's hold on its mother's apron strings and will also never feel overshadowed by its sibling on the social scene. Aquarius likes to be at the centre of a busy and often noisy environment, while Cancer likes peace and quiet and can be quite content with its own company. As they grow older, each starts to appreciate the other's qualities. Aquarius will certainly be a tower of strength to Cancer when it comes to being out and about, and Cancer will prove a great listener when the latest attempt at rebellion has bitten the dust.

Aquarius and Leo

Aquarius Child/Leo Mother

Leo and Aquarius are opposite signs in the zodiac and embody very different attitudes, most particularly the Leo ego versus the Aquarian's humanitarian nature. To start with, the Leo mother loves to show off her little Aquarian, delighting in its natural curiosity about life, its friendliness and its clear determination to be a law unto itself. Aquarius loves the fact that its mother is well organised, has a wonderfully large personality and is never likely to thrust anything haphazard into the equation. Leo, however, likes to be boss and always knows best and it's not long before she realises that her child has no intention of being ordered around. Aquarius is independent, has a searching mind and a contrariness that completely baffles its mother. Whilst never disobedient, Aquarius always wants reasons for doing things and rarely responds well to the 'do as I say because I say so' scenario. This infuriates Leo who thinks Aquarius should acknowledge her superiority in all fields! Leo can also be incredibly snobbish and is often very impressed by outward show. Her Aquarian child, who will genuinely like people just because they're great fun or thoroughly interesting, often appals its mother in its choice of companion, and there can be much upset and disagreement when Leo lays down the law as to who is, or is not, the right sort of friend. However, she is nothing if not magnanimous and often she'll bow to her child's wishes and start to trust her Aquarian's judgment. (This is not, after all, Pisces who is forever coming home with the world's lame ducks!) Both Leo and Aquarius like the status quo and can be very inflexible. Over something that really matters to her, Leo can become intolerant and dogmatic, only to find that her child's intransigence is equally formidable. Whatever difficulties these two might face, Leo's emotional and financial generosity to her child will be heart-warming, while Aquarius will show loyalty and friendship to its mother through thick and thin.

Aquarius Child/Leo Father

The Leo father, as befits the head of the family, likes to think that his child will fall into line quickly and quietly as soon as raises his little finger. Not so with an Aquarian son or daughter. He soon finds out that his Aquarian child can be as stubborn as he can be didactic and if it wasn't for his basic broadmindedness and the warmth of his personality, as well as his child's natural friendliness, many an impasse could be reached between these two. Aquarius loves its father's flair and capacity for enjoyment but gets embarrassed at its frequently over the top behaviour in his efforts to be centre stage. Leo is equally puzzled by his child's cool detachment and constantly rebukes Aquarius for not entering into the spirit of things. Where this father/child does prosper, of course, is in the teacher/pupil role. Aquarius, who revels in its father's ability to put his subject across, quickly picks up Leo's enthusiasms. Once Aquarius learns to play the game of keeping Leo on its throne and feigning obedience while taking its own very individual path, this relationship will head for success. Two intransigent personalities, on the other hand, can end up at loggerheads.

Aquarius/Leo Siblings

This sibling relationship will never be predictable and these two will probably yo-yo between great highs and lows, with the certainty that when the dust settles they'll face the world, and any consequences, as a formidably united duo. Aquarius sometimes resents Leo's rather pushy behaviour while the Lion cub frets at its sibling's aloof attitude and tendency to change its game plan at the last minute. Leo can also find the Aquarian's need to move boundaries and its individualism highly trying, whilst Aquarius thinks the Leo boasting and bossiness is thoroughly tiresome. Both, however, tend to look at life's bigger picture and are thoroughly sociable. The Aquarian inventiveness is an excellent match for Leo's expansive and creative personality, just as much as Aquarius is often grateful for Leo's brilliant organisational skills. With both signs liking the status quo and sticking to their guns come hell or high water, this is often a relationship of noisy arguments and silent tensions just as much as it is about laughter, friendship and a strong sense of loyalty.

Aquarius and Virgo

Aquarius Child/Virgo Mother

Although these two signs are radically different, this is often a relationship that prospers despite the odds being stacked against it. The little Aquarian will certainly feel very secure in its mother's well-organised environment, and Virgo will love her child's intelligence and friendliness, which endear it to all and sundry. She probably won't be quite so happy with the Aquarian penchant for doing its own thing from a very early age: she likes her routines and a disciplined lifestyle and Aquarius soon shows its independent nature and tendency not always to fall in with exactly what its mother has planned. Virgo finds it tiring in the extreme forever having to debate everything with a three-year-old, although it's the same interest in communication and learning that binds these two strongly together. Aquarius, who tends to look at life's bigger picture and is fascinated by the world in general, often feels cramped in Virgo's much smaller world, to say nothing of its mother's certainties and her fixation with the practical realities of life. Aquarius feels that everything, from friendships, to the nearest town, to the other side of the world, is up for exploration and that life is a mystery waiting to be unravelled. Virgo is also happiest ticking all the right boxes in exactly the right order. Her child is the zodiac's free spirit and quickly becomes irritated by Virgo's sometimes nit-picking and fussy manner just as much as Aquarius unnerves its mother with its unpredictability and contrariness. Neither is really comfortable with their feelings. Virgo buries them in work and in being busy while the Aquarian glare and decision to stand apart is often the child's only signal that strong emotions are churning around. Thus these two never really give or receive much at a deeper level and rarely develop a truly comfortable and relaxed relationship, but the child's strong sense of loyalty will override any feelings of wanting to run from its mother's grip and Virgo will always be a fount of practical support to her child.

Aquarius Child/Virgo Father

Virgo is conservative by nature and comfortable in the practicalities of life. For his son or daughter, it's ideas and a new outlook that matter. Virgo likes to take a diligent approach to everything it takes on and, for the father to watch his little Aquarian tackle games, puzzles and, later, homework without real practical application brings him out in a rash of nit-picking and fussiness. Aquarius also finds it difficult to show overt affection which, to this tactile man, comes as a shock. It takes time for him to realise that his youngster's affection is expressed in words – whilst usually standing at a distance! Where these two will gel is in the realms of education. Virgo is an excellent teacher and his Aquarian a willing pupil and these two will often be found in earnest conversation. During the teenage years, Aquarius craves independence and tends to become perverse and Virgo racks up the criticism and worries intensely. Sometimes Virgo completely loses patience with his contrary little Aquarian, while his child sees its father as too conventional and obsessed with a safety-first lifestyle. Generally, however, Virgo is stalwart in its support and Aquarius supremely loyal.

Aquarius/Virgo Siblings

As with any sibling relationship that involves two relatively incompatible signs of the zodiac, this is often an all or nothing situation. On the plus side, both are intellectually gifted and love discussion. Virgo often lends practical common sense to the Aquarian's original ideas while Aquarius enlivens Virgo by taking it out of a rather confined comfort zone. Despite being less inventive in its thinking, Virgo is far quicker than Aquarius at sussing out situations and getting out of trouble. Aquarius is far more open and friendly than Virgo and can be of enormous help to its sibling on the social scene. Virgo, however, is the more discriminating of the two and often saves Aquarius from getting into friendships or situations that spell nothing but trouble. At home, Virgo is king or queen of the domestic environment while Aquarius craves independence and the wider world, so neither treads on the other's toes. These two may never be really close but, if given enough space to grow up out of the other's shadow, usually value each other as loyal friends.

Aquarius and Libra

Aquarius Child/Libra Mother

Both Aquarius and Libra are air signs and value the exchange of ideas and communication generally. Aquarius will love the sound of its mother's voice and Libra will chat along to her baby even when she is getting no discernible reply at all! The very young Aquarian feels relaxed and comfortable within a good routine and, despite its later unpredictability, not too much in the way of sudden changes. Libra, who finds decision-making a trial and hates to upset anyone, often dithers about and disrupts her baby's timetable – much to its distress. Of course, her baby's social life will be second to none, which will definitely appeal to Aquarius, who is one of the friendliest people around and loves being out in the wider world. Mother and child usually have a large circle of friends, enjoy getting involved in art and music groups and quickly sign up for library cards. Libra's tendency to worry, however, about what people think and her inclination to pander to the strongest personality around is thoroughly annoying to Aquarius, who, at a very young age, has an insight into people that its mother definitely lacks. Libra resents having her friendships questioned by a five-year-old! Her easy-going nature, on the other hand, is bliss for her Aquarian: Libra won't lose too much sleep over her child's contrariness and she'll be relatively sympathetic to its need for independence. Her touch on the reins will be sure, but very light. Sometimes these two suffer from planning much, but doing very little, as well as a lack of genuine understanding. Neither is particularly strong on the emotional front and both prefer to take decisions from the head rather than the heart. Although Libra might occasionally wish that her Aquarian wasn't quite such an individual, and took more interest in a stylish appearance, she'll always take pride in its humanitarian outlook and honest approach. In turn, Aquarius knows its mother will never choose to rock any boats and will always be there with a kind word and a lot of home comforts.

Aquarius Child/Libra Father

The arrival of an Aquarian child to the Libran father is the start of what is usually a lifetime companionship, although not always an easy relationship. The Libran father prides himself on his charm, his laid-back personality and the fact that diplomacy is his forté. His Aquarian son or daughter takes a more open and honest approach to everything and is more of an individual than its father will ever be. Hence Libra finds himself constantly apologising for his child's sometimes rather perverse behaviour, to say nothing of its ability to be centre stage with an unusual selection of clothes. Libra is also ambitious and often frets at his child's ideas for the future, totally unable to understand its humanitarian instincts and its need for achievements well away from the more conventional career ladders. These are small problems in what is, on the whole, a very chatty and lively friendship. Both love being out and about, and Libra will make it his business to involve Aquarius in many of his cultural interests. He'll love his child's inventive thinking and loyalty just as much as his Aquarian will bask in its father's genuine affection and admiration.

Aquarius/Libra Siblings

With two air sign siblings it's very often a case of each having much to say to the other and yet very little in the way of real emotional understanding. Although Aquarius can be stubborn, detached, and fiercely independent and seems to be the stronger character, it is frequently the charming Libran who wields the power behind the dazzling smile and the butter-wouldn't-melt expression. As young children, Aquarius frequently takes the rap for Libra's misdemeanours, and Libra then takes even more advantage of the Aquarian's natural willingness to help. On the other side of the coin, Aquarius gets irritated at Libra's indecision and what it sees as its superficial and frivolous concerns. Far more important is the Aquarian's fury at seeing its sibling so gullible, and then having to step in and save it from going down totally the wrong road. Generally, however, this is a relationship that is epitomised by much fun and laughter and a genuine friendliness that survives all manner of dramas.

Aquarius and Scorpio

Aquarius Child/Scorpio Mother

As 'intractable' describes both Aquarius and Scorpio, it is inevitable that this is going to be a relationship of stalemate situations, deep feelings and seething resentments on the one hand, and abiding loyalty on the other. To start with, mother and baby seem to have a lot in common. Aquarius loves Scorpio's fixed routines and thrives in her determination to get things right as far as her child is concerned. She is thrilled with her willing and friendly youngster who soon becomes the centre of a lively group of playmates and loves to help her around the home. Both also have great fortitude and together make an excellent team when problems arise. The five-year-old Aquarian will come up with the right answers and calm down its more emotional mother, who, in turn, shows her child what a sense of purpose will achieve! Scorpio is focused, persistent and highly imaginative but lacks the original and inventive Aquarian thinking, and this contrast soon takes effect. Her child's intellectual approach, thirst for knowledge and independent stance often makes Scorpio feel as though she's not good enough for Aquarius, especially as it just loves to talk to everybody around, especially other adults. Her imagination, possessiveness and jealousy go into overdrive and conjure up scenarios that are in no way based in reality. She then claws Aquarius back into what she sees as safer territory and re-exerts control, prompting it to rebel. She also finds it very difficult to cope with her child's rather detached emotional nature and its tendency to distance itself from both sensitive discussions and her sometimes rather manipulative behaviour, seeing her child's airy disregard for her passions and concerns as a rebuff. In addition, Scorpio becomes infuriated with her Aquarian child's unpredictable nature and decidedly contrary behaviour, which goes against her more conventional grain. At best these two are wonderfully steadfast and forgiving towards each other, but this is usually a relationship that goes through many difficult moments.

Aquarius Child/Scorpio Father

The Scorpio father likes to have things organised, including his son or daughter, and finds it very difficult to cope with a child who seems to have its own very definite, independent agenda, which in no way coincides with his plans! Whilst Scorpio is brilliant with his young Aquarian, making sure he spends time with his son or daughter and acting as a loving but perhaps rather strict teacher, as his child gets older and becomes more opinionated, arguments and obstinacy abound. The more frustrated Scorpio becomes with his youngster the more he indulges in dogmatism and the more Aquarius distances itself from the proceedings. Scorpio is also quite a conventional sign and certainly very ambitious and the father rarely understands his child's erratic thinking, unpredictable behaviour and certain knowledge that it doesn't want to be guided/forced down any particular path. On the plus side, of course, neither father nor child will hear a word said against the other and the discerning Scorpio will always find an ally in the honest Aquarian. Sometimes this relationship bites the dust, but with time and effort it can, and does, blossom.

Aquarius/Scorpio Siblings

Aquarius and Scorpio siblings usually have a very dynamic but uneasy relationship. Although Aquarius talks a lot about change, both in fact like the status quo and neither really wants to rock the sibling boat (although they frequently do!). They are, however, incredibly obstinate and get themselves into major stand-offs. It's usually the more logical Aquarian who has to dip its toe gently into Scorpio's emotional depths and turn the situation around. Aquarius is also bemused by its sibling's constant suspicions about people's motives just as Scorpio looks askance at Aquarius' basic trust in human kindness. Within the family neither invades the other's territory as Scorpio is usually quite possessive of its parents while Aquarius is far more focused on the wider world. Loyalty is often the key to this relationship, despite Aquarius losing patience with the secretive and devious Scorpio who, in turn, gets thoroughly rattled by its sibling's perverse behaviour. At best, they present a united front to the world, their grievances well and truly hidden.

Aquarius and Sagittarius

Aquarius Child/Sagittarius Mother

An Aquarian baby born to a Sagittarian mother will quickly feel at home. Both are very sociable and value their independence and it is therefore as natural to the mother to introduce her baby to family, neighbours, friends – anyone in fact who comes into her orbit – as it is a delight to her baby to have such a stimulating lifestyle. The Sagittarian mother is certainly not going to feel unloved or unwanted when her little Aquarian shows interest and affection to other people in the vicinity. Her teaching skills are also avidly seized upon by her baby, who is usually quick to learn and shows a natural curiosity about life. Where Sagittarius can misread the Aquarian nature is in failing to realise that her baby needs much more in the way of routine than she expects, and the happy and positive demeanour of her Aquarian can also blind her to its obstinacy. She takes a far more adaptable approach to life than the Aquarian who, despite a seemingly insatiable appetite for the new and the different, is secretly rather attached to the status quo. It takes the Sagittarian mother some time to realise that her baby needs the security of a daily timetable within which it can explore its brave new world. She also finds out that she's treading a fine line between an over-restrictive routine and one that is too flexible and will often complain that her Aquarian child is a law unto itself – which invariably it is! Nevertheless, these two, more often than not, get on extremely well and a great understanding between them frequently develops during the child's teens. The Sagittarian mother is well able to cope with the Aquarian's need to rebel and will also be a great champion of its humanitarian and idealistic thinking. As well as this relationship being intellectually exciting to mother and child, they also benefit from mutual interests, a sense of fun and, most important of all, a respect for each other's individualism and need for freedom.

Aquarius Child/Sagittarius Father

Sagittarians relish a meeting of minds, and with his Aquarian child the Sagittarian father will experience just that! Debate between these two will be endless and, for the most part, productive. However, the father will find his offspring's sometimes fixed opinions somewhat trying, just as the Aquarian will see its father as careless with people's emotions and blindly optimistic about future grand plans. Aquarius also likes to be in the right over everything and this stance begins early in life. It takes all the Sagittarian father's wisdom to prove his child wrong without engendering a display of the Aquarian obstinacy. Despite the above, this father/child relationship jogs along extremely well. They both enjoy being out and about, have a get-up-and-go attitude to life and thrive in a fairly relaxed and open environment, although Sagittarius needs to remember that his Aquarian child develops best when it can see the boundaries. Although the father may well despair of his child's sometimes eccentric lifestyle, he'll always be sure of the Aquarian loyalty and, deep down, will admire his child's spirit and idealism. In turn, Aquarius needs its father's philosophical and optimistic outlook.

Aquarius/Sagittarius Siblings

Sagittarius can be extremely patronising and capricious and Aquarius insufferably opinionated and unpredictable, and when both siblings are showing these negative traits, there is no easy or safe middle ground. Luckily, this relationship has more to unite it than divide it. On an intellectual level Sagittarius and Aquarius have much in common. Both relish the acquisition of knowledge and will love trips to museums and places of historical interest, getting books from the library or accessing information from the internet. They are also very sociable and, best of all, are likely to share a great sense of humour, which, when all else is failing miserably between them, will definitely save the relationship. Sagittarius also encourages its Aquarian sibling to take a few chances in life while Aquarius lends some rational and analytical thinking to the Sagittarian grandiose plans. These two (as children or adults) will never be in each other's pockets, but will be there for one another when the going gets tough.

Aquarius and Capricorn

Aquarius Child/Capricorn Mother

To the organised, disciplined Capricorn who just wants her baby to be happy in her well-managed household, the little Aquarian can come as a shock. Aquarius craves freedom and independence and whilst it certainly needs the set boundaries within which it can define its life, it becomes incredibly frustrated with its mother's over-protective manner and, sometimes, strict routines. She, therefore, can't understand why her baby is stressed and scratchy as Aquarius frets at its lack of opportunity to put its inquisitive nature to good use. Much more than its mother, the baby loves to be out and about and chatting to all and sundry, which is all a bit worrying to Capricorn who likes to control her child's social life. With the Aquarian intransigence coming up against the Capricorn need to be in charge, these two are soon locked in a battle of wills. Capricorn likes to be busy and is goal orientated: she has a list of things to do, which she must complete. Her baby, on the other hand, likes to explore in its own time and in its own way and doesn't take kindly to set playtimes and a lack of opportunity (even at the crawling stage) to do its own thing. Capricorn, therefore, gets irritated with a child she sees as uncooperative, and Aquarius becomes bored, angry and frustrated. The Aquarian's short attention span also rattles its Capricorn mother, who is diligent in the extreme and expects her child to persevere. As the child grows older the natural rebel in Aquarius comes up against the more conventional Capricorn and communication can completely break down during the teenage years. On the plus side, however, the baby Aquarian benefits hugely from the secure environment provided by its mother and her innate reliability. In turn, Capricorn can find life becoming much more exciting in the company of her Aquarian and she often learns to take a more flexible attitude. She is usually, also, a happy beneficiary of her child's great sense of loyalty.

Aquarius Child/Capricorn Father

At the birth of an Aquarian child, the ambitious, rather proper, Capricorn father is faced with the zodiac's true individual who gives nothing for convention and will be as contrary as its father is reliable. The father usually finds it very difficult to understand the motivations of his Aquarian and certainly loses patience with what he sees as its obstinacy and belief that it is right about everything. Equally, Aquarius finds its father bossy, demanding and too concerned with correct behaviour. Money is also a bone of contention: Capricorn expects pocket money to be spent, saved or both, whilst Aquarius sees nothing wrong with issuing an IOU and borrowing! The father often despairs of his Aquarian offspring, feeling that he or she will get nowhere in the world, and Aquarius resents being pushed down paths it doesn't want to tread. With a bit of thought, however, Capricorn will realise that his child is naturally curious about the world, and will enjoy being out and about with its father. Aquarius, in turn, will be grateful for its father's support through most of the more difficult times and will encourage Capricorn to look at the world with new eyes.

Aquarius/Capricorn Siblings

As neighbouring signs of the zodiac tend to be incompatible, these two can either be intrigued or utterly bemused by their differences. It's often the case that Capricorn spends a lot of its time clearing up after Aquarius, in one way or another, whilst the Aquarian sibling uses up a lot of energy getting its sibling to let its hair down and to take pleasure in life. Aquarius has a much more friendly nature and is good at dragging its brother or sister into the social scene. It takes effort, however, for these two really to get on, especially as Capricorn tends to be bossy and Aquarius stubborn. Frequently Aquarius sees its sibling as miserly and a 'wet blanket', and Capricorn looks askance at the Aquarian perversity and natural urge to rebel. Educational outings, however, can definitely be a source of pleasure for both and they'll probably take an interest in each other's hobbies. If left to their own devices, these two often start to appreciate each other's qualities. Aquarius admires the Capricorn hard-working ethos while Capricorn benefits from its sibling's inventive approach to life.

Aquarius and Aquarius

Aquarius Child/Aquarius Mother

Many mothers and children are keen to think that they are each other's best friend. In the case of the Aquarian mother and her Aquarian baby, this is very likely to be true as all the best Aquarian relationships are based on a very deep friendship. Therefore, the mother looks at her new baby and knows she has a companion and ally for life, and, in its own way, her child also appreciates this from the moment of birth. These two are locked into a wonderful, open and potentially very exciting relationship, one built on loyalty and honesty and a deep understanding of each other's individuality, cool detachment and, above all, need for space. Like its mother, the Aquarian baby will be very sociable, very independent and look at life with a natural curiosity. The two of them will enjoy a slightly haphazard lifestyle contained within certain structures and, as both tend to like the status quo, the mother will understand that her baby responds best to changes that are introduced slowly. Of course, with two Aquarians there can be a major stand-off or two as neither backs down quickly: the terrible twos, and the teenage years, can be particularly troublesome for this duo. However, these two talk endlessly and both respond well to reason so harmony is frequently restored after a lengthy chat. Whether, of course, they ever really communicate is another story. Neither is comfortable in the realms of feelings and, despite thinking they know each other extremely well, they can often feel totally misunderstood. Outings (including the occasional demonstration!) and many common interests lead these two to have some great times together, and both will admire each other's inventive approach to life and indulge each other's eccentricities! Rarely does this mother/child relationship go wrong. If it does, it's usually because familiarity (in the case of two identical personalities) breeds contempt.

Aquarius Child/Aquarius Father

The relationship between an Aquarian child and an Aquarian father can be both a joy and a struggle. For a start, the father is much more likely than the Aquarian mother to take an inflexible and autocratic attitude which can bring out the innate stubbornness in the son or daughter and result in brooding silences. The father's fixed opinions can also drive the young Aquarian to distraction, especially when he or she believes that the father should be just as unconventional and modern in outlook as the child. Well, he was, but that was a few years ago! Certainly this is a lively combination, and the Aquarian father will do everything in his power to develop his child's potential and will take a keen interest in its education. Although father and child will chatter away endlessly, neither gives anything away on the emotional front. Whilst both are grateful to the other for not intruding, it eventually leads to very little real understanding of the other. However, the Aquarian child's innate need to be different from the rest, its humanitarian interests and friendly demeanour will all be fostered by its father who, in return, will receive much loyalty and love from his offspring.

Aquarius Siblings

Two Aquarian children can either become great friends, egging each other on to bigger and better adventures and loyally supporting each other through thick and thin, or can take the independent, contrary stance just a bit too far and end up as two individuals living under the same roof. Usually some kind of happy medium is achieved, giving both of them a certain amount of freedom and yet engendering companionship and an understanding of each other's original thinking and behaviour. Both can be extremely wilful and at times each will tiptoe around the other, but both are rational and open to reason and talking things over invariably sorts out the problems. These two will thrive in a busy social scene, will make lots of friends and generally need to keep mentally occupied. Bored or uninterested Aquarian children will use their vivid imaginations to get up to no good at all! Generally, much wit and laughter is part and parcel of this sibling relationship and, although never emotionally close, they'll take a life-long interest in each other's progress.

Aquarius and Pisces

Aquarius Child/Pisces Mother

For the gentle and highly sensitive Piscean mother, the arrival of her rather contrary and fiercely independent Aquarian baby can be a jolt to the system. She likes to go through life on a bit of a wing and a prayer and rather hopes things fall into place, whereas her little Aquarian makes it clear from the start that it's going to thrive in a set routine and an organised environment. Many problems can dog these two at the beginning because of the Aquarian need for a timetable and order and the Piscean horror of anything that stops its rather vague and unworldly swim through life. As Pisces is the more adaptable of the two, it is usually the mother who initially has to make all the concessions although, later on, her little Aquarian, who has a real yen for the unpredictable and different, will be thoroughly entertained by its mother's spur of the moment decisions and sudden trips to the swimming pool, art gallery or craft shop. She will also be a wonderfully creative presence in the life of her Aquarian and will certainly encourage its inventive and original thinking. As Aquarius finds with the other water signs (Scorpio and Cancer), these two invariably miss out on an emotional level. The airy Aquarian coolness and the detached way it deals with its feelings (usually with a glare and a determination not to let anything get in the way of its rational mind) is a completely mystery to the more open Pisces, whose tears and emotional highs and lows are so much a part of her everyday life. She feels rebuffed by her child's seeming indifference to her woes whilst Aquarius frets at the absence of an intellectual response to its worries. Pisces also finds her child's obstinacy difficult to deal with while Aquarius despairs of its mother's indecision and confusion. On the plus side, Pisces is invariably vastly entertained by her loyal, intelligent and witty Aquarian who, in turn, values its kind and compassionate mother. At worst, they bumble along in much misunderstanding while keen to improve the situation.

Aquarius Child/Pisces Father

The Piscean father is often puzzled by the innate curiosity and intellect of his Aquarian child and finds its endless questions and need for debate thoroughly draining. Pisces hates to be tied down to anything, and his youngster often becomes extremely frustrated at its father's penchant for swimming away from commitments. He does, however, love his child's honesty, loyalty and independent stance and is usually greatly entertained by the Aquarian wit and its sometimes slightly eccentric behaviour. With Pisces, the great thespian of the zodiac, Aquarius doesn't have to worry too much about embarrassing its father! The Aquarian obstinacy and lack of flexibility generally can often irritate Pisces but at the same time he is brilliant at defusing situations and makes a real effort to understand his child's worries. An Aquarian daughter often finds it easy to open up to her Piscean father, although a son will usually clam up in the face of his more openly emotional stance. Despite their differences, these two often learn to respect each other. If they drift apart it's because neither has bothered to nurture the relationship.

Aquarius/Pisces Siblings

Zodiacal neighbours usually have little in common but, with a little care and consideration, can use their differences to mutual benefit. The Piscean can be very helpful to its Aquarian sibling in coping with its emotions: Aquarius is very rational and learns a lot from Pisces about listening to its heart rather than always making decisions from the head. Aquarius is equally protective of its more vulnerable and gentle brother or sister, coming to its rescue when it's got itself into another impossible situation! Of course, Aquarius becomes exasperated with its sibling's indecision and rather weak-willed attitude and resents having to prop it up, while Pisces cannot understand the Aquarian determination to be different almost for the sake of it. Pisces often has to smooth troubled waters in the wake of its sibling's perverse comments or behaviour. Both, however, are very concerned with the welfare of others and it's not unusual for these two to be heavily involved in environmental or humanitarian issues from an early age. These two often turn out to be good companions and each other's saving grace.

PISCES

The Pisces Child 0-5 Years

The Pisces child views the world through beautiful eyes and the far-away look of the zodiac's natural dreamer and escapist, who truly believes that the grass must definitely be greener somewhere else. This is the last sign in the astrological circle and, as well as being the most unworldly, compassionate and intuitive, is often one of the most difficult to deal with. The Piscean symbol is two fishes swimming in opposite directions, suggesting that members of this sign find it difficult to be straightforward, to concentrate for any length of time and to make lasting commitments. It is this rather vague perception of the self, however, that makes them remarkably creative: all Pisceans possess artistic talent of some kind or other, and it is the birth sign of Chopin, Handel, Renoir, Michelangelo and that luminary of the Hollywood A list, Elizabeth Taylor, with her two Oscars, eight marriages and remarkable violet eyes.

From the very beginning Pisces is over emotional: tears are part and parcel of its make-up and it cries over anything and everything whether happy, sad, cross or racked with indecision. The newborn Pisces won't just make its feelings known about hunger, pain or needing a nappy change, but will also be highly susceptible to atmosphere, picking up on tensions and anything akin to unhappiness. Even in the earliest days, the Piscean intuition is working and it's not long before that sixth sense becomes obvious to anyone who chooses to see it. It's as though this young child knows exactly what is going to happen, whether it's a meal it's not going to like, a sudden argument brewing in the home or the arrival of a favourite relative. Secret smiles or a sad little face often tell a very big story. Along with this strong intuitive nature goes a tendency to experience the most amazing dreams. A three-year-old Piscean talking about strange things that have happened, places it's visited and people it's met should not necessarily be told it has an over-active imagination. A dream is probably being related in all its glory.

The artistic and creative talents of the Pisces child, however, are very much linked to this wonderful imagination, and somewhere along the line his or her talents will emerge. Sometimes a bent for music, art or dance will be obvious at a very young age, but by the time Pisces goes to school it could be interested in making up short stories, photography, flowers, icing buns – anything in fact that allows its creative mind to run riot. Chiefly, however, Pisces is invariably the most brilliant little actor (probably only outshone by a Sagittarian on a good day!). He or she loves to entertain and will blossom in front of an appreciative audience, its natural and rather sweet shyness going right out of the window as it indulges in mimicry or acts out a dance routine or other short scenario. A well-stocked dressing up box is often a favourite possession. As well as a highly developed imagination, the little Piscean is also born with an escapist nature – always looking to get away from the grim realities of life and into a beautiful environment somewhere else! It's often accused of daydreaming and vagueness but this 'out of it' pose is merely its way of indulging that escapism just as its artistic pursuits are another way of achieving a beautiful world. The third link with the unworldly Piscean nature is a relatively high dependency factor, whether it's on stronger characters or jelly beans. At worst the young Pisces can get itself into all sorts of trouble through a weak-willed willingness to go along with people and situations that it knows, intuitively, are doing him or her no good at all.

Pisces, like the other water signs (Scorpio and Cancer), is a child of hidden depths, strong currents, and often choppy but unfathomable seas, and this highly emotional and sometimes very complex character is a total mystery to the more pragmatic. At times it seems to live in state of muddle at best, and total confusion at worst. Tidiness and neatness are not in this child's vocabulary but every last possession has a purpose and a special meaning and cleaning up or clearing out is never going to be easy for the little Fish. Practical this child is not, and getting itself organised for school, going out to tea or packing kit for a swimming lesson (a wonderful activity for Pisces) is usually accompanied by major dramas. The compassionate side of the Piscean nature is wonderfully obvious in the child's fascination with lame ducks of all sorts, whether it's the fledgling that's fallen out of the nest, the child with no real friends at nursery or its instinctive empathy with someone in trouble. It will also be the first member of the family to pick up on its mother's worries or upsets. Asking for a cuddle is often not for its own comfort but to give reassurance and love to someone else. This, after all, is one of the kindest and most loving members of the zodiac and its starts in the cradle.

Gentle massage with oils, quiet music and subdued lighting all work wonders in soothing this baby's sometimes tearful equilibrium, and, as with any water sign, Pisces often gains much benefit from that particular element. This is a baby who will love its bath and get very fractious when the evening routine is cut short for any reason and it's rushed through its splashing, playing with the ducks and general fun in the water. Toy boats, fish and other sea creatures are often Piscean bath-time favourites, and this is also a child who will wait avidly for the book at bedtime.

All Piscean children tend to need a rock around which they can swim, but at the same time they do not respond well to strict rules, routines and too much discipline which they find thoroughly unsettling. For parents of the little Fish it's often a fine balancing act between giving their child stability and security on the one hand and a slightly laissez-faire and flexible environment on the other. This is, on the whole, a very gentle child who tends to hate anything robust, whether it's sports or just a noisy and slightly boisterous party. It also thrives on kind and sympathetic treatment and sensitive communication but at the same time needs firm guidance, as Pisces is gullible, impressionable and easily led. He or she, in a wonderfully unworldly manner, wants to believe the best about everyone and feels that the whole population is worthy of its love. Pisces is famous for its very caring nature (this is the child who wears a stethoscope and plays at being doctor). From two or three years old, the young Fish will be talking to the homeless on the street (and probably offering a bed for the night) and organising a charity collection. Teaching a Piscean about life's more precarious situations can be heartbreaking as its idealism and natural faith in human goodness often seem to be shattered. Although many Pisces children will say that certain situations 'didn't feel right' and it's clear their intuition has come to their rescue, they are youngsters who rarely think logically about the realities and need a lot of help in this regard.

A little Fish can be secretive and fairly economical with the truth when it suits him or her. Lies are often an embellishment of a story rather than a downright untruth, but sometimes it's difficult to know where fantasy ends and fact begins. There can also be a real sense of negativity around a Pisces child who will turn molehills into mountains at the slightest whim and feel thoroughly downhearted at its own imagined disasters. Again, this is a child who needs an occasional grounding in the here and now if its vivid imagination is not to get out of control.

Pocket money and Pisces are quickly and easily parted! It is rarely a big spender but has got frittering away its cash down to a fine art. Teaching a young Piscean to save is often an uphill struggle but can be a very valuable lesson for a five-year-old who frequently wastes money and complains bitterly about its financial problems. Generosity, however, is another story: this is a child who would give its last penny to help someone out – even if it had to arrange an IOU in order to keep its promise!

The Pisces child is one of the most winning and charming in the zodiac. Vague, idealistic and totally impractical it may be, to say nothing of frequently being walked over by stronger personalities, but it has a wonderfully calm and tender temperament and a genuine humility and selflessness that is truly remarkable. Its artistic flair, sensitivity and ability to lend a compassionate ear to anyone in trouble (and come up with some amazingly perceptive solutions) makes it a joy to be with. At the school gate it will not, like perhaps Aries and Leo, noisily take control and order people about, but will probably be the quiet one at the back who, one by one, the rest of the class come to realise is an absolute diamond. This is the one who will have a kind word for everyone, bring the box of tissues when needed and cheer up friends (and foes for that matter) with a song, dance or funny story. A star in the making.

Pisces and Aries

Pisces Child/Aries Mother

The energetic and forthright Aries mother is delighted at the arrival of her gentle Piscean but, after the first few months, realises that she and her baby are very different. Aries is probably the most straightforward sign in the Zodiac and Pisces one of the most mysterious. Pisces thrives in a quiet, relaxed and generally very flexible environment and is floored by its busy mother and her somewhat boisterous lifestyle. Aries is far too busy to spend hours trying to fathom exactly what her baby might be thinking and Pisces can't cope with being harried and hurried and the whole notion of instant action. Pisces retreats into tears and Aries into annoyance and, the more Aries pushes for answers, the more her youngster becomes secretive and vague. This baby, from the start, is highly emotional and lives by its feelings, imagination and intuition, all of which are an enigma to Aries. It can also seem to be very dependent which, again, is a concept far removed from Aries' freedom-loving spirit. It doesn't take long, either, for Pisces to realise that its mother's wishes are paramount, but the little Fish can go along with those as it is totally selfless and would rather be walked all over than try to call the shots. Pisces will genuinely admire its pugnacious mother who has no fears about going into battle to protect her son or daughter, just as much as she'll be enchanted by her child's creativity and genuine kindness and will do much to encourage the Piscean talents. She'll also be grateful for her youngster's wonderful ability to soothe when her confidence hits rock bottom. Even as a three-year-old, Pisces knows the right things to say and how to listen. Aries will always get irritated at her child's slightly weak-willed attitude, escapism and idealism, just as Pisces won't appreciate its mother's impatience and impulsive behaviour, but despite many potential problems these two usually manage to remain lifelong friends. The Fish may swim away from time to time but, when in need of a champion, back it comes.

Pisces Child/Aries Father

For the Aries father, his Piscean child is an absolute delight as here, clearly, is someone who will look up to him as a knight in shining armour. Pisces looks forward to weekend adventures with its very enterprising father (especially if water sports are involved), though sometimes wishes he would go in for more gentle playground pursuits rather than rush towards the highest slide or most dangerous ropewalk! It doesn't take long, of course, for Aries to realise that his Piscean son or daughter just doesn't have his derring-do attitude and begin to get annoyed at what he sees as wimpish behaviour. He can't stand the constant Pisces tears and emotionalism but hasn't the time to talk through his child's vulnerabilities and worries. In turn, Pisces comes to see its father as bossy, unfeeling and egocentric. However, once Aries finds out where his Piscean's interests lie, he'll move heaven and earth to advance his child and, at the same time, be amazed at the Piscean intuition and proud of its artistic flair. He'll never understand why his son or daughter is so gullible, just as Pisces shrinks at its father's hurtful remarks. Both frequently give up on the other, but not for long.

Pisces/Aries Siblings

The straightforward Aries and the secretive Pisces are, on the face of it, totally incompatible. Aries hates the Piscean retreats into moody silences and its secretive and very idealistic approach to life, while Pisces is horrified at its sibling's pushy, egocentric behaviour and terrible impatience. Aries always feels it has to chivvy its sibling into getting anything done, just as much as Pisces spends its time apologising for its sibling's insensitive remarks. As with all neighbouring signs, however, each has much to offer the other if only they can see it. Pisces usually watches in both amusement and amazement as Aries dashes off on a new adventure, but is marvellous at soothing its sibling's dented ego when it all goes wrong. Aries does much to encourage Pisces' creative talents (and probably acts as a very efficient agent!) and is brilliant at persuading its sibling to face life's realities. Aries often stops Pisces going down a totally unsuitable road while Pisces acts as counsellor and referee when Aries oversteps the mark. These two usually act as a lifetime counterweight.

Pisces and Taurus

Pisces Child/Taurus Mother

The placid and patient Taurean mother is exactly right for the unworldly little Pisces. This is often a magical and very supportive relationship where Pisces flourishes in its mother's well-organised home and knows from the start that she is utterly reliable. Taurus is charmed by her undemanding baby, who instinctively feels very safe and protected and free to develop its sensitivity, compassion and imagination. Both mother and child are creative and they'll spend many happy hours together painting, gardening, cooking and, because Taurus usually has a lovely voice, in all sorts of musical activities. Taurus is also the perfect mother to comfortably ground her Piscean: she certainly won't ignore her child's vivid imagination nor fret at its sometimes rather secretive and vague nature, but will help her son or daughter to direct its talents in a very constructive way and encourage it to talk about its innermost feelings. She will do her best, too, to understand the Piscean intuition, which, as an earth sign and used to dealing with the tangible, she finds more difficult but rarely dismisses as folly. The young Piscean is also grateful for a mother whose opinions are so wonderfully fixed. Taurus is happy to let her child float ideas past her and is grateful that Pisces listens, respects what she has to say and doesn't want to argue every point. Sometimes the more adaptable Piscean can get a bit annoyed with its mother's inflexibility and her rather stubborn manner just as she, in her stoic way, cannot understand why Pisces has to cry at every turn. Her child's vagueness and gullibility can also be a puzzle when she is so certain about everything, but she is an excellent guide and rock to her little Fish when it gets itself into situations that are way out of its depth. Most of all, Taurus will never try to rationalise her child's dreams and emotions and Pisces will always value its mother as a wonderfully stable harbour as it makes its often rather muddled way through life.

Pisces Child/Taurus Father

The father/daughter relationship often fares better than that between father and son. The gentle Pisces girl is the strong Taurean father's idea of a damsel in distress, in need of protection, guidance and probably saving from herself as well. She, of course, worships her strong, opinionated father and, in a winsome manner, gets her own way every time. A Piscean son, on the other hand, can be difficult for a Taurean father who sees his child as unreliable, over-sensitive and far too emotional, and worries that he'll never hold down a proper job! Both son and daughter, however, feel very secure with Taurus and love the way he takes them out for snacks, introduces them to good food and allows them to experiment in the kitchen when he is acting as chef. He, in turn, loves his child's vivid imagination and actively encourages its acting skills and artistic talents. Taurus is as affectionate and warm-hearted as his child is kind and compassionate and neither really wants to rock the boat. Whatever goes on in the life of his young Piscean, Taurus will always be there, but often despairing of its latest dream for the future!

Pisces/Taurus Siblings

This is usually a very solid and affectionate relationship: neither is looking to upset any apple carts and both function best in a calm, stable environment without too much interference from each other. Taurus occasionally gets mad at the Piscean tendency to brood silently or to come up with totally unrealistic plans, while Pisces cannot comprehend its sibling's intransigent attitude and opinionated views. For a little Bull, who likes everything in its place, the Fish's muddle and confusion is extremely irritating, but Pisces can get just as annoyed by the Taurean self-indulgence and laziness. On the plus side, Taurus is brilliant at dealing with Pisces' tears and emotions: it doesn't get involved but is good at sorting the wheat from the chaff and finding a solution to problems. Pisces is very sensitive to its sibling's worries about change, and is often very helpful, understanding and sympathetic when Taurus is faced with a major crossroad, such as starting school. Their combined artistic talents, too, make them their own concert party and one on which the curtain rarely comes down.

Pisces and Gemini

Pisces Child/Gemini Mother

Pisces likes to muddle and dream its way through life while Gemini (often called the butterfly of the zodiac) loves to touch on an object for a few minutes before moving onto another, more interesting opportunity. Thus mother and baby are both happy to enjoy a take-it-as-it-comes daily routine and, in the early months, these two seem made for each other. Gemini organises a busy social life for them both and, whether at home or in nursery, she'll ensure her little Piscean is never bored. The mother's thirst for knowledge usually makes her a mine of interesting information and she's in her element teaching and reading to her child. Pisces will never say no to a session with a good book, but unfortunately it's usually far more attuned to the paint brush, a drum kit or making a pasta picture, and often there is a little bit of early friction as the mother goes with the intellect and the child with its creative imagination. Pisces is all heart and feelings while Gemini is entirely the rational mind, and the mother finds it very difficult to deal with the endless Piscean tears and deep emotions: she's often tempted down the 'pull yourself together' route when no amount of her sensible and logical comments succeed in comforting her youngster. Pisces, with its feelings trampled on or misunderstood often retreats into sulky and secretive silence, which further irritates its more open mother. Gemini is not particularly tactile, which also comes as a problem to a young Pisces, who is often much in need of a hug and a cuddle when its delicate sensibilities have been hurt. Although both can be changeable, and often talk much but communicate little, this relationship can survive many difficulties, not the least of which is the fact that neither is likely to be totally honest with the other. Pisces embroiders the truth while Gemini can say one thing and mean another! However, the Pisces kindness and compassion (and particularly it's acting abilities) are captivating to Gemini, whose own wit and energy are inspirational to her child.

Pisces Child/Gemini Father

Whilst Pisces is adaptable and willing to go along with everyone and everything, even this child finds the pace set by its Gemini father almost too hot to handle. Pisces likes to take life at a gentle trot and gets thoroughly unnerved by the sudden Gemini decisions and, worst of all, the continual changes of plan. The father, in turn, can get very frustrated at his child's idealistic notions about the world, which are in stark contrast to his more intellectual views, and worries about his son or daughter being a little too weak-willed. Although Pisces is fascinated by its father's range of knowledge, it also feels at times that it's being lectured, while Gemini cannot fathom his child's over the top emotions and general vagueness. However, Gemini is usually bowled over by his child's sensitivity to people and situations and just loves its highly developed imagination. On the social scene these two can make quite an impact with the Gemini wit and mimicry allied to Pisces' thespian skills. This relationship often improves with age, once both start to appreciate each other's qualities rather than focus on their differences, and is usually easier for a Gemini father and a Pisces son.

Pisces/Gemini Siblings

Despite great differences, these two usually get on better than expected. Pisces, for a start, is a wonderful listener (which is just as well as its sibling rarely stops chattering) and Gemini is very confident in its abilities to talk the Fish out of its crazier plans. The Gemini logic and talent for language combined with the Piscean artistry and imagination make them a formidable pair when they are planning to entertain parents or friends, and Pisces is particularly understanding of Gemini's short attention span. However, neither sibling is particularly straightforward and both suffer enormously from being let down when each realises the other has either lied or opted out of taking responsibility. Gemini also gets thoroughly irritated when Pisces goes into one of its silent and secretive moods, just as much as the little Fish resents its sibling's endless questions and superficiality. Whilst Gemini will never understand its sibling's deep feelings and Pisces will never work out why Gemini has to live on its nerves, these two often jog along companionably together.

Pisces and Cancer

Pisces Child/Cancer Mother

Both Pisces and Cancer are water signs and from the very beginning there is usually a tremendous sense of harmony between mother and child. Both happily function on the intuitive level, having an unspoken understanding that rarely lets either of them down. The Pisces baby is a natural actor at heart and blossoms in front of an appreciative audience, and its number one fan will be its mother who is delighted to find herself with a baby who prefers a flexible timetable, loves the comfort she provides and values hugs and tenderness way above the delights of the world at large. For once she need not feel either worried or guilty if the practicalities of life take second place to their wonderful relationship! It therefore comes as a surprise to Cancer that her baby Piscean is prone to tears. Pisces tends to be more emotional than all the other signs put together and expresses all its feelings (from ecstatic joy and deep unhappiness to seething anger) in this very watery manner. The Piscean baby is no exception, but soothing baths, gentle massages, quiet music and subdued lighting can work wonders for its equilibrium Whilst the Pisces child doesn't fare well within a rigid routine, it does need a lot of attention and a well-ordered day (something the Cancer mother is well able to give and organise) if time-wasting is to be avoided. The natural Piscean artistic talents are usually also encouraged by a Cancerian mother. The danger in the Cancer mother/Pisces child relationship is an excess of emotion and an overactive imagination combined with an impractical attitude to life and a dearth of sensible solutions to problems. At worst these two can drift around in a mass of misunderstandings. But generally the Piscean baby gazes at its Cancerian mother through dreamy, beautiful eyes and the life-long love-in has begun!

Pisces Child/Cancer Father

There are likely to be few difficulties between the Cancer father and his Piscean child early on, especially if Cancer gets involved with swimming lessons, or anything else to do with water, and artistic ventures which help his child's imagination to flourish. Both will also understand the other's sensitivities. Later on, however, Cancer will fret about the Piscean's lack of punctuality, the chaotic state in which it lives and its total lack of ambition. Money matters also prove a bone of contention. Cancer likes to feel there are a few nest eggs around and Pisces manages to fritter away the cash. The Piscean nature is to swim somewhat haphazardly through life and this is rarely understood by its Cancer father who takes his responsibilities very seriously. Cancer will definitely have some sympathy with his child's emotional attitude to life but will be baffled by its 'what will be will be' approach. Rarely do these two have a major bust-up: if problems persist they gently distance themselves from one another. On the whole, however, they usually develop a very loving relationship and enjoy having a good old moan together about being misunderstood!

Pisces/Cancer Siblings

Generally these two find they enjoy many of the same interests and both thrive in a strong domestic unit. Emotionally they are also in tune but, because each sees its own vulnerability in the other, tensions and arguments arise and neither forgets what has been said or done. At worst, both can harbour grudges for a lifetime. Cancer can also become irritated at its Piscean sibling's inability to stick at anything and Pisces often thinks of Cancer as 'Mummy's darling'. Both have an innate ability to be economical with the truth, a situation that ultimately leads to both of them suffering the occasional injustice – all of their own making. In the land of emotional drama, these two are in a league of their own but at the same time are each other's champion and lavish kindness and protection on each other when feelings have been hurt or dreams shattered. Distance can sometimes lend enchantment but neither will really want to cut cords. This duo often relate better when they are older, which is a comfort to parents of a sulking Crab and a silent Fish!

Pisces and Leo

Pisces Child/Leo Mother

The Leo mother looks at her Piscean baby's beautiful eyes, and Pisces gazes at its well-organised and very elegant mother, and both think that this is going to be a wonderful relationship. And so it will be for a few months, as Leo gives her baby the security that comes from an orderly routine, and revels in her baby's natural gentleness and what seems to be an inborn talent for putting on a bit of a show and being a little star. It doesn't take long, however, for the Leo/Pisces differences to emerge. It soon becomes obvious that the brisk, ordered and efficient Leo is up against a child who loves to muddle through life and to whom the idea of tidying up its room or toys is a complete anathema. She soon finds, too, that she can't rely on Pisces to complete tasks, or even to start them for that matter, let alone remember which kit to take to school or whether there's a class outing. Leo breezes through life in a big-hearted, open and broadminded way but her Piscean tends to be secretive, sensitive and, in its mother's view, has no real backbone. Pisces, in turn, thinks its mother ignores its feelings, is bossy in the extreme and never really listens to what it has to say. The Piscean tears are also beyond Leo's comprehension: she's positive, active and gets on with life and she's not at all comfortable with what seems to her to be negativity and a tendency to hide away from life's realities. On the plus side, of course, both are highly creative and very sociable and, with its mother's encouragement, Pisces swims happily into new groups and develops its artistic talents. The Pisces intuition also quickly picks up on its mother's more vulnerable feelings and Leo is charmed by her child's natural compassion and kindness. At worst Pisces can feel quite intimidated by its mother's confidence and intolerance, while Leo is worried by her child's inability to face reality and infuriated at its dissemblance when the going gets tough. It takes a lot of tolerance and a long learning process for this relationship to prosper.

Pisces Child/Leo Father

The Pisces child is usually enormously proud of its Leo father, valuing his opinions and learning a lot from him about confidence, magnanimity and generosity. A Pisces daughter often worships her own King of the Jungle, who will be very protective and love the fact that she is naturally gentle, sensitive and compassionate. He probably won't be so thrilled with the way she tries to fob him off with all sorts of excuses when she's forgotten yet another small task, and certainly won't be best pleased when he always seems to be rescuing her from her own follies. A Pisces son, however, is quite another story for the Leo father, who often fails to appreciate his child's selfless and unworldly nature and loses patience with its vague ideas, secretive behaviour and tendency to trifle with the truth. To start with, his son looks up to him but can soon start to see its father as bullying, ambitious and very intolerant. Luckily, a wonderful imagination and mutual creativity often save this relationship, with both daughter and son, and Leo is the first to applaud his child's artistic success. When all else fails Leo and Pisces understand the benefits of a spending spree!

Pisces/Leo Siblings

As with any Pisces/Leo relationship, this is never going to be a naturally comfortable situation. For the competent and efficient Leo it's annoying in the extreme to have to deal with a sibling who seems to live in a state of complete confusion and who can be thoroughly unreliable. Pisces, in turn, gets furious with the Leo conceit and often rather pompous behaviour, and hates being pushed around by its more confident sibling. It's often Pisces, however, who has the last laugh, slipping away out of trouble when problems arise and being much better at making up the story as it goes along. On the plus side, both are very creative: the Leo showmanship allied to the Piscean imagination can make them a formidable double act. Leo is often grateful, too, for its sibling's sixth sense and compassion when another grand plan goes to pot, while Pisces benefits from Leo's ability to organise its rather muddled existence. Forced to live in each other's pockets, this can become a stressful relationship for both. Given space, they often learn to value each other.

Pisces and Virgo

Pisces Child/Virgo Mother

Virgo is a practical, reliable earth sign and therefore a perfect stabilising mother for the idealistic and sometimes weak-willed little Fish. She is also her baby's opposite number in the zodiac, which suggests a relationship that will go through highs and lows as they try to accommodate each other. At the birth of her baby (especially if it's her first) Virgo will start to worry about getting everything right, and Pisces intuitively picks up on her distress. Both are then unsettled and it isn't until Virgo gains confidence in her abilities that both mother and baby become comfortable and happy in their roles. Pisces, to start with, will thrive in its mother's daily routines but it won't be long before it begins to chafe against Virgo's busy schedule and thoroughly well-organised day. Virgo, of course, is a natural teacher and she'll do much to encourage her child to develop its talents, but her child needs time to exercise its wonderful creative imagination. A little Fish starts to fret if its waking hours are so well planned that there is no time for simple, creative play or for it to gaze into space and daydream. Virgo finds this secretive part of her child's life both irritating and incomprehensible: she can't get a handle on it and it's not rational! She's also wary of her Piscean's elaborate stories and, after some disillusionment, learns to be a little sceptical about her child's version of events. As with all earth signs, she's a pragmatist and frequently loses patience with her child's tearful negativity, to say nothing of the messy clutter her child thinks is essential for its well-being. Pisces, of course, tends to feel useless in the face of criticism and swims off into a silent sulk as it'll rarely make a battle royal about anything. Generally, this relationship works well despite the glitches. Virgo loves her child's sensitivity and kindness (a young Piscean will always put its mother's needs before its own) and delights in her child's ability to entertain, while Pisces is thankful for its mother's common sense and wholeheartedly loving support through thick and thin.

Pisces Child/Virgo Father

Virgo likes routine and order and is known for his meticulous approach to life. His little Fish seems to be a byword for disorganisation and, even, chaos, and he quickly finds himself in the role of critic par excellence. Although he is caring and loving of his very gentle son or daughter and appreciates its artistic flair, he finds his child's vagueness, reluctance to fight its corner in the playground and endless expectation of him to dry the tears and sort out the problems thoroughly irritating. In turn, Pisces sees its father as finicky and very demanding in his pursuit of excellence and perfection. Ever reluctant to get into a debate with its father (knowing that Virgo will probably shred the Piscean views) his child tends to back away from its father and retreat more and more into its vivid imagination. On the plus side, of course, both father and child are very adaptable and Pisces is better than most at dealing with Virgo's tendency to put work before pleasure and change arrangements. Much love and mutual admiration usually keep this relationship on the rails. Pisces is forever grateful for its father's common sense, while Virgo is very proud of his child's compassion and talent to amuse.

Pisces/Virgo Siblings

The Piscean kindness and gentleness is a wonderful balm to the slightly fussy Virgo who worries endlessly about anything from a slight cut on the finger (obviously a case of tetanus in the making) to a playground misdemeanour for which it hasn't owned up. Pisces listens, soothes and often comes up with the right solutions, although probably shies away from going into battle on Virgo's behalf. Pisces in turn values its sibling's practical skills and common sense, which invariably help the Fish get out of trouble: Virgo is also pretty astute at seeing through the Fish's tall stories! However, Virgo can get irritated at always having to remember everything for its Pisces sibling, who can't seem to focus on the nitty-gritty of life, while the Fish wonders why Virgo has no imagination whatsoever. Determination and resolve, however, are lacking and sometimes this relationship goes around in muddled circles especially when decisions have to be made. Nevertheless, these two usually help each other out for years.

Pisces and Libra

Pisces Child/Libra Mother

This is a relationship between the two great romantics and idealists of the zodiac and is a seemingly wonderful match. Both happily drift their way through the early months, mother and child taking a very relaxed attitude to life and enjoying a close and loving bond. The totally selfless little Pisces instinctively feels at home with its easy-going and refined mother, who is more than happy to accommodate the Fish's gentle ways. Neither mother nor child relishes conflict and, from an early age, Pisces works out how to keep its mother happy: this is not a sign without a certain amount of guile! Problems arise for these two when routines have to be organised, plans made and decisions taken. Pisces is vague and Libra vacillating, and sometimes these two rush around in ever-decreasing circles, achieving nothing. When Pisces is again late for a party, or misses out on a swimming lesson, it may not go into a temper tantrum but will sulk in silence (probably with a pout to match) and withdraw. Libra apologises and is desperate to get back in her child's good books, promising much in the way of recompense, and then fumes at being taken for a (usually financial) ride by her son or daughter. Both can also be very gullible and want to believe the best in everyone: mother and child can spend a lot of time wondering how they ever got into such regrettable situations! Socially Libra will do much for her little Pisces, as she is normally very popular and her child will be equally welcome as it is such an entertaining addition to the group. Mother and child usually also enjoy artistic pursuits of all kinds. As Pisces gets older, it finds real communication with Libra somewhat difficult as she keeps trying to rationalise her child's very emotional take on life and, ultimately, feels drained by the Fish's very deep feelings and its somewhat negative attitude. Differences between these two are usually brushed under the carpet and if either is going to brood over problems it's Pisces: Libra never complains at having to mend fences!

Pisces Child/Libra Father

Libra is ambitious but its desire to get to the top is often hidden behind a veil of rather charming indifference. His Piscean child is probably going to be far happier swimming its way gently through life and, if it gets to the top, well that'll be more by luck than judgment! Charmed though the Libran father will be with his imaginative and sensitive child, he'll nevertheless become exasperated with its secretive and vague nature, to say nothing of its tendency to dissolve into tears at every turn. He worries intensely about his child's future! Pisces, however, never feels harried or pushed into things by its laid-back father and gets a lot of praise for its artistic endeavours and generally very entertaining demeanour. Both father and child are idealistic and often sit together wondering what the world is coming to! Libra loves the fact that Pisces is so sensitive and unworldly and delighted that money falls through his child's fingers as much as it does his own! This is invariably a very loving but sometimes slightly elusive relationship between a changeable father and a little Fish who so often slips right out of Libra's grasp.

Pisces/Libra Siblings

As both Pisces and Libra will do anything for a quiet life, this is never going to be a relationship fraught with loud arguments and much noisy door slamming. If anyone is likely to take umbrage, it's more likely to be Pisces, and then it'll be more tears than tantrums. Libra just seethes silently! Neither sibling is likely to bear a grudge and, whatever gripes they may have with one another, they invariably put up a united front at home and on the social scene. Libra is particularly good at listening to the Piscean woes and worries and making it see sense, while Pisces encourages Libra to talk about its resentments and anger brought about by its own indecision and need to please. Both tend to be gentle and kind, although Libra sometimes despairs of its sibling's tendency to bring home all sorts of lame ducks, while Pisces cannot believe that Libra has fallen for yet another sob story. The Piscean intuition often saves the day for both of them. Both can be inadvertently thoughtless but these siblings usually enjoy a very loving friendship for life.

Pisces and Scorpio

Pisces Child/Scorpio Mother

When the Scorpio mother's piercing gaze meets her Piscean baby's beautiful eyes, she is immediately aware of a deep emotional bond and often a real sense of destiny with this particular child. The little Fish instinctively feels very safe and secure with Scorpio, who will not only provide her child with an organised domestic scene but will also truly understand its vulnerabilities. Mother and child have highly developed intuition and Scorpio knows precisely what her Piscean is feeling: these two communicate instinctively rather than rationally. The Piscean tears probably don't flummox her at all: she knows how to put things right. They are also both highly imaginative: Scorpio makes sense of her Piscean's dreams, is usually particularly tolerant of its make-believe friends, its idealism and even its escapist nature. While she is in control she knows her child will not be easily led into anything! It is this control, however, that also causes problems between them. Scorpio is determined and persistent and Pisces tends to be rather vague and weak-willed, and she frequently loses patience with what she sees as her child's lack of purpose and a tendency to drift. The more she tries to order and to interfere, the more Pisces tends to slip away, usually into a lengthy silence accompanied by much sulking. It takes time for her to realise that Pisces needs a very gentle touch. Pisces is very affable and as trusting about people as Scorpio is suspicious. There are often heated discussions between them about the suitability of friends and acquaintances! Scorpio can also be extremely obstinate and when she lays down the law there is no room for negotiation. That works for a time with Pisces, but the more adaptable Fish can later be very devious when it comes to outmanoeuvring her and, having done that, then soothes and comforts Scorpio. This is a relationship that rarely founders: even when Pisces drives its mother to distraction, Scorpio's loyalty never wavers.

Pisces Child/Scorpio Father

In the early years of this relationship Pisces feels immensely protected by its father, who usually manages to bring a sense of structure and order into his child's life. Because he exudes a tremendous sense of power the little Fish is often in awe of Scorpio, but rarely afraid of him. As with any two water signs, they'll often be the first ones at the swimming pool, mucking about in boats or quietly fishing together and Scorpio will also do much to foster his Piscean's imagination. With a Piscean daughter, Scorpio can become a jealous and possessive father and will want to vet her friends from three onwards! On the other hand, a daughter is brilliant at encouraging her father to listen to his gut instinct, something he takes time to realise is usually right. For his Pisces son, Scorpio can also make life difficult once he twigs that the Fish doesn't have his determination and thirst for success. A didactic father, however, finds during the teenage years that his Piscean starts to ignore him and silently swims away into less turbulent waters. This relationship usually endures, though not without a few blips along the way.

Pisces/Scorpio Siblings

There can be a lot of game playing in this relationship, with Scorpio being manipulative and Pisces secretive and slightly devious. Scorpio is invariably the stronger personality and yet it is often far too clever for its own good, many of its plots and plans coming to grief. The gentler Pisces is a balm to the wounded Scorpio feelings and, although never being in quite the stalwart league of, say, Taurus, will be very kind and sympathetic to its sibling before swimming off and denying all knowledge of the latest bit of misbehaviour! These two understand each other at a very deep level, often feeling they are telepathic, and are also highly imaginative. On the plus side, they concoct wonderful artistic masterpieces of all kinds but, at worst, let their thinking go into overdrive and drown in negativity and depression, with the more adaptable Pisces invariably having to drag Scorpio out of a very black mood. Pisces rarely understands Scorpio's need for privacy, but this relationship is usually very loving, caring and supportive and there for the long term.

Pisces and Sagittarius

Pisces Child/Sagittarius Mother

The Pisces baby is a little actor at heart and, right from the start, feels the need to give a great performance. Its Sagittarian mother is more than happy to go along with her enchanting child and bask in all the reflected glory. Both mother and child also function best within a fairly flexible timetable, although the Sagittarian soon finds out that, like all Pisceans, her baby needs a rock around which it can swim and she is perhaps not the best at providing that safe and solid ground in the form of a slightly more structured day. The beautiful Piscean eyes have a far-away look and the baby is a natural dreamer. To its active Sagittarian mother, who rarely has time to stand and stare, the Piscean inability to 'get a grip' and to get on with things can be exasperating, and in turn her little Fish becomes tearful and distracted by the constant activity and its mother's lack of understanding of its more sensitive nature. The Piscean tears are invariably a mystery to the happy-go-lucky Sagittarian, who, not being terribly in touch with her emotions, fails to realise that her baby picks up, and is affected by, every nuance and every undercurrent. In this relationship, Sagittarius needs to learn to give her Piscean calm, quality time, to develop her baby's creative skills, of which there are usually plenty, and to listen carefully to her child's fears and worries. Pisces cannot just be jollied out of its cares and woes. At worst, these two rub each other up completely the wrong way. The confident Sagittarian is usually oblivious to her child's vulnerabilities and driven to distraction by Pisces' muddled, emotional and naïve approach to life. Pisces feels swamped by its exuberant mother and disheartened by her unfeeling remarks. At best, however, these two gain a great deal from each other: Pisces learns to be more self-assured and Sagittarius to be more thoughtful. Best of all – this mother and child can be guaranteed to put on a great show of genuine togetherness and affection whenever the occasion demands.

Pisces Child/Sagittarius Father

Sagittarius is a sign synonymous with activity, a can-do attitude, frankness and optimism and his gentle, caring and unworldly Piscean child is none of those things. It therefore takes time for the father fully to appreciate the very different gifts of his son or daughter. However, both signs are interested in the arts; music is often a shared passion, as is the stage. A sport such as skiing can also bring father and child together. The biggest problem for the Sagittarian is the general aimlessness of the Piscean, who, in turn, feels his or her tender feelings have been trampled on by a father who doesn't want to know about insecurities and worries. The Piscean gullibility also tends to infuriate Sagittarius, who is known for his good judgment. The more open-minded Sagittarian father can, in time, develop a good relationship with his Piscean, but the more macho Sagittarian will find it almost impossible to find common ground with this compassionate and impressionable child. This relationship often works best between a Sagittarian father and a Piscean daughter in whose artistic skills, sensitivity and caring behaviour he can easily take great pride.

Pisces/Sagittarius Siblings

This sibling relationship is not one of the easiest. At best they reach adulthood having signed a truce and are at least on speaking terms. At worst, they come a cropper early on and no amount of trying to heal the wounds makes the situation any better. The emotional and sensitive Piscean often finds it really difficult to cope with his or her Sagittarian sibling who is oblivious to its finer feelings and can be tactless and irresponsible in the extreme. In turn, the Sagittarian finds Pisces to be wimpish, indecisive and weak-willed and not up to joining in with its rather noisy and boisterous way of life. A shared sense of humour can be a life-line to these two, as can the teenage years when the Piscean's caring nature can be a balm to the Sagittarian's wounded pride and frequently broken heart! Equally, Sagittarius is able to lend some objective and sensible distance to the Piscean's problems and to give some excellent and wise guidance. On the plus side, both are sociable and adaptable and, as both are wanderers by nature, each fully understands the other's rather commitment-phobic behaviour.

Pisces and Capricorn

Pisces Child/Capricorn Mother

Those beautiful Piscean eyes focus adoringly on its mother and the baby knows full well that it will feel very secure with a Capricorn. She, in turn, knows she has a thoroughly amenable and gentle baby who will thrive in her busy and organised lifestyle. That is the theory! In reality it's not always so straightforward. Pisces is highly emotional and whilst not given to tantrums or digging in its heels, expresses any kind of upset or discomfort with copious tears. Because the whole notion of letting her feelings come to the surface is never in the Capricorn mother's game plan, she finds it very difficult to understand the Piscean vulnerabilities, and cannot fathom why her child can't 'pull itself together'. She also finds out very quickly that her Piscean has a thoroughly underdeveloped sense of time management. For a woman who prides herself on being everywhere on time, she can become exasperated at the Piscean dilly-dallying and total disorganisation. For its part, her child can often feel pressurised and hassled. It likes to drift through life, not run to efficient timetables, and the more it feels it has to achieve targets, the more distracted it becomes. So, Capricorn sees her child as dreamy, vague and impractical, while Pisces frets at its mother's pragmatism and exacting standards. If Capricorn can encourage her child's artistic talents and take the pressure off, she'll bring out the innate sensitivity, kindness and adaptability of Pisces. She'll also find that her child is able gently to tap into her own emotions: many Capricorn mothers and Pisces children find they are able to communicate at a very deep level. Through its mother's efforts, Pisces starts to live in less confusion, learns to become more decisive and understands about standing up for itself. These two will probably never totally see eye to eye but this relationship is usually one of much affection, though often a lot of worry on the mother's part – even when her child is an adult!

Pisces Child/Capricorn Father

With a Piscean daughter, who he probably sees as being delightfully feminine and artistically talented, the Capricorn father can be the picture of indulgence. He may well carry on alarmingly about her spendthrift ways and idealistic notions, but usually thoroughly enjoys her company and will take her swimming and drop her off at her ballet and drama classes. She sees him as the perfect father figure, although, from time to time, can get a bit tearful at his inflexibility and over-conventional stance. For a Piscean son, however, the situation can be very different. Capricorn gets exasperated with his son's emotional sensitivity and escapist tendencies. For a sign like Capricorn, firmly rooted in the practical and pragmatic, a Piscean son who does not thrive on hard work, duty and ambition is a total mystery. Pisces sees his father as bossy, controlling and demanding. With Capricorn's encouragement, rather than approbation, his son can flourish within the father's firm boundaries and sensible routines. Joint interests often make life that much easier too. In time, these two can become good friends, but usually only when Pisces has achieved something tangible in life.

Pisces/Capricorn Siblings

On the surface, these two have little in common. Pisces lives in something akin to chaos and Capricorn needs an orderly environment. Capricorn is practical and sensible and values all things tangible, whereas Pisces is an artistic dreamer living in the realms of feelings and intuition. However, the Piscean has the potential truly to understand its Capricorn sibling and get behind that very conventional, and often worried and pessimistic, façade. In Pisces, Capricorn has a wonderfully kind and sympathetic listener who, seemingly out of nowhere, comes up with the right answers. Capricorn is also able to offer Pisces plenty of practical help and sort out its rather jumbled thinking. More importantly, it will always be there for its sibling. Problems arise when Capricorn constantly has to help its sibling get its life together and Pisces feels crushed by the Capricorn control and tendency to shatter its dreams. At best, Pisces can soften Capricorn's rather rigid outlook, whilst Capricorn can focus the Piscean talents.

Pisces and Aquarius

Pisces Child/Aquarius Mother

The Aquarian mother is usually both puzzled and delighted at the arrival of her Piscean baby: it's dreamy eyes and generally calm nature make her think that looking after this child is going to be a doddle, but she quickly realises that this new arrival is probably as much of an enigma as she is herself. Two unfathomable personalities can either live in a state of total muddle and misunderstandings or in unmitigated bliss. Over the years, the Aquarian mother and Pisces baby will tend to wander between both ends of the spectrum and discover both outer limits. The Aquarian's quick intellect, independence and certainty about life are in direct contrast to the little Piscean, who is idealistic, intuitive and extremely vague about everything. While the fish just likes to swim gently through babyhood, its Aquarian mother is bustling about, organising lots of social occasions and probably changing her plans at a moment's notice. Whilst all Piscean children are pretty adaptable, all this activity, and particularly the noise, is thoroughly unnerving to Pisces, who uses tears, rather than tantrums, to express its feelings. Its Aquarian mother, used to dealing with all problems logically and rationally, is completed fazed by her over-emotional baby, who lives in the realm of the senses and doesn't seem to appreciate her efforts at all. The Piscean charm, however, wins her over. A natural actor at heart, the baby learns stagecraft very early on and his or her performance just melts the Aquarian. The escapist tendencies of Pisces also come up against the more rigid views of its Aquarian mother, and her basically loyal and honest nature is also frequently put to the test by her more secretive child who has a great talent for embroidering the truth. However, neither sign is looking for trouble and both are naturally kind-hearted: for the most part, this mother/child relationship usually comes through the storm-tossed years battered but unbowed.

Pisces Child/Aquarius Father

Frequently this is a relationship of exasperation on the one hand and a great sense of wonder on the other. The vagueness, emotionalism and sometimes weak-willed attitude of his Piscean child, to say nothing of the chaos that seems to surround his son or daughter, drives the Aquarian father to distraction. Equally, the child is frequently alarmed by its father's contrary attitude, unpredictable behaviour, tactless remarks and what is sometimes seen as an inability to grow up! However, the Aquarian also grudgingly approves of his child's sensitivity, artistic talent and unworldly attitude. The Piscean, in turn, is intrigued by its father's kindness, original thinking and ability to communicate with all and sundry, although a Piscean daughter might wish her father was slightly more tactile. Interests in common can be a great bond between this father and child as can, in later years, a joint appreciation of the good things in life. Whilst an easy flow of understanding between them is never likely to materialise, a mutual pride in each other's achievements and qualities can ultimately resonate through this relationship.

Pisces/Aquarius Siblings

These very different siblings either decide they have nothing in common at all or realise they have much to learn from each other. The Aquarian's logical and intellectual mind-set can provide an excellent framework for its Piscean sibling who frequently lives in a mass of confused thoughts and feelings. Whilst both signs tend to be kind, friendly and sympathetic, Pisces can teach the Aquarian about sensitivity to others and, more importantly, introduce its sibling to the notion of speaking from the heart rather than rationalising every single emotion. Artistic creativity and inventive thinking are hallmarks of each sign, and frequently these two enjoy the same cultural pursuits. Both are also imaginative, a quality that draws them together when life gets tough and they need to brazen out a situation! Arguments, however, can prove difficult to resolve: Aquarius becomes intractable and perverse, Pisces swims off into deep waters and remains mute. At worst the relationship founders in contrariness and indecision. At best these two help each other along brilliantly.

Pisces and Pisces

Pisces Child/Pisces Mother

Whilst this mother/child relationship must be one of the most selfless in the zodiac, it is also likely to suffer from confusion, secrecy and a lot of unrequited dependency. At the beginning, of course, they live in a happy little bubble of contentment, each intuitively aware of the other's caring, compassionate nature and extreme sensitivity to atmosphere and feelings. The fact that there is little organisation and a rather fluid timetable is not a problem at all as they begin to enjoy the company of friends and family and the mother starts to develop her child's creative talents. They share the copious Piscean tears together, whether from happiness or despair, and there is often much cuddling and comfort as they go through life's ups and downs. Once the little Pisces is toddling, however, and in need of some relatively firm guidance, it's not always easy for the mother to impose anything in the way of discipline and her child can run charmingly out of control. The Piscean youngster is never likely to test the boundaries as much as, say, an Aries or Gemini, and responds well to a lighter touch, but even that can be missing. The mother frequently gives in to the easy life and as soon as her child latches onto this, the Fish's tendency to embroider the truth to get itself out of scrapes comes to the surface. As both mother and child have vivid imaginations and are inclined to colour black and white pictures in vivid hues, there can be many misunderstandings and disappointments. Secrecy is another problem, and although these two may talk a lot, there is sometimes the feeling that neither is giving anything away. In the standard Piscean muddle, getting her child to school on time, to the right appointments and to a promised treat is also a matter of luck. At worst, these two swim around in a pond of hidden depths and conflicting currents, each unable to depend on the other and never fully trusting each other. At best this is a relationship of gentleness, creativity and great kindness, which is the key to much mutual happiness.

Pisces Child/Pisces Father

At his best, the Pisces father can be a wonderful companion and fount of inspiration. His Pisces child is a most appreciative ally and frequently these two have a great time together, whether it's at the swimming pool, inventing games in the playground or dreaming up some entertainment for the family. But, both father and child can be vague and weak-willed, and there is often much confusion, and ultimately disappointment, when either the father has forgotten a commitment to his child or, as happens as the child gets older, it has found something else to do – usually at the beck and call of a stronger personality. Of course, the father will never berate his child for untidiness or for thriving in chaos, because he does exactly the same but he might despair at seeing his child easily led into situations better left alone. A Piscean father and son often become great buddies because each understands the other's great sensitivity, intuition and unworldly approach to life. Usually this relationship is a joy to both, despite the difficulties of the teenage years when father and child refuse to face issues.

Pisces Siblings

Pisces siblings either spend a lot of time rushing around helping each other out or expend a great deal of emotional energy seething and sulking about being let down and having their delicate sensitivities crushed. They will happily live in a chaotic state of clutter, enjoy using their vivid imaginations and, as a twosome, being wonderful entertainers, often using their skills to cover up a situation that does not show them in their best light! The compassion and kindness that are inherent in Pisces children are normally put to good use in bringing home wounded birds, making sure the neighbour's cat is fed or visiting a friend who is ill. Their greatest fault is their tendency to be economical with the truth, although with a Pisces sibling it is often difficult to get away with it. Each just knows when it's being conned! Both can also be weak-willed: often a duty to a sibling takes a back seat to a more interesting proposition. Whatever their childhood difficulties, however, these two invariably swim back to each other again and again.